Om Saha Nau-Avatu |
Saha Nau Bhunaktu |
Saha Viiryam Karavaavahai |
Tejasvi Nau-Adhiitam-Astu Maa Vidvissaavahai |
Om Shaanti Shaanti Shaanti ||

Om, May God protect us both (the teacher and the student),
May God nourish us both,
May we work together with energy and vigour,
May our study be enlightening, not giving rise to hostility,
Om, Peace, Peace, Peace.

— Taittiriya Upanisad

Constitution of India, Professional Ethics and Human Rights

Thank you for choosing a SAGE product!
If you have any comment, observation or feedback,
I would like to personally hear from you.
Please write to me at **contactceo@sagepub.in**

Vivek Mehra, Managing Director and CEO, SAGE India.

Bulk Sales

SAGE India offers special discounts
for bulk institutional purchases.

For queries/orders/inspection copy requests
write to **textbooksales@sagepub.in**

Publishing

Would you like to publish a textbook with SAGE?

Please send your proposal to **publishtextbook@sagepub.in**

Get to know more about SAGE

Be invited to SAGE events, get on our mailing list.

Write today to **marketing@sagepub.in**

Constitution of India, Professional Ethics and Human Rights

Praveenkumar Mellalli

*Assistant Professor, Sri Krishna Institute
of Technology, Bangalore*

SAGE | TEXTS
www.sagepublications.com
Los Angeles • London • New Delhi • Singapore • Washington DC

First published in 2015 by

$SAGE | TEXTS

SAGE Publications India Pvt Ltd
B1/I-1 Mohan Cooperative Industrial Area
Mathura Road, New Delhi 110 044, India
www.sagepub.in

SAGE Publications Inc
2455 Teller Road
Thousand Oaks, California 91320, USA

SAGE Publications Ltd
1 Oliver's Yard, 55 City Road
London EC1Y 1SP, United Kingdom

SAGE Publications Asia-Pacific Pte Ltd
3 Church Street
#10-04 Samsung Hub
Singapore 049483

Published by Vivek Mehra for SAGE Publications India Pvt Ltd, typeset in 10.5/12.5 pts Stone Serif by Diligent Typesetter, Delhi and printed at Repro India Ltd, Mumbai.

Library of Congress Cataloging-in-Publication Data

Mellalli, Praveenkumar, author.
  The Constitution of India : professional ethics and human rights / Praveenkumar Mellalli, Assistant Professor, Sri Krishna Institute of Technology, Bangalore.
    pages cm
  Includes index.
1. India. Constitution. 2. Constitutions—India 3. Constitutional law—India.4. Human Rights—India. 5. Professional ethics. I. Title.
KNS1744.5195.M45   342.54—dc23   2015   2015035667

ISBN: 978-93-515-0771-0 (PB)

The SAGE Team: Amit Kumar, Indrani Dutta, Vandana Gupta, Anju Saxena and Ritu Chopra

Dedicated to

my mother and father
and to
those who read it with dedication

CONTENTS

LIST OF TABLES

LIST OF FIGURES

PREFACE

I am immensely delighted to present this book to all first/second semester students of Bachelor of Engineering (B.E.) courses (all branches) of the Visvesvaraya Technological University (VTU), Balagavi, Karnataka.

The book has been written with an intention to provide more sophisticated study material for the students to assist them to pass the examination and successfully achieve the objectives and outcomes of this subject in the most efficient and effective manner, and that too in the easiest way.

I have been conversant with this subject for the last seven years. As an aspirant of Civil Services, I have earned in-depth knowledge and understanding of this subject through my pertinacious self-study. I have been teaching this subject for the last six years, with great pleasure, to aspirants of Civil Services, B.E. students and other students. Thus, the high level of my studies, knowledge, understanding and experience colligated with this subject tremendously have helped me write this book.

Striking a sagacious balance between the requirements of the examination for the students and the objectives and outcomes of the syllabus of the subject was one of the main difficulties before me whilst writing the book. I have applied an innovative strategy in the structure, content and representation of this book, which has helped me in successfully overcoming the above-mentioned difficulties. I have also tried my best to give a lucid explanation of the syllabus and used diagrams and tables wherever necessary to provide clearer and easier presentation.

I am confident that this book will be extremely helpful for the students to pass the examination and thus accomplish the objectives and outcomes of the syllabus in an easy way.

I am very open to all constructive remarks and welcome all concrete suggestions from the readers of this book.

'End is fixed at Beginning', so have a good beginning to get a good end to your engineering course. All the best for your studies!

Praveenkumar Mellalli

PREFACE

CPH: OBJECTIVES, SYLLABUS AND OUTCOMES

OBJECTIVES

1. To provide basic information about the Indian Constitution.
2. To identify individual role and ethical responsibility towards society.
3. To understand human rights and its implications.

SYLLABUS

Module 1

Introduction to the Constitution of India, the Making of the Constitution and Salient Features of the Constitution. **(2 Hours)**

Preamble to the Constitution of India; Fundamental Rights and Its Limitations. **(3 Hours)**

Module 2

Directive Principles of State Policy; Relevance of Directive Principles of State Policy and Fundamental Duties. **(2 Hours)**

Union Executives: President, Prime Minister, Parliament, Supreme Court of India. **(3 Hours)**

Module 3

State Executives: Governor, Chief Minister, State Legislature, High Court of State. **(2 Hours)**

Electoral Process in India; Amendment Procedure 42nd, 44th, 74th, 76th, 86th and 91st Amendments. **(3 Hours)**

Module 4

Special Provision for Scheduled Caste and Scheduled Tribe; Special Provision for Women, Children and Backward Classes; Emergency Provisions; Human Rights—Meaning and Definitions, Legislation, Specific Themes in Human Rights and Working of National Human Rights Commission in India. **(3 Hours)**

Power and Functions of Municipalities; Panchayats and Cooperative Societies. **(2 Hours)**

Module 5

Scope and Aims of Engineering Ethics; Responsibility of Engineers; Impediments to Responsibilities. **(2 Hours)**

Risks, Safety and Liability of Engineers; Honesty, Integrity and Reliability in Engineering. **(3 Hours)**

OUTCOMES

After studying the course, you will be able to:

1. Have general knowledge and legal literacy, thereby taking up competitive examinations.
2. Understand state and central policies, fundamental duties, electoral process and special provisions.
3. Understand powers and functions of municipalities, panchayats and cooperative societies.
4. Understand engineering ethics and responsibilities of engineers.
5. Have awareness on basic human rights in India.

GUIDELINES TO READ THE BOOK

Follow the below guidelines before you start reading this book:

1. Read chapters consecutively or sequentially; it will help you save your time, efforts and memories, because chapters are arranged in an analogous or corre-spondent manner, such as both the Prime Minister and the Chief Minister have been discussed within the same section (Section IV).

2. If you wish to just gain basic knowledge of the subject and pass the examina-tion, then just focus on the content denoted with **BOLD LETTERS**; they are very important from the VTU's examination point of view. And while studying, make personal synopsis and review it during the time of examination, instead of reading all material again; this will help you save your time and efforts. Also, solve the model question papers after completing each chapter and during the examination period.

3. This subject is compulsory for most competitive examinations. If you wish to take up the competitive examinations in the future, it is necessary to have a good knowledge and understanding of this subject, so please read each sen-tence of the book thoroughly.

Praveenkumar Mellalli is an Assistant Professor at Sri Krishna Institute of Technology, Bangalore. He teaches the Constitution of India, professional ethics and human rights (CPH).

ACKNOWLEDGEMENTS

I would like to put forward a very emotional and respectful note to my mother Mrs Vishalaxi Dayanand and my father Mr Dayanand Mellalli. They have been standing behind me in my all endeavours, providing unconditional support and instilling confidence by playing a divine role in all my ideas, goals, thoughts and work that make most of my efforts a success at the end, which includes this book as well. I would like to thank my brother for extending his support. I am also thankful to Shri Sadashiv Mahaswami, a seer of Hukkeri Math, Haveri, Karnataka, for his blessings that have kept me motivated to write this book.

I am very grateful to my prospective supervisor of Doctoral studies, Professor Dr Gerald Schneider, Chair of International Politics, Department of Politics and Public Administration, University of Konstanz, Germany, for motivating me to work hard. His excellent publications and articles inspired me to write this book. I am also thankful to Professor Dr Dayanand Mane of Mysore University, Mysore, Karnataka, and Assistant Professor Jagadeesh Babu K. of Karnataka State Open University, Mysore, Karnataka, for their support.

I am obliged to many eminent constitutional experts and political scientists, especially Dr Subhash C. Kashyap and M. Laxmikant, whose works have had a significant impact on me, and in some way or other have inspired me to write this book.

Heartfelt thanks to my dear friend, Mr Nithish, Doctoral Research Scholar, Kuvempu University, Shimoga, Karnataka, who criticized positively, supported and encouraged me to write this book. I am also thankful to a few other friends namely Mr Inder Mani, Inspector of Revenue Department, Government of India, New Delhi; Mr Kiran, Assistant Commissioner of Police, Indo Tibetan Border Police; Mr Praveen B., Sub Inspector, Central Industrial Security Force, Pune; Dr Nanjunda; Kusunur; Ms Trinidad; and Ms Maryana. They have helped me in having thoughtful insight into this subject, and have given timely emotional support and motivation to complete this book.

I am thankful to my colleagues at the Raj Reddy Institute of Technology, Bangalore, especially Ganesh M., Dr Venkatesh K., Laxmi Devi, Asha and Dr Shankarananda, and also those of the Sri Krishna Institute of Technology, Bangalore, especially Dr Manjunath (Principal), Shankar B. S., Nagesh V. N., Dr Manju, Kalpana G., Veeresha S. and Manjunath, for their help, support and encouragement to write this book.

I am also thankful to the team of SAGE Publications, New Delhi, especially Amit Kumar, Indrani Dutta, Vandana Gupta, Niranjan Jha, Anju Saxena and Ritu Chopra for putting munificent and tremendous efforts day and night to publish the book on time.

Praveenkumar Mellalli

Section I

Introduction to the Constitution of India

1

The Concept of the Constitution

What is the foundation of the cricket game? Why are there only six balls in an over? Why should there be only two batsmen on the crease, not four? Why does the scoring shot to boundary give only four and six runs, why not eight or ten? Why are there total three umpires in cricket? This is all because, it is written in the rules of cricket. The rules are the foundation, without which there could be no cricket. The rules are fundamental to all games or sports.

In the same way, the Constitution is also fundamental to a nation and its governance. For instance, think: Why is India a democratic country? Why do we have the parliamentary form of government, not the presidential form of government like in the USA? Why do we have two Houses in the Parliament? Why is India a secular country? Why do Indians have Fundamental Rights? Why is the Prime Minister the most powerful person in India? Why don't we elect the Governor of a state? Why do the governments work for the welfare of the people? This is all because, it is written in the Constitution of India, which is a tool that makes the government system work. It is a living document. It connects the land, the people and the governments of India.

The term 'Constitution' has been originated from the **Latin word 'Constituere', which means 'to establish', or 'to construct' or 'to form'.** Later in French, it found its use as 'Consitutio' for regularities and orders. The New Oxford American Dictionary defines Constitution as 'a set of fundamental principles or established precedents according to which a state or other organization is governed'. According to Greek philosopher Aristotle, 'Constitution is the way in which citizens, who are component parts of the state are arranged in relation to one another.'[1]

The Constitution of India means 'a set of fundamental principles or established precedents according to which the Indian state is governed'. **The Constitution of India is 'the mother law' or 'the basic law' or 'fundamental law' 'the supreme law (the law of all laws)' of the nation.** This is because of the following reasons: (a) all other laws are based on this, that is, all laws, rules and regulations must be in line with the Constitution of India; (b) it is the source of power

---

[1] Aristotle (384–322 BC) was a Greek philosopher and scientist. He gave this definition in his famous work *Politics*.

to the government, that is, it determines the form, structure, governance, powers and functions of the governments; (c) in India, no one is above the Constitution, that is, everyone including the President and the Prime Minister has to follow the Constitution and must work under the Constitutional provisions; and (d) the people of India are the source of power to the Constitution, that is, the Constitution derives its power from the people (Figure 1.1).

FIGURE 1.1
THE BASIC CONCEPTS OF THE CONSTITUTION OF INDIA

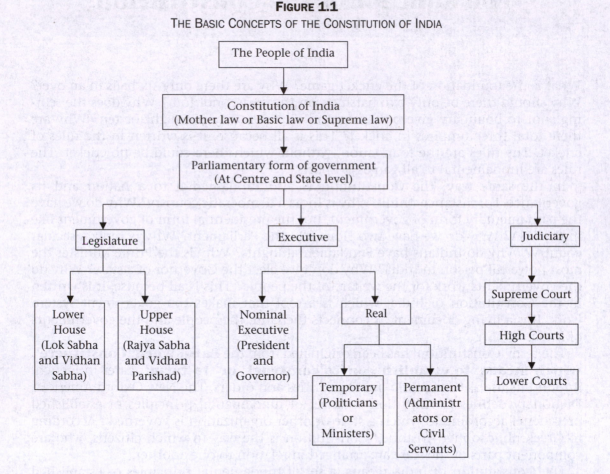

2

The Making of the Constitution

The making of the Indian Constitution can be studied under two heads: first is the evolution of the Constitution and second is the Constituent Assembly.

THE EVOLUTION OF THE INDIAN CONSTITUTION

The Indian Constitution has evolved over a period of time and is in a document form. Its nascent steps can be traced back to the British rule. Table 2.1 chronologically briefs the important landmarks in the Indian constitutional development during the British rule in India.

CONSTITUENT ASSEMBLY

Generally, a 'Constituent Assembly (CA)' means a group of persons that draft a constitution for a country. Over a period of time, most of the Indian freedom fighters demanded the British Government to form a Constituent Assembly in order to frame the Constitution of India. The historical development of the Constituent Assembly is as follows:

1934: **M. N. Roy was** the **first person** to propose a Constituent Assembly to frame the Constitution of India.

1935: For the first time, the **Indian National Congress (INC)** officially demanded for the creation of a Constituent Assembly to the British Government.

1940: **In principle,** the British Government accepted to form a Constituent Assembly to frame the Constitution of India in the **'August Offer of 1940'.**

1946: Finally, under the provision of the **'Cabinet Mission Plan-1946',** the British Government created the Constituent Assembly to frame the Constitution of India.

According to the Cabinet Mission Plan-1946, the strength of the Constituent Assembly was to be 389. The Constituent Assembly was to be a **'partly elected'** (296 members were to be indirectly elected by British India) and **'partly nominated'** (93 members were to be nominated by the princely states) body. Interestingly, **Mahatma Gandhi** did not join the Constituent Assembly.

At the first meeting of the Constituent Assembly, that is, on 9 December 1946, it elected **Dr Sachchidanand Sinha,** the oldest member, as **the temporary President** of the Constituent Assembly. On 11 December 1946, it elected **Dr Rajendra Prasad as the President** and **H. C. Mukherjee as the Vice-President** of the Constituent Assembly. **Sir B. N. Rau** was appointed as the **'Constitutional Advisor'** to the Constituent Assembly. Two days later, the **'Objectives Resolution'** was moved by **Jawaharlal Nehru** in the Constituent Assembly, which was later accepted as **the Preamble to the Constitution** in its modified form.

The Constituent Assembly not only framed the Constitution of India, but also worked as **a legislative organ** till the first Parliament was elected in 1951. As the legislative organ, the Constituent Assembly performed certain important functions, which are as follows:

1. It confirmed India's membership in the **Commonwealth of Nations** in May 1949.
2. It adopted the **National Flag** on **22 July 1947.**
3. It adopted the **National Anthem and National Song** on **24 January 1950.**
4. It elected **Dr Rajendra Prasad** as the **first President of India** on 24 January 1950.

The Constituent Assembly took **'2 year, 11 months and 18 days'** and had **11 sessions** to complete the process of writing the Constitution of India. **On 26 November 1949,** the Constitution of India was adopted. The members and the President of the Constituent Assembly signed on the Constitution of India. It contained **a Preamble, 22 Parts, 395 Articles and 8 Schedules** on the day it was adopted. It **came into force on 26 January 1950.** This day is referred to as the **'Date of Commencement of the Constitution of India'** and is celebrated in India as the **'Republic Day'.**

India commenced its Constitution on 26 January and celebrates this day as the Republic Day because of the historical importance of this date. It was on **26 January 1930,** when the **First Independence Day or** *Purna Swaraj* **(complete independence)** was celebrated.

The Constituent Assembly constituted various committees to deal with different works. Of them, the **'Drafting Committee'** was the most important one as it prepared the draft of the new Constitution. It included the following **seven members:**

1) Dr B. R. Ambedkar as its Chairman.
2) Alladi Krishnaswamy Iyer
3) Dr K. M. Munshi
4) T. T. Krishnamachari
5) N. Madhava Rau
6) N. Gopalaswamy Ayyangar
7) Sir Syed Muhammad Saadulla

Other important committees and their chairpersons are listed in Table 2.2.

Dr B. R. Ambedkar (first Law Minister), played a very important role in drafting the Constitution of India. He is recognized as the **'Father of the Constitution of India'** or **'Chief architect of the Constitution'.**

TABLE 2.1
CONSTITUTIONAL LANDMARKS AND THEIR IMPORTANT PROVISIONS DURING THE BRITISH RULE IN INDIA

Constitutional Landmarks	Important Provisions
Regulating Act of 1773	• First step of the British Government to control the affairs of the East India Company (EIC). • Designated the Governor of Bengal as the Governor General of Bengal. The first Governor General of Bengal was Lord Warren Hastings. • This Act established the Supreme Court in Calcutta (now Kolkata).
Pitt's India Act of 1784	• Indian affairs came under the direct control of the British Government. • Distinguished the commercial and political functions of the EIC. • Established the 'Board of Control' to manage political affairs and allowed the 'Court of Directors' to manage commercial affairs of the EIC. So this Act established 'Double Governments' in India.
Charter Act of 1833	• Designated the Governor General of Bengal as the Governor General of India. The first Governor General of India was Lord William Bentinck. • Created the Government of India for the first time having authority over British India. • Ended the activities of the EIC as a commercial body.
Charter Act of 1853	• Separated the legislative and executive functions of the Governor General's Council. • Created the 'Central Legislative Council (CLC)' that functioned as a 'mini-Parliament'. • For the first time, this Act introduced local representation in the CLC. • Introduced the open competition system to recruit civil servants.
Government of India Act of 1858 (enacted after the 'First War of Independence' in 1857)	• Rule of the EIC ended and the British Crown started to rule India directly. • Changed the Governor General of India title to 'Viceroy of India'. The first Viceroy of India was Lord Canning. • Ended the system of 'Double Governments'. • Secretary of State for India was appointed who had complete control over the administration of India.

(Table 2.1 Contd)

(Table 2.1 Contd)

Constitutional Landmarks	Important Provisions
Indian Councils Act of 1861	• Initiated the process of decentralization. • Seeds of representative institutions or parliamentary system sown in India. • Introduced Indians as non-official members of the legislative council. • Gave ordinance making power to the Viceroy of India.
Indian Councils Act of 1892	• Introduced indirect elections. • Enlarged functions of the legislative council.
Indian Councils Act of 1909 (or Morley–Minto Reforms)	• Change the name of the CCL to 'Imperial Legislative Council (ILC)'. • For the first time, it associated Indians with the Executive Councils of the Viceroy and the Governor. Satyendra Prasad Sinha was the first Indian to join this council. • Introduced the communal representation of Muslims by accepting the 'separate electorate' for them. It legalized communalism. Lord Minto is called the father of communal electorate.
Government of India Act of 1919 (or Montagu–Chelmsford Reforms)	• Introduced direct election for the first time in India and gave voting rights to a few people on the basis of property, tax or education. • Separated provincial and centre subjects. • Provincial subjects were divided into. First, the 'transferred subjects' (administered by the Governor with the help of state ministers responsible to the state legislature); second, the 'reserved subjects' (administered by the Governor and his Executive Council without any responsibility towards the state legislature). This dual system of government is called 'dyarchy'. • For the first time, it introduced bicameralism at the Centre, that is, the ILC was replaced by the Upper House and Lower House. • Established the Central Public Service Commission in 1926.
Government of India Act of 1935	• Provided for the establishment of 'All-India Federation'. • Introduced three lists, that is, federal, state and concurrent subject lists. • Abolished dyarchy in provinces and introduced it at the Centre. • It gave provincial autonomy and established responsible governments at provinces. • It introduced bicameralism at provincials. • Established the Reserve Bank of India (RBI).
Indian Independence Act of 1947	• Ended the British rule in India and declared India as an independent and sovereign state from 15 August 1947. • Divided British India and created two independent dominions, that is, India and Pakistan. • Gave options for the Indian princely states to join either India or Pakistan or to remain independent.

TABLE 2.2
THE IMPORTANT COMMITTEES OF THE CONSTITUENT ASSEMBLY AND THEIR CHAIRPERSONS

Chairpersons	Committees
Sardar Vallabhbhai Patel (the 'Iron Man of India' and the first Home Minister)	• Provincial Constitution Committee • Advisory Committee on Fundamental Rights and Minorities
Jawaharlal Nehru (the first Prime Minister of India)	• Union Powers Committee • States Committee • Union Constitution Committee
Dr Rajendra Prasad (the first President of India)	• Rules for Procedure Committee • Steering Committee

Salient Features of the Constitution

The salient features of the Constitution, as stands today, are as follows:

1. Lengthiest Written Constitution in the World

Constitutions are classified into two categories: a **written Constitution,** which is codified, such as the Indian Constitution or the American Constitution; and an **unwritten Constitution,** which is not codified, such as the British Constitution.

Originally, that is, in 1949, the Indian Constitution contained **a Preamble, 22 Parts, 395 Articles and 8 Schedules.** Currently, it contains **a Preamble, 25 Parts, about 465 Articles and 12 Schedules.** No other nation's written Constitution is as elaborate, detailed and comprehensive as that of India. So, the Constitution of India is the **lengthiest of all written Constitutions in the world.** The American Constitution is the oldest and shortest written Constitution in the world. It contains only seven Articles.

2. Universal Adult Franchise (UAF)

The British Indian Government adopted the principle of limited franchise, that is, it gave voting rights to only men, the rich and educated people, not to all. But the Constitution of India incorporated the principle of UAF, according to which **all citizens who have completed 18 years of age have the 'Right to Vote'** without any discrimination on the basis of religion, cast, race, sex, wealth, literacy and so on.

3. Secular State

The Constitution of India has no religious colour. It equally respects and promotes all religions and does not discriminate between any two religions. The Constitution of Pakistan, on the other hand, is not secular as it promotes only the Islam. It also implies that a non-Muslim cannot become the President of Pakistan.

4. Borrowed from Various Sources

The founding fathers of the Indian Constitution studied Constitutions of various nations and the Government of India Act 1935, and borrowed some important provisions; details are given in Table 3.1.

5. Neither Rigid nor Flexible but a Blend of Both

Modern Constitutions are also classified into rigid and flexible. **A rigid Constitution** is the one to which making any amendment or change is very difficult as it requires a special procedure, such as the USA Constitution. **A flexible Constitution** is the one to which making any amendment or change is easy as it requires a simple procedure, such as the British Constitution.

The Indian Constitution is neither rigid nor flexible, but a blend of both, because some provisions of it can be amended by a special or complex procedure like **'special majority'** (the support of a majority of more than 50 per cent of the total membership of the House and/or the majority or support of two-thirds of the members of the House present and voting) in the Parliament and ratification by half of the total states in India; both are difficult tasks, for example, making any amendment to the Fundamental Rights. On the other hand, some other provisions of the Constitution can be amended by a simple procedure like **'simple majority'** (the support of a majority of more than 50 per cent members of the House present and voting) in the Parliament, for instance, the creation of new states.

6. Quasi-federal System

Based on the nature of the relation between the national government and regional governments, modern governments are mainly classified into the **'federal system of government'** and the **'unitary system of government'**. A **'federal government'** is the one where the Constitution itself divides the powers between the national government and the regional governments, and both governments function independently in their respective jurisdictions, for example, the USA, Canada, Brazil and Russia.

A **'unitary government'** is the one where the Constitution vests all powers only in the national government, and if at all regional governments exist, they derive their powers and authority from the national government, not by the Constitution, for example, Britain, Japan, Spain and China (see Figure 3.1).

The Indian Constitution provides the provision for the federal system of government. Important federal characteristics of the Indian Constitution are as follows:

(i) **Written constitution:** The Indian Constitution is a codified one, that is, it is systematically arranged with assigning a number to its each provision, such as Parts and Articles.

(ii) **Bicameralism:** The Indian Constitution provides for two Houses in the Parliament, that is, the Rajya Sabha (representing the states at the national level) and the Lok Sabha (representing the people of India). A **unicameral system** means, having only one House in the legislature.

(iii) **Division of powers:** The Constitution of India divides the power between the Centre and the states through three lists; they are as follows:

    (a) **Union list:** It consists of **100 subjects** on which the Central government has the exclusive powers to make laws, for example, railways, passport and Visa, defence, external affairs and so on.

FIGURE 3.1
ILLUSTRATING THE CONCEPT OF FEDERAL GOVERNMENT AND UNITARY GOVERNMENT

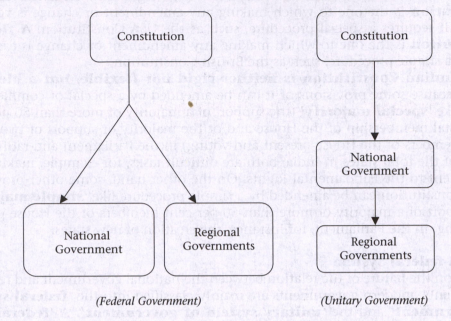

(b) **State list:** It consists of **61 subjects** on which the state governments have the exclusive power to make laws. For example, police, local governments, agriculture, intoxicating liquor, libraries and so on.

(c) **Concurrent list:** It consists of **52 subjects** on which both the Central and the state governments have the common powers to make laws. For example, criminal laws, forests, education, health and so on. **In case of any conflict between a Central law and a state law on any subject in the concurrent list, the Central law prevails.**

If any subject does not come under these three lists, then it is considered as **'residuary subject'** and the Indian Constitution has **vested residuary powers on the Central government.**

(iv) **Supremacy of the Constitution:** In India, the **Constitution is Supreme;** no one is above the Constitution. Each aspect of governance, laws, executive actions, judicial function and so on must be in line with the Constitution. Conversely, in Britain, the Parliament is supreme, not the Constitution.

(v) **Independent judiciary:** Our Judiciary derives its powers directly from the Constitution and its independence from the legislative and the executive organs of the government.

(vi) **Rigid Constitution:** Some provisions of the Constitution are very difficult to amend.

(vii) **Dual polity:** It means having two governments: one at the national level (Central government) and another at the regional level (state governments). But now, the Indian Constitution provided for the third-level of governments, that is, the local governments.

The Indian Constitution also has certain characteristics of the **unitary government.** These are as follows:

(i) **Single Constitution:** Unlike in a federal country, where the Centre and states have their own Constitutions, India has only one Constitution that is commonly applied for both the Centre and the states.

(ii) **Single citizenship:** A citizen is the one who enjoys the **'civil and political rights'** of a country. In India, the people have **only single citizenship, that is, 'Indian citizenship'** and all Indian citizens enjoy the same civil and political rights all over the country. But in the USA, there are two citizenships: one is American citizenship and another is state citizenship.

(iii) **Strong Central government:** Although the Indian Constitution divides the powers between the Centre and the states, **the Centre is more powerful than the states.** For instance, the Central list has more and important subjects, the Centre's law can override the states' laws and so on.

(iv) **Destructible states:** The Central government can divide any existing state, reunite two or more states, rename any state, abolish and create any state and alter the boundaries of any state. Hence, the state governments in India do not enjoy territorial security as they are destructible by the Central government. But in the USA, states are indestructible.

(v) **Flexible Constitution:** Some provisions of the Indian Constitution are simple to amend.

(vi) **All India services:** There are three kinds of services in India. First is the **'state service'** where a person works for the state government throughout his/her career, for example, *Tehsildar*, Village Accountant, State Road Transport Corporation bus drivers and so on. Second is the **'Central service'** where a person works for the Central government throughout his/her career, for example, employees of Indian Railways, India Post, army personnel and so on. Third, **'all India service'** where a person can work for both the Central and the state governments during his/her career, for example, Indian Administrative Services, Indian Police Services and Indian Forest Services; these people hold top-level positions in the administration, for example, Secretary, Police Commissioner and so on; they are appointed by the Centre that has ultimate control over them, but the state governments have only immediate control.

(vii) **Appointment of the Governor:** The Governor is the head of the states and he also acts as an agent of the Centre in a state. The President has the power to appoint and remove a Governor. The Governor has Veto powers over the state legislature bills. But in the USA, the Governor is elected by the people.

(viii) **Emergency provisions:** During a 'national emergency' period, the Indian government may transform itself into the unitary form of government as the Central government becomes more powerful.

(ix) **Integrated judicial system:** Each level of courts in India, that is, the Supreme Court, the High Courts and the Lower Courts are organized on the principle of hierarchy and all of them interpret both the Central and the state laws. This is also called the **single system of courts.** In the USA, there is a double system of courts where, the state-level courts interpret only state laws and the Federal Court only Central laws.

(x) **Integrated audit system:** Audit means the inspection or verification of financial accounts. The Comptroller and Auditor General (CAG) of India, who is appointed by the President, audit both the Centre and the state accounts. **He also acts as an agent of the Parliament**.

(xi) **Integrated election system:** The Election Commission of India conducts elections for the Parliament as well as the state legislatures. The Central government has power over this Commission, but the state government does not.

Therefore, as the Indian Constitution has both the 'federal and unitary governments' characteristics', it is described it as **'quasi-federal', 'cooperative federalism'**, 'bargaining federalism', 'federation with strong centralizing tendency' and 'federal in form, but unitary in spirit'. Interestingly, **the term 'federation' has nowhere been used in the Indian Constitution**.

7. Parliamentary Government

On the basis of the kind of relation between the executive and the legislature, the contemporary democratic governments are classified into two. One is the **presidential form of government,** in which, the **executive is not accountable or responsible to the legislature** and both organs work independent of each other on the principle of **'separation of powers',** for example, the USA, Brazil, Chile and so on.

The other is **the parliamentary form of government or the prime Ministerial government,** in which, the **executive is accountable or responsible to the legislature** and both organs work on the principle of **'cooperation and co-ordination',** for example, India, Japan, Britain, Pakistan, Mongolia and so on.

The parliamentary government is also known as **'Westminster model of government'** because the name of the place where the British Parliament is located in London is 'Westminster'. Also, the parliamentary government was originated in the Kingdom of Great Britain.

The Constitution of India established the parliamentary form of government in India. Its important features are as follows:

(i) **Collective responsibility:** The Central Council of Ministers (executive) is collectively responsible to the Parliament (legislature) particularly to the Lok Sabha.

(ii) **Majority party rule:** A political party that enjoys the majority in the Lok Sabha can form the government at the Centre.

(iii) **Dual executives:** It means the presence of the **'nominal executive'**, that is, the President and the Governor; and **'real executive'**, that is, the Prime Minister (PM) and his Council of Ministers.

(iv) **Double membership:** A member of the executive (a minister) is also a member of the legislature (the Parliament).

(v) **Leadership of the PM and the CM:** The PM is the leader of the nation and the CM is the leader of the state.

(vi) **Dissolution of the Lower House:** This means ending the term of the Lower House (Lok Sabha or Vidhan Sabha) after the end of their terms or in other cases. The Upper House is a permanent body, so it is not subjected to dissolution.

8. Three-level governments

Originally, the Constitution of India provided for only dual polity, that is, the Centre and the state governments. But the 73rd and 74th amendments added the third-level governments, that is, the local governments, such as panchayats and municipalities. Such a feature is not found in any other Constitutions of the world.

9. Constitutional Bodies

A Constitutional body is the one that is **directly established by the Constitution** itself and that derives power from the Constitution, not by the Centre or the states. They are independent from the executive, the legislature and the judiciary. For examples, the Election Commission of India, the State Election Commission, Union Public Service Commission (UPSC), Karnataka Public Service Commission (KPSC), National Commission for SC and so on.

10. Fundamental Rights: Please refer to Chapter 5.

11. Directive Principles of State Policy (DPSP): Please refer to Chapter 6.

12. Fundamental Duties: Please refer to Chapter 7.

13. Judicial system: Please refer to Chapters 19 and 20

14. Emergency provisions: Please refer to Chapter 24.

TABLE 3.1

SOURCES FROM WHERE THE PROVISIONS HAVE BEEN BORROWED AND THEIR CONTRIBUTIONS
TO THE INDIAN CONSTITUTION

S. No.	Source	Borrowed Features
1.	Government of India Act 1935	– Judiciary – **Public Service Commissions** – Federation system – **Office of Governor** – **Emergency provisions**
2.	British Constitution	– **Parliamentary system** – **Single citizenship** – **Cabinet system** – **Prime Minister and Council of Ministers** – **The rule of law** – **Bicameralism and Lower House more powerful** – Legislative procedure – **Writs** – **Council of Ministers responsible towards the Lok Sabha** – Parliamentary privileges
3.	USA Constitution	– Written Constitution – **Fundamental Rights** – **Judicial review** – **Independence of judiciary** – Removal of Supreme Court and High Court Judges – Post of Vice-President
4.	Australian Constitution	– **Concurrent list** – **Centre–state relationship** – **Joint sitting of the two Houses of the Parliament**
5.	Soviet Constitution (erstwhile USSR, now Russia)	– **Fundamental Duties** – Ideals of justice (social, economical and political) in the Preamble
6.	German Constitution	– **Suspension of Fundamental Rights** during emergency
7.	South African Constitution	– **Procedure for amendment of the Constitution** – Election of a Rajya Sabha member
8.	Japanese Constitution	– Procedure established by law – **Federation with the strong Centre** – Appointment of the Governor of a state
9.	Canadian Constitution	– **Vesting residuary powers in the Central government** – Advisory jurisdiction of the Supreme Court
10.	Irish Constitution	– **Directive Principles of State Policy** – Method of election of the President – Nomination of members to the Rajya Sabha
11.	French Constitution	– **Republic** – **Ideals of liberty, equality and fraternity** in the Preamble

THE PARTS OF THE INDIAN CONSTITUTION AT A GLANCE

S. No.	Parts	Subject	Articles
1.	**I**	The Union and its territory	1–4
2.	**II**	Citizenship	5–11
3.	**III**	Fundamental Rights	12–35
4.	**IV**	Directive Principles of State Policy	36–51
5.	**IVA**	Fundamental Duties	51A
6.	**V**	The Union Chapter I—The Executive Chapter II—Parliament Chapter III—Legislative Powers of the President Chapter IV—The Union Judiciary Chapter V—The Comptroller and Auditor-General of India	52–151 52–78 79–122 123 124–147 148–151
7.	**VI**	The States Chapter I—General Chapter II—The Executive Chapter III—The State Legislature Chapter IV—Legislative Power of the Governor Chapter V—The High Courts in the States Chapter VI—Subordinate Courts	152–237 152 153–167 168–212 213 214–232 233–237
8.	**VII**	Repealed by Const. (7th Amendment) Act, 1956	
9.	**VIII**	The Union Territories	239–242
10.	**IX**	The Panchayats	243–243O
11.	**IXA**	The Municipalities	243P–243ZG
12.	**X**	The Scheduled and Tribal Areas	244–244A
13.	**XI**	Relations between the Union and the States Chapter I—Legislative Relations Chapter II—Administrative Relations	245–263 245–255 256–263
14.	**XII**	Finance, Property, Contracts and Suits Chapter 1 - Finance Chapter 2 - Borrowing Chapter 3 - Property, Contracts, Liabilities, suits, obligations and rights Chapter 4 - Right to Property	264–300A 264–291 292–293 294–300 300A
15.	**XIII**	Trade, Commerce and Intercourse within the Territory of India	301–307
16.	**XIV**	Services under the Union and the States Chapter I—Services Chapter II—Publics Service Commissions	308–323 308–314 315–323
17.	**XIVA**	Tribunals	323A–323B
18.	**XV**	Elections	324–329A

(Table Contd)

(Table Contd)

S. No.	Parts	Subject	Articles
19.	**XVI**	Special Provisions Relating to Certain Classes	330–342
20.	**XVII**	Official Language Chapter I–Language of the Union Chapter II—Regional Languages Chapter III—Language of the Supreme Courts, High Courts, etc. Chapter IV—Special Directives	343–351 343–344 345—347 348—349 350—351
21.	**XVIII**	Emergency Provisions	352–360
22.	**XIX**	Miscellaneous	361–367
23.	**XX**	Amendment of the Constitution	368
24.	**XXI**	Temporary, Transitional and Special Provisions	369–392
25.	**XXII**	Short Title, Commencement [Authoritative Text in Hindi] and Repeals	393–395

THE SCHEDULES OF THE INDIAN CONSTITUTION AT A GLANCE

Schedules	Subject
First	The list of states and union territories.
Second	Provisions relating to the allowances, emoluments, privileges and so on of the President, Governors of States, Speaker and the Deputy Speaker of the House of the People and the Chairman and the Deputy Chairman of the Rajya Sabha and so on.
Third	Forms of Oaths and Affirmations for ministers, MPs, Judges and so on.
Fourth	The allocation of seats to the states and union territories in the Rajya Sabha.
Fifth	The administration and control of scheduled areas and scheduled tribes.
Sixth	The administration of tribal areas in the states of Assam, Meghalaya, Tripura and Mizoram.
Seventh	Division of powers between the Centre and the states through the Union list, the states list and the concurrent list.
Eighth	List of **22 recognized languages** — Assamese, Bengali, Bodo, Dogri, Gujarati, Hindi, Kannada, Kashmiri, Konkani, Maithili, Malayalam, Marathi, Meitei, Nepali, Oriya, Eastern Panjabi, Sanskrit, Santali, Sindhi, Tamil, Telugu, Urdu.
Ninth	Validation of certain Acts and Regulations.
Tenth	Disqualification of MPs, MLAs/MLCs on the ground of defection.
Eleventh	The powers, authorities and responsibilities of panchayats.
Twelfth	The powers, authorities and responsibilities of municipalities.

Section II

Constitutional Framework

4
CHAPTER

Preamble to the Constitution of India

INTRODUCTION

The Preamble means, a preliminary introduction to a Constitution usually explaining its purpose. The introductory part of the Indian Constitution, that is, the Preamble, underscores **the objectives, goals and basic principles** of the Constitution. The Preamble is a modified form of the **'Objectives Resolution' moved by Jawaharlal Nehru in the Constituent Assembly in 1946**. The entire Constitutional framework is **based on the** basic **philosophy and fundamental values of the Preamble.** The Preamble is the expression of **dreams, ambitions and inspirations** of the founding fathers of the Constitution. It is for these values of the Preamble that Indian freedom fighters made immense scarification. Because of this, now we are enjoying these values. The Preamble is described as the **'identity card of the Constitution', 'key to the Constitution', 'the soul of the Constitution'** and **'the horoscope of our sovereign, democratic and republic nation'.**

'We, **THE PEOPLE OF INDIA**, having

Solemnly resolved to constitute India into a

SOVEREIGN SOCIALIST SECULAR DEMOCRATICS REPUBLIC and

To secure to all its citizens:

JUSTICE, Social, Economical and Political;

LIBERTY of thought, expression, belief, faith and worship;

EQUALITY of status and of opportunity; and to promote among them all;

FRATERNITY assuring the dignity of the individual and the unity and *integrity* of the Nation;

IN OUR CONSTITUENT ASSEMBLY this **twenty-sixth of November, 1949,**

do HEREBY ADOPT, ENACT ABD GIVE TO OURSELVES THIS CONSTITUTION.'

According to Laxmikanth,

The Preamble discloses the following four important things:

(i) **Source of authority of the Constitution:** The Preamble states that, the Constitution derives its authority from **the people of India.**

(ii) **Nature of Indian state:** That is, sovereign, socialist, secular, democratic and republican polity.

(iii) **The objective of the Constitution:** That is, to deliver justice, liberty, equality and fraternity for all the people of India.

(iv) **Date of adoption:** The Constitution of India was adopted on **26th November 1949.**[1]

The Government derives its powers from the Constitution, not by the Preamble. **The Preamble is non-justiciable,** which means that citizens cannot seek justice in the courts of law based on the Preamble. The Supreme Court in the Kesavananda Bharti Case in 1973 held that **the Preamble is a part of the Constitution,** and it is subjected to the amending powers of the Parliament. Using this power, the Parliament enacted the **42nd Constitutional Amendment Act in 1976,** which added **three new words: 'Socialist', 'Secular' and 'Integrity'** to the Preamble.

THE IMPORTANT WORDS OF THE CONSTITUTION

The following are the important terms of the Indian Constitution:

(i) **Sovereign:** India is a sovereign country, which means that it is not dependent on any other country. It is completely independent to carry out its internal and external affairs. And for Indians, there is no authority above the Indian Constitution.

(ii) **Socialist:** In simple words, socialism means that a state or the government has the ownership of all the means of production and distribution of areas, such as capital, industry, service sector and so on. In **'communistic socialism',** there are no private properties at all, and all means of production and distribution are owned by the state, for example, the former Soviet Union.

India has **'democratic socialism'** where both private sectors and the State have the ownership of the means of the production and distribution of some areas, for example, education, health, telecast, food and the like. However, in some areas, private entities are strictly prohibited and that are completely owned by the State, for example, atomic energy, Indian Railways and so on. Indian socialism has the features of both Marxism and Gandhism, but it is largely tilted towards Gandhism.

---

[1] M. Laxmikanth (2010), *Indian Polity for Civil Service Aspirants*, 3rd edition, McGraw-Hill Publications, New Delhi, p. 4.1.

(iii) **Secular:** India has no official religion like that of Pakistan and Nepal, as it is a secular country, that is, it does not preserve or promote any one religion. The Constitution of India has a positive concept of secularism; accordingly, it equally gives respect to all religions, irrespective of their strengths and weaknesses.

(iv) **Democratic:** A democratic nation is the one where the **people possess the supreme power.** Democracy means the **rule of the people or the majority rule.** There are two kinds of democracy. First is the **'direct democracy'** in which the people rule directly by using their supreme power, through tools such as referendum (a popular vote by the electorate whether to approve a specific legislative Act), recall (the act of removing an elected person by the people) and plebiscite (a vote by the electorate determining the public opinion on a question of national importance), for example, in Switzerland. Second is the **'indirect democracy or representative democracy'** in which the elected persons rule the people as the people delegate their supreme power to these persons through periodic elections for a fixed term; for example, in India, the Members of Parliament and the Members of Legislative Assembly rule the country on behalf of the people.

India has the **'representative (or indirect) parliamentary democracy'**; accordingly, the people elect parliamentarians through periodic elections, to rule the country for a fixed term, and **the executive is responsible to the Parliament for its acts.** The USA has 'the representative (or indirect) presidential democracy'; accordingly, the people elect the President through periodic elections to rule the country for a fixed term, and the President (executive) is not responsible to the Parliament for its acts.

(v) **Republic:** In a **monarchy,** the position of the head of the State held by a person is based on hereditary rights like that in the UK. In a **republican country,** the position of the head of the State held by a person is based on the mandate or will of the people, not on hereditary rights. It also means that the people possess political sovereignty, not the king or the queen. **India is a republican country, which means that** the **head of the Indian State, that is, the President of India,** is elected by the people through periodic election for a fixed term and that position does not belong to any hereditary succession and is open to all Indian citizens.

(vi) **Justice:** Justice means, 'the quality of being just or fair'. The Constitution of India gives fair treatment to all the people of India without any discrimination on the basis of religion, caste, sex, race, wealth, place of birth and so on. Justice involves punishing wrongdoers, to prevent illegal activities or crimes in future and to provide relief or compensation to the victims of wrong acts. The Constitution of India ensures social, economic and political justice to all its citizens:

(a) **Social justice** implies equal treatment to all citizens and the absence of privileges to any one section of the society on the basis of religion, caste, sex, race, wealth, place of birth and so on, and uplift of the weaker section of the society, such as the Scheduled Caste, Scheduled Tribe, Other Backward Class, women and children.

(b) **Economic justice** implies non-discrimination between the people on the basis of their economic status and treating all equally, irrespective of one's property, income and wealth, and providing opportunities for the economically weaker people to improve their economic conditions.

(c) **Political justice** implies that all citizens should have equal political rights and equal opportunity to get all political offices and have equal voice in government affairs. It politically empowers the weaker sections of the society. Because of this provision, even a tea seller could become the Prime Minister of India.

(vii) **Liberty:** It implies the **freedom of choice** or **immunity from the arbitrary exercise of authority.** The Indian Constitution does not restraint on individual activities and provides opportunity for all to **develop their personalities;** and it gives the liberty of thought, expression, belief, faith and worship through Fundamental Rights. But our liberty is not absolute and qualified or restricted on reasonable grounds.

(viii) **Equality:** It implies to provide equal opportunity and status to all citizens without any discrimination and **absence of special rights** or provisions for any section of the society. The Preamble provides for equality of status and opportunity. Generally speaking, in India, around 70 per cent of the all forms of wealth are with just 20 per cent of the population, 70 per cent of the population have 30 per cent of wealth and the rest 10 per cent of the population have nothing. This is also applicable to political or social fields. This is called unequal society. It is the duty of the government to reduce this inequality as stipulated by the Constitution.

(ix) **Fraternity:** It implies the **sense of brotherhood** or friendship and mutual support within a group of people. Through this concept, the Preamble ensures the following: first, **the dignity of individual;** and second, **the unity and integrity** (territorial and psychological) of India. As all Indian citizens are the children of *Bharat Mata* or mother India, we are also siblings to each other. The Constitution of India promotes a feeling of fraternity by providing the **'single citizenship'** to all Indians.

5

Fundamental Rights and Their Limitations

INTRODUCTION

Part III of the Indian Constitution—**from Articles 12 to 35**—is about the Fundamental Rights (FRs). In **1255, King John of England** issued **Magna Carta,** that is, the first ever written 'Charter of Rights' that gave certain political rights to rebellious English barons. So, **Part III of the Indian Constitution** is described as the **'Magna Carta of India'** as it gives certain written FRs to the people of India. These rights are called fundamental because of the two reasons. First, these rights are **directly given and protected by the mother law of the land, that is, the Constitution of India** itself to its people. In other words, these rights are neither given by the legislature nor by the executive, not even by the judiciary, but by the Constitution of India. Second, these rights are very essential for the overall development (intellectual, material, moral and spiritual) of individuals.

The FRs are the issues between the State[1] and the people. That is, there are certain limitations on the power of the State to provide certain basic rights to the people. The FRs are intended to **prevent authoritarian, dictatorship or the despotic rule** in the nation; and to **protect the freedom and liberties** of the people against the encroachment by the State. They promote **'political democracy'** and seek to establish **'a government of laws and not of men'**. Because of this, **the FRs are superior to ordinary laws.**

Originally, the Indian Constitution provided a total of **seven FRs**, but the **44th Amendment Act 1978 erased the 'Right to Property' as a FR** and now it is just a **legal right** under Article 300-A. There are a total of **six FRs**. The overview of the six FRs has been given in Table 5.1.

---

[1] According to Article 12 of the Constitution, the term 'the State' means the Government of India, the governments of states, the Parliament, the state legislature, all local and other authorities within the territory of India and under the control of the Government of India.

CHARACTERISTICS OF THE FUNDAMENTAL RIGHTS

The important characteristics of the FRs are as follows:

1. They are **justiciable,** that is, these rights can be enforceable by the law of the courts. The **Supreme Court and the High Courts act as the protector, defender and guarantor of the FRs of the people** against arbitrary actions of the executives and acts of the legislature. **In case of the violation of the FRs, one can directly approach either the Supreme Court or a High Court to seek justice.**
2. **The FRs are guaranteed against the State only.** In case of violation of any FRs by an individual or private person, the ordinary legal remedies are available, but not the Constitutional remedies under Article 32.
3. These rights are **not absolute, but qualified,** which means that the State can impose reasonable restrictions on them. But these restrictions can be reviewed by the courts. To illustrate, Section 66A of 'the Information and Technology Act 2000' enacted by the Parliament prohibited the people to make any objectionable comment in social media, such as the Facebook, Twitter and so on. However, the Supreme Court declared Section 66A as unconstitutional or *ultra-vires* as it was against the 'Right to Speech and Expression' of the people.
4. The **Parliament has the power to amend any FRs;** so the FRs are not permanent.
5. The FRs can be **suspended** during a national emergency period, except **the rights given under Articles 20 and 21.**
6. The application of the FRs is limited to armed forces, intelligence agencies (RAW and IB) and where the martial rule or military rule is imposed.
7. Non-Indians like foreigners in India also enjoy few FRs given under Articles 14, 20, 21, 23, 25, 27 and 28, but not all six FRs.
8. Some FRs are negative in the sense that they impose certain restrictions on the State, such as those provided by Articles 14, 15(1) and 20, and some FRs are positive, such as those provided by Articles 25, 29(1) and 30(1) as these confer certain privileges on the people.

AN OVERVIEW OF THE FUNDAMENTAL RIGHTS

In the following, we have provided a brief overview of the FRs provided by the Indian Constitution:

RIGHT TO EQUALITY

Article 14: Equality before Law and Equal Protection of Law

According to Article 14, the State shall not deny equality to any person before the law or the equal protection of the laws within the territory of India. This right is based on the **'Rule of Law'.** According to it, no man shall be punished except for a breach of law and all are equal before the law.

Equality before the law means that all persons are equal before the law: no special privileges are there for any one person; there is equal subjection of all people to the ordinary laws of the land; and no person (rich or poor, male or female, official or non-official) is above the law. **Equal protection of law implies** right to equality of treatment in equal circumstances; the similar application of the same laws for all the people who are in similar situations should be treated alike without any discrimination.

Exceptions:

1. **The President of India and the Governors of states**

   (a) Enjoy immunity from criminal proceedings in all courts of laws, but they do not enjoy immunity from civil proceedings.
   (b) Cannot be arrested or imprisoned during their term of office.
   (c) Are not answerable to any courts for their use of powers and performance of duties.

2. **Foreign officials:** The heads of the states, ambassadors, diplomats and the officers of International Organization such as the United Nations enjoy immunity from criminal and civil proceedings in India.

3. **MPs, MLAs and MLCs:** They are not liable to any proceedings (civil or criminal) in any courts for anything said or any acts in their respective houses.

4. **Media persons:** They are not liable to any proceedings (civil or criminal) in any courts for publishing true reports on the business of the Parliament or the state legislatures.

Article 15: Prohibition of Discrimination on Certain Grounds

According to Article 15, the State shall not discriminate against any citizen on the grounds of **religion, race, caste, sex or place of birth.** It also prohibits discrimination against the people in public places, such as shops, hotels, restaurants, theatres, public wells, tanks, roads, parks and so on by both the State and private individual. This is intended to eliminate the abuse of Indian social systems. However, the State can make discrimination between the people on other than these grounds and in certain exceptions.

Exceptions:
The State can make special provisions for the improvement of conditions of **Scheduled Castes (SCs), Scheduled Tribes (STs), women and children**. For example, free elementary education for children, reservation for women in elections of the local governments, reservation for SCs and STs in all the elections and jobs and so on.

Article 16: Equality of Opportunity in Matters of Public Employment

Article 16 provides the provision for the **equality of opportunity in public employment** for all citizens without any discrimination on the grounds of religion, race, caste, sex, descent and place of birth or residence. It also means that the State can make discrimination on other than these grounds, such as education, physical qualities, and professional experience and technical expertise and the like.

Exceptions:

1. The Parliament can prescribe **residential condition** for certain employment for the advancement of backward regions. For example, Article 371-J provides a special status to the Hyderabad–Karnataka region, under which governments should provide reservations for candidates belonging to this region in the state government jobs.
2. The State can provide or reserve jobs for people of a particular religionin their respective **religious institutions.** For example, in the Wakf Board of the Government of Karnataka, most jobs are allocated for the Muslim people.
3. The State can provide reservations for **backward classes, such SCs, STs and OBCs,** in government jobs if they are not adequately represented in the states.

In any government recruitment, the total quota of reservation **should not exceed 50 per cent of total vacancies;** out of this, **27 per cent is reserved for OBCs, 15 per cent for SCs and 7.5 per cent for STs.** The '**creamy layer**' (well-advanced section within the OBCs) is excluded from the reservation quota. At present, the income limit for the OBC category **is 6 lakh per annum.**

Article 17: Abolition of Untouchability

Article 17 abolishes 'untouchability' in all forms. Under the Protection of Civil Rights Act 1955, any form of practice of untouchability is a punishable offence. A person convicted under this act is disqualified for the election of the Parliament or state legislatures.

Article 18: Abolition of Titles

Article 18 prohibits the State to confer titles **(except military and academic titles)** on anybody, that is, either to an Indian or to a foreign national. It also prohibits Indians from accepting any titles from any foreign state and a foreigner in India should get the consent of the President of India to receive any title from a foreign country.

Under this Article, the hereditary titles, such as Maharaja, Rai Bahudur, Raja Bahadur, Dewan and so on are banned. However, civilian awards, such as Bharat Ratna, Padma Vibhushana and so on are not considered as titles under this Article, and these awards are prohibited to use as a suffix or prefix with the name.

RIGHT TO FREEDOM

Article 19: Protection of Six Rights

Article 19 provides **six FRs** in the nature of freedom **only to the Indian citizens; however, the State can impose reasonable restrictions on these rights** on certain grounds. The six rights are as follows:

1. **Article 19(1): Freedom of Speech and Expression**
   According to it, all citizens have the right to express freely their opinions, beliefs, views in the verbal and non-verbal forms. This right includes freedom of silence, freedom of press, right to safeguards against telephone tapping, right to telecast (like electronic media), right to the demonstration, **but not, right to strike,** right to support a bandh called by political or other organizations, right to know about Government work and so on.
   Restrictions: The sovereignty and integrity of India, security of the State, friendly relations with foreign states, public order, decency or morality, contempt of court, defamation and incitement to an offence.

2. **Article 19(2): Freedom of Assembly**
   All citizens have the **right to assemble peacefully and without arms in public places;** these include right to hold public meetings and demonstrations.
   Restrictions: Sovereignty and integrity of India and public order that also involves maintaining of traffic in the concerned areas.

3. **Article 19(3): Freedom of Association**
   All citizens have the **right to form associations and unions, including** the formation of companies, political parties, societies, trade unions, clubs and so on.
   Restrictions: Sovereignty and integrity of India and public order and morality.

4. **Article 19(4): Freedom of Movement**
   All citizens have the **right to move freely throughout the territory of India.**
   Restrictions: Interest of general public and the protection of interest of any ST.

5. **Article 19(5): Freedom of Residence**
   All citizens have the **right to reside and settle in any part of the country either temporarily or permanently.**
   Restrictions: Interest of general public and the protection of interest of STs.
   Articles 19(4) and 19(5) imply that India is one unit with regard to Indian citizens, and it helps to promote fraternity and national feeling among Indians.

6. **Article 19(6): Freedom of Profession, Occupation, Trade or Business**
   All citizens have the **right to practise any profession, to do any occupation, business or trade.** This right does not confer right to practise illegal, immoral and dangerous work.
   Restrictions: Prescribing professional or technical qualifications that are necessary for practising any profession or carrying on any occupation, trade or business, enabling the State to carry on any trade, business, industry or service to the exclusion (wholly or partially) of citizens.

Article 20: Protection in Respect of Conviction for Offences

Article 20 provides three provisions to protect the rights of all accused and convicted persons. These are as follows:

1. **No ex-post facto law:** It means that no person shall be punished or convicted retrospectively; in other words, an accused person shall be convicted according to the present law that is in force. It also means that no greater punishment shall be given for an offence than prescribed by the law in force.
2. **No double jeopardy:** It means that no person shall be prosecuted and punished for the same offence more than once.
3. **No self-incrimination:** It means that no person accused of any offence shall be compelled to be a witness against himself. It implies two things: first, prosecution must prove guilty of accused and second, an accused person need not make any statement against his/her own will.

Article 20 **cannot be suspended** even during an **emergency period.**

Article 21: Protection of Life and Personal Liberty

This Article guarantees to all citizens and non-citizens that **no person shall be deprived of his life or personal liberty except according to the procedure established by law.** It is covered against arbitrary or illegal activities of **both the executives and the legislature.** The Supreme Court declared that following rights are the part of Article 21.

Right of women to be treated with decency and dignity; right to health; right to emergency medical aid; right to timely medical treatment in government hospitals; right to privacy; right to shelter; right to livelihood; right to live with human dignity; right to decent environment and protection against hazardous industries; right to free legal aid; right to against solitary confinement; right to speedy trial; right to information; right to travel abroad; right against delayed execution; right against handcuffing; right against inhuman treatment; right against bonded labour; right to fair trial; right of prisoner to have necessities of life; right against public hanging; right to hearing; right to reputation; right to not to be driven out of the State; right against custodial harassment.

Article 21-A: Right to Education

The **86th Constitutional Amendment Act 2002** added **new Article 21-A** to the Constitution, which provides for **'free and compulsory education' for all children between the age of 6 and 14 years.** This is a significant step to achieve the nation's aim to educate all children as it made elementary education as an FR.

Article 22: Protest against Arrest and Personal Detention

Detention of persons without a trial was common practice in the colonial rule. But the Indian Constitution provided for the following safeguards to the people in case of arrest and detention:

1. No person shall be arrested and/or detained **without informing about ground of arrest** and detention.
2. Arrested/detained person has the **right to consult and defended by a lawyer.**
3. Arrested/detained person **should be produced before the nearest magistrate within 24 hours by** the authorities.
4. Authorities should release an arrested person within 24 hours if the magistrate does not authorize for further detention.

However, these rights are not applicable in case of preventative detention[2] and aliens.

RIGHT AGAINST EXPLOITATION

Article 23: Prohibition of Traffic in Human Beings and Forced Labour

This Article protects citizens and non-citizens against the **State and private** person from **traffic in human beings** (means **selling or buying** of men, women and children like goods; *devadasis;* **slavery** and immoral traffic in women and children including prostitution), **forced labour** (means compulsory work without remuneration). However, the State can impose limitations on these rights for public purpose or service like military service for which it is not bound to pay.

Article 24: Prohibition of Employment of Children in Factories, etc.

This Article **prohibits the employment of children below the age of 14 years in factories, mines and in other hazardous places like construction**

---

[2] Preventative detention means, detaining a person by authorities for a specific period of time may be a day, one week or three months, in order to prevent him/her from committing any offence or crime.

work, etc.[3] However, the employment of children in non-hazardous places is not prohibited but regulated by the Government. Also, the employment of children in restaurants, hotels, dhabas, resorts, teashops, theatres and so on is banned.

RIGHT TO FREEDOM OF RELIGION

Article 25: Freedom of Conscience and Free Profession, Practice and Propagation of Religion

According to this Article, all persons are equally entitled to the freedom of conscience (inner freedom to mould relation with God or creatures), freely profess (declaration of religious belief freely and openly), practice (performance of religious worships, rituals, ceremonies and so on) and propagation (spreading of one's religious beliefs to other). However, freedom to propagate religion **does not include any right to forcible conversions** of religion and it is a punishable offence.

Article 26: Freedom to Manage Religious Affairs

Under this Article, every religious denomination and sections has the right to **establish and maintain institutions** for religious and charitable purpose, to manage their own affairs in matters of religion, to acquire own and administer property.

Rights under Articles 25 and 26 are subjected to public order, morality, health and other provisions related to the FRs.

Article 27: Freedom Not to Pay Taxes for Religious Promotion

Article 27 says that **no person shall be compelled to pay any taxes for promotion and maintenance of any particular religion or religious denomination.** Also, the State can use the collected tax to promote all religions as it is in line with the secularism.

Article 28: Freedom Not to Attend Religious Instruction

Article 28 completely **forbids providing any religious instruction in any educational institution, wholly owned by the State.** In other recognized institutions and aided by the State, there will be freedom for all to participate or not to participate in religious instructions and worships.

---

[3] The Government has planned to completely prohibit the all forms of employment of children below the age of 18 years by enacting 'Child and Adolescent Labour (Prohibition) Act 2012'.

CULTURAL AND EDUCATIONAL RIGHTS

Article 29: Protection of Interests of Minorities

Article 29 guarantees all citizens, residing anywhere in India and having a distinct language, script or culture, the right to conserve the same. No citizen shall be denied admission to any educational institutions maintained or aided by the State on grounds of religion, race, caste or language. This article provides protection to both religious minorities and linguistic minorities.

Article 30: Right of Minorities to Establish and Administer Educational Institutions

Under this Article, all minorities (linguistic or religious) have the right to **establish and administer** educational institutions of their choice and the State shall not discriminate against any educational institutions run by minorities in granting aid. However, **the State can regulate these institutions** in order to protect the public interest.

RIGHT TO CONSTITUTIONAL REMEDIES

This is the sixth FR. **Article 32** provides for such a mechanism. It made **the Supreme Court and the High Courts as a defender and guarantor of the FRs** of the citizens. Under this Article, right to protect the FRs and seek remedy for their violations, is also an FR in itself. **Dr B. R. Ambedkar** described Article 32 as 'an article without which this Constitution would be a nullity. **It is the very soul of the Constitution and the very heart of it'.**

The provisions of Article 32 are as follows:

1. In case of the violation of the FRs, an aggrieved citizen has the **right to directly move to the Supreme Court or a High Court** by appropriate proceedings to protect his/her FRs and get a remedy.
2. The Supreme Court (under **Article 32)** and the High Courts (under **Article 226)** has the **power to issue WRITS,** direction or orders for the enforcement of any FR. There are total five writs (a written order of the Courts) in India. They are as follows:

   (i) **Habeas Corpus:** The literal meaning of 'Habeas Corpus' is **'to have the body of'.** This writ can be issued by the **higher courts (the Supreme Court** and High Courts) against **the public as well as private persons to produce the body** of detained persons. The objective of this writ is to **bring the detained person before the court and examine the legality of detention; if the detention** of a person is found to be illegal, then the courts will set that person free. This writ is a **bulwark of individual liberty against arbitrary** or illegal or forced detention.

(ii) **Mandamus:** The literal meaning of 'Mandamus' is, **'we command'.** It is a command issued by the **higher courts to public officials or body (not for a private person)** including inferior courts, asking them **to do their public duty that they have refused or failed to do.**

(iii) **Prohibition:** The literal meaning of 'Prohibition' is, **'to forbid'. This writ is issued by a higher court to a lower court or a tribunal to prevent it from exceeding its jurisdiction or usurping a jurisdiction that it does not possess. This writ is available only against judicial and quasi-judicial bodies and not available** against the legislative and the executive bodies and a private individual or body.

(iv) **Certiorari:** The literal meaning of 'Certiorari' is, **'to be certified' or 'to be informed'. This writ is issued by a higher court to a lower court or a tribunal, either to transfer a case pending before a lower court to itself or squash (nullify) the order of lower courts. This writ is available only against the judicial, the quasi-judicial and the executive bodies and not available** against the legislative and a private individual or body.

Unlike 'Prohibition', which is only preventative (prevent the wrongdoings of lower courts), 'Certiorari' is both preventative and curative (give relief in case of wrong judgement of lower courts).

(v) **Quo-Warranto:** The literal meaning of 'Quo-Warranto' is, **'by what authority or warrant'. This writ is issued by a higher court to examine the legal claim of a person to a public position or office. It prevents** a person holding a public office which he/she is not legally entitled or qualified to hold. This write **can be claimed by any person** whether he/she is personally aggrieved or not. This write can be issued against substantive public office, not against a ministerial or private office.

TABLE 5.1
OVERVIEW OF SIX FUNDAMENTAL RIGHTS

No.	Fundamental Rights	Article No.	Details
	General	12	Definition of State
		13	Laws inconsistent with or in derogation of the FRs
		14	Equality before law and equal protection of law
		15	Prohibition of discrimination on the basis of religion, race, caste, sex or place of birth
I	**Right to Equality** (Articles 14–18)	16	Equality of opportunity in matters of public employment
		17	Abolition of untouchability
		18	Abolition of titles

(Table 5.1 Contd)

(Table 5.1 Contd)

No.	Fundamental Rights	Article No.	Details
II	**Right to Freedom** (Articles 19–22)	19	Protection of certain rights like the freedom of speech
		20	Protection in respect of conviction for offenses
		21	Protection of life and personal liberty
		22	Protection against arrest and detention in certain cases
III	**Right against Exploitation** (Articles 23 and 24)	23	Prohibition of traffic in human beings and forced labour
		24	Prohibition of employment of children in factories, etc.
IV	**Right to Freedom of Religion** (Articles 25–28)	25	Freedom of conscience and free profession, practice and propagation of religion
		26	Freedom to manage religious affairs
		27	Freedom as to payment of taxes for promotion of any particular religion
		28	Freedom as to attendance at religious instruction or religious worship in certain educational institutions
V	**Cultural and Educational Rights** (Articles 29 and 30)	29	Protection of interests of minorities
		30	Right of minorities to establish and administer educational Institutions
VI	**Right to Constitutional Remedies** (Article 32)	32	Remedies for enforcement of rights conferred by this Part

6
CHAPTER

Directive Principles of State Policy

INTRODUCTION

Part IV of the Constitution—**from Article 36 to 51**—is about the Directive Principles of State Policy (DPSPs). The DPSPs are **directions given by the Constitution to the Government** to implement certain policies whenever it can in future. The purpose of the DPSPs is to set up **certain social and economic goals** before the lawmakers with a view to establish **social-economic democracy** in the country. **Dr B. R. Ambedkar described the DPSPs as 'novel features'** of the Indian Constitution. It is also described as **'Conscience of the Constitution'**.

THE CHARACTERISTIC OF THE DPSPs

The important characteristics of the DPSP are as follows:

1. The DPSPs resemble the **'Instrument of Instructions'** of the **Government of India Act 1935.**
2. The DPSPs are meant to promote **the welfare state** and are aimed at **realizing the ideals of justice, liberty, equality and fraternity** as **mentioned in the Preamble** of the **Constitution.**
3. **The DPSPs are 'fundamental to the governance of the country'** and 'it shall be the duty of the State to keep in mind about these principles while making policies and laws'.
4. **The DPSPs are non-justiciable,** which means that they are not legally enforceable in a court for their violation. So the Government cannot be forced to implement them; this is because in order to implement all the DPSPs, the State should require lots of financial resources, which is not possible to get in a limited period.

SANCTIONS BEHIND THE DPSPs

Although the DPSPs impose **moral obligation on the Government** to apply them, what if the Government ignores these DPSPs while making laws and policies as stipulated in the Constitution? What if the Government does not implement these policies? It is clear that the DPSPs are non-justiciable, so one cannot approach a court to enforce them. The answer is: The real sanction behind the DPSPs is **'political sanction', that is, the public opinion.** Dr B. R. Ambedkar said, 'A government which rests on popular vote can hardly ignore the DPSPs while shaping its policy. If any government ignores them, it will certainly have to answer for that before the electorate at the election time.'

CLASSIFICATION OF THE DPSPs

On the basis of the content, the DPSPs are divided into the following three categories:

1. **Socialistic Principles:**
   These principles are based on the socialism and aim to **promote social and economic justice,** and establish the **welfare state** and **democratic socialist state.** They direct the state:

   (i) To promote the **welfare of the people** by promoting a social order permeated by social, economic and political justice and to **reduce inequality** in income, status, facilities and opportunities.

   (ii) To secure the right to an adequate means of livelihood for all citizens, men and women equally, as well as **equal pay for equal work for both men and women.** The State should work to prevent the concentration of wealth and the means of production in a few hands, and try to ensure that the ownership and control of the material resources are distributed to best serve the common good; and opportunities for children to development in a healthy manner; and the preservation of the health and strength of workers and children against forcible abuse.

   (iii) To provide **free legal aid to the poor.**

   (iv) To secure the right to work, to education and to public assistance for unemployed, old-aged, sick and disabled persons.

   (v) To make provision for just and **humane condition of work and maternity relief.**

   (vi) To secure **living wage, social and cultural opportunities** for all workers and a **decent standard of life.**

   (vii) To promote the **participation of workers in management** affairs in industries.

   (viii) To improve the **public health** and to increase the level of nutrition and the living standard of the people.

2. **Gandhian Principles:**
   These principles are derived from the **Gandhian ideology.** Some of the dreams and ideas of our Father of Nation were incorporated into the DPSPs. They direct the State:

   (i) To organize **village panchayats** with providing sufficient powers to them so that they can function as units of self-government.

(ii) To promote **cottage industries** on an individual and the co-operation basis in rural areas.

(iii) To protect the **weaker section of the society** (SCs, STs, OBCs, women and children) from social injustice and exploitation and promote their educational and economic development.

(iv) To ban the consumption of **intoxicating drugs and drinks** like alcohol, cigarettes, opium and so on, which are injurious to health.

(v) To **prohibit the slaughter of cows, cattle, calves** and improve their breed.

3. **Liberal–intellectual Principles:**
   These principles are based on the ideologies of liberalism. They direct the State:

   (i) To secure the **Uniform Civil Code (UCV)** for all citizens throughout the country. The UCV means that **a codified civil law that is commonly applicable to all Indian citizens, irrespective of their religions, castes, races, places and so on;** for instance, at present, there are different laws on marriage for Hindus and Muslims in India, but under the UCV, there will be a similar law on marriage for all Indian citizens, irrespective of their religions, castes, races, places and so on.

   (ii) To provide **early childhood care and education** for all children until they complete 14 years.

   (iii) To promote **agriculture and animal husbandry** on modern scientific lines.

   (iv) To protect and improve the **environment,** including forests and wildlife.

   (v) To protect the important **historic and national monuments,** places and objects.

   (vi) To **separate the judiciary and the executive** in the public services of the State.

   (vii) To promote **international peace, security;** maintain good relation between nations; to respect international law, treaty and obligation; to support the settlement of international disputes by arbitration.

CONFLICT BETWEEN FUNDAMENTAL RIGHTS AND DIRECTIVE PRINCIPLES

On the one hand, the State has a moral obligation to implement the DPSPs that are non-justiciable, whereas, on the other hand, the Supreme Court acts as a protector of the FRs that are justiciable. So when the State wants to implement a DPSP and if it affects any FRs, it gives rise to a conflict between the Parliament and the Supreme Court.

In the Champakam Dorairajan Case 1951, the Supreme Court held that, in case of a conflict between the FRs and DPSPs, the FRs prevail over the DPSPs, and the Parliament can amend or take away any FRs in order to implement any DPSPs'. But in the Golakanath Case 1967, the Supreme Court held that the Parliament cannot amend or take away any FRs in order to implement any DPSPs.

In the famous **'Kesavananda Bharti Case 1973',** the **Supreme Court laid down the 'Basic Structure' of the Constitution,** and in the **Minerva Mills Case 1989,** the Supreme Court declared that 'the Indian Constitution is founded on the bedrock of the **balance between the FRs and the DPSPs'.**

Thus, **the present status** of the conflict between the FRs and the DPSPs is that the **FRs are superior to the DPSPs and the Parliament can amend or take away any FRs in order to implement any DPSPs but without disturbing the Basic Structure of the Constitution.**

RELEVANCE OF THE DPSPs

Although the DPSPs do not have a legal force to enforce, they are highly relevant to the overall interest of the country. As Dr B. R. Ambedkar rightly said, 'The DPSPs have great value because they lay down that; the goal of Indian polity is **'economic democracy'** as distinguished from political democracy.' M. C. Chagla, a former Chief Justice of India, had said, 'If all these principles are fully carried out, our country would indeed be a heaven on the earth.'

The following points illustrate the relevance of the DPSPs:

1. They (DPSPs) lay down the **basic framework for the governance** and **social and economic goals** of the country and act as **a friend, guide and philosopher to the Government.**
2. They act like a general recommendation for the Constitution to the all Indian authorities and keep reminding them about **our social and economical goals.**
3. They **help the Courts to interpret laws** in complex situations.
4. They **provide stability to the Government policies** despite the change of the political party in power in the country over a period of time.
5. They serve as a **barometer to measure the performance of the Government** and facilitate the speedy implementation of social democratic and economic policies in the country.
6. They empower the opposition parties to exercise control over the ruling party if the latter deviates from the DPSPs.

7

CHAPTER

Fundamental Duties

INTRODUCTION

Fundamental Duties (FDs) means the moral work given by the mother law of the nation (Constitution) that needs to be obliged by all the citizens. Although rights and duties go hand in hand, the **original Constitution of India (in 1949) did not contain FDs** but only the FRs. In other words, the original Constitution gave only FRs to the people and not any FDs. But after the experience of Emergency in 1975, the then political leaders decided to include certain FDs in the Constitution.

So based on the recommendation of the **'Sardar Swaran Singh Committee 1976'**, the Government of India incorporated the FDs in the Constitution by enacting the **42nd Constitutional Amendment Act in 1976.** This act **added a new part,** that is, **PART VI-A,** to the Constitution, which consists **only one Article,** that is, **Article 51-A.** This act added 10 FDs to the Constitution, but 86th Constitutional Amendment Act in 2002 added one more FD. At present, **Article 51-A involves total 11 FDs** for all Indian citizens; they are as follows:

1. To **abide by the Constitution** and respect its **ideals and institutions,** the **National Flag** and the **National Anthem.**
2. To cherish and follow the **noble ideals** which inspired our **national struggle for freedom.**
3. To uphold and protect the **sovereignty, unity and integrity** of India.
4. To defend the country and render **national service** when called upon to do so.
5. To promote **harmony and the spirit of common brotherhood** amongst all the people of India, transcending religious, linguistic and regional or sectional diversities, and to **renounce the practices derogatory to the dignity of women.**
6. To **value and preserve** the rich heritage of the country's composite **culture.**
7. To protect and improve the **natural environment,** including forest, lakes, rivers and wildlife, and to have compassion for living creatures.
8. To develop the **scientific temper, humanism and the spirit of inquiry** and **reform.**

9. To **safeguard public property** and to **abjure violence.**
10. To **strive towards excellence in all spheres** of individual and collective activity so that the nation constantly rises to higher levels of endeavour and achievement.
11. To **provide opportunities for education** to his child or ward between the age of 6 and 14 years.

All the 11 FDs are **'non-justiciable';** so the government cannot take legal action against someone if any citizen fails to perform any one of these duties as **they are not enforceable in any court of law.** However, the FDs may be enforceable by law if the Parliament provides provisions for that. For instance, according to the Prevention of Insults to National Honour Act 1971, it is a punishable offence to show disrespect to the Constitution, the National Flag and the National Anthem.

These FDs impose **moral and civic duties** on the citizens, so it is the citizens' **moral (not legal) obligation to perform these duties.** Moreover, these duties are not new to the Indian society as these values are already there in Indian tradition, religion and mythology. Unlike the FRs, **the FDs are applicable to only Indian citizens,** not to non-citizens or foreigners. Thus, being Indian citizens, while enjoying our FRs, we must also be conscious about our FDs in order to facilitate the overall development of the nation.

Section III

Union Legislature, State Legislature and Electoral Process in India

8
CHAPTER

The Parliament

INTRODUCTION

The Parliament is the legislative organ of the Union Government, which enacts laws for the nation. India has the **'parliamentary form of government'** (also known as **'the prime ministerial government'** or the **'Westminster model of government'[1]**) where **the executive is responsible to the legislature.** The Parliament of India has a pre-eminent and key position in the Indian democratic political system. **Articles 79–122 of Part V** of the Constitution cover various aspects of the Parliament.

The Parliament consists **three parts,** namely **the President of India, the Lok Sabha and the Rajya Sabha. The President of India is an integral part of the Parliament, though he is not a member of either the Rajya Sabha or the Lok Sabha.** The Indian Parliament is **'bicameral legislature'** as it consists of two houses, that is, the Rajya Sabha and the Lok Sabha.

LOK SABHA

The Lok Sabha is also known as **'the house of the people', 'the lower house', 'the popular house' and 'the First Chamber'. The Lok Sabha represents the people of India as whole at the national level.** In other words, nearly 1.25 billion people of India are represented in the Lok Sabha.

The maximum strength of the Lok Sabha is **552 as fixed by the Constitution,** out of which **530** members represent the states, 20 the union territories (UTs) and **two members are nominated by the President** from the **Anglo-Indian community. At present,** the Lok Sabha consists in **545 members,** of whom **530** members represent the states, 13 members represent the UTs and **two** members represent the Anglo-Indian community.

The people of **India directly elect the members of the Lok Sabha** from **'territorial constituency'** from their respective states and UTs, according to the **'Universal Adult Franchise'.** Here, the **proportional representation system**

---

[1] The Westminster model of government was originated in Britain; the place where the British Parliament is located in London is known as 'Westminster', so the parliamentary form of government is also called 'The Westminster model of government'.

is not adopted. There is **a reservation for SC and ST people** in the election of Lok Sabha according to their population ratio.

Unlike the Rajya Sabha, **the Lok Sabha is not a permanent body but a temporary body as it is subjected to dissolution after the end of its term** or in other cases. **The term of the Lok Sabha as well as the term of its members is five years.** In other words, after the end of the five-year term of the Lok Sabha, all the 545 members of it will lose their membership, and they need to get the fresh mandate of the people through a General Election.

RAJYA SABHA

The Rajya Sabha is also known as **'the council of states', 'the upper house', 'the house of elders' and 'the Second Chamber'.** The Rajya Sabha **represents the states and UTs of India at the national level** and work for the interests of their people.

The maximum strength of the Rajya Sabha is **250** as fixed by the Constitution. Out of this, **238** members represent the states and the UTs (only Delhi and Puducherry) and **12 members are nominated by the President,** who are eminent personalities in the field of **literature, art, science and social service** (LASS). The **allocation of seats in the Rajya Sabha** to the states and UTs is mentioned in the **4th Schedule** of the Constitution.

The **members of the Rajya Sabha are indirectly elected,** that is, elected members of Vidhan Sabha or State Legislative Assemblies elect their respective representative member of the Rajya Sabha. For example, the representative members of Karnataka in the Rajya Sabha are elected by the MLAs of Karnataka.

The election to the Rajya Sabha is conducted according to the **'proportional representation system'** by means of **'single transferable vote'.** The seats in the Rajya Sabha are allocated to the states **based on their populations.** So more populous states such as Uttar Pradesh and Bihar have more representatives and less populous states like Tripura have fewer representatives in the Rajya Sabha (Table 8.1).

It must be noted that **the Rajya Sabha is a permanent body,** that is, a **continuing chamber** and **not subjected to dissolution.** But **one-third members of the Rajya Sabha get retired after every second year;** a retired member is eligible to become a member again. **The term of a member of the Rajya Sabha is six years, but there is no term for the Rajya Sabha** as it is a permanent body.

QUALIFICATIONS TO BECOME A MEMBER OF PARLIAMENT (MP)

In order to become a member of either the Lok Sabha or the Rajya Sabha, one should:

1. Be **a citizen of India.**
2. Have completed **30 years** of age in case of the **Rajya Sabha** and **25 years** of age in case of **the Lok Sabha.**
3. Have any other qualification as stipulated by the Parliament.

DISQUALIFICATIONS OF A MEMBER OF PARLIAMENT (MP)

An MP may lose his position if he/she

1. Holds any **office of profit** in the Government.
2. Voluntarily acquires the **citizenship of any other nation.**
3. Is an undercharged **insolvent.**
4. Is found to have **an unsound mind** by a court.
5. Gets the **imprisonment of two or more years** for any convicted offences; also, such person will be barred to contest any election for the **next six years** after the completion of his/her imprisonment.
6. Is proved to be the **guilty of corruption** or any other offences in the election.
7. Fails to provide details of **election expense** in a given time to the Election Commission of India.
8. Gets convicted of **encouraging enmity between** different groups.

Under the above circumstances, the **President of India** decides on the disqualification of an MP in consultation with the Election Commission of India and **his decision stands final.**

The **Speaker of the Lok Sabha** and **the Chairman of the Rajya Sabha** decide on the disqualification of their respective house members in case of **'defection',** but this decision is **not final** and can be questioned in the courts. If any MP voluntarily resigns from the political party from which he/she was elected, if he/she fails to follow the direction of his/her political party with regard to vote in the house, if any independent member or nominated member joins any political party, then such an MP may be disqualified under the **10th Schedule of the Constitution.**

CONDITIONS WHEN AN MP VACATES HIS/HER SEAT

An MP vacates his/her seat in the Parliament under the following conditions:

1. If he/she gets the **two Memberships,** that is,
   (i)   If a person is elected to both the Lok Sabha and the Rajya Sabha, his/her seat in the Rajya Sabha gets vacant if he/she does not indicate his/her preferred house within 10 days.
   (ii) If one member of a house is also elected to another house, his/her seat in the first house gets vacant.
   (iii) If one person secures two seats in any house, he/she will lose both the seats in case if he/she fails to indicate his/her preference to the house.
   (iv) If one person is elected to both the Parliament and a state legislature and does not vacate his/her seat in the state legislature within 14 days, then his/her seat in the Parliament gets vacant.

2. If he/she is **disqualified** under the **anti-defection law or 10th Schedule of the Constitution.**
3. If he/she **resigns** voluntarily for his seat in the house.
4. If he/she **does not attend meetings** of the house for 60 days without the permission of the house.
5. If his/her election to the house is declared void by the courts.

PRESIDING OFFICERS OF THE PARLIAMENT

Speaker of the Lok Sabha

The presiding officer of the Lok Sabha is the Speaker. Generally, when the term of the existing Lok Sabha ends or it is dissolved, the Speaker does not lose his office and continues till just before the first meeting of a new Lok Sabha. When the newly elected Lok Sabha meets for the first time, then the President of India appoints the senior most member of that house as **'the Speaker Pro Tem'** just to **administer the oath ceremony of the newly elected members and to make arrangements for the election of a new Speaker.**

The Lok Sabha elects the Speaker (also the Deputy Speaker) from amongst its members. The Lok Sabha is the sole authority to remove the Speaker (also the Deputy Speaker) **by passing a resolution** by an absolute majority with regard to that; thus, the Speaker **enjoys the security of tenure.** The Speaker can **resign** by submitting **his resignation** to the Deputy Speaker and vice versa.

As the presiding officer of the Lok Sabha, the Speaker's decision with respect to **parliamentary affairs is final** and cannot be questioned in the courts. He acts as the representative and Chief Spokesperson of the Lok Sabha and the protector of the power and privileges of the members of the Lok Sabha. He has the vested powers and responsibilities to smoothly conduct the business of the house. All the Chairmen of the Parliamentary Committees in the Lok Sabha are appointed by the Speaker and he directs their functions. (A list of the Speakers of the Lok Sabha has been provided in Table 8.2.)

The **Deputy Speaker acts as the Speaker** and performs his duties when the Speaker's position is **vacant** or the Speaker is **absent.** In other times, the Deputy Speaker takes part in the business of the house as an ordinary member. (Table 8.3 provides a list of the Deputy Speakers of the Lok Sabha.)

The Chairman of the Rajya Sabha

The presiding officer of the Rajya Sabha is the Chairman. **The Vice-President of India is the Chairman of the Rajya Sabha.** Whosoever becomes the Vice-President of India, he automatically becomes the Chairman of the Rajya Sabha, that is, the Vice-President of India is the *ex-offico* **Chairman** of the Rajya Sabha. **The Chairman of the Rajya Sabha is not a member of the Rajya Sabha.** It is possible to remove the Chairman of the Rajya Sabha from his office **only after removing him from the Vice-President position.** In case of **resignation, he submits the resignation to the President of India.** (In Table 8.4, a list of the Chairmen of the Rajya Sabha have been given.)

The powers and functions of the Chairman of the Rajya Sabha are similar to those of the Speaker of the Lok Sabha. As the presiding officer of the Rajya Sabha, the Chairman's decision with respect to the parliamentary affairs in the Rajya Sabha is final and cannot be questioned in the courts. He acts as a representative and Chief Spokesperson of the Rajya Sabha and the protector of the power and privileges of the members of the Rajya Sabha. He has the vested powers and responsibilities to smoothly conduct the business of the house. All the Chairmen of the Parliamentary Committees in the Rajya Sabha are appointed by the Chairman of the Rajya Sabha and he supervises their functions.

But the Speaker of the Lok Sabha enjoys **two special powers** that are not available to the Chairman of the Rajya Sabha. Those are as follows:

1. The Speaker of the **Lok Sabha decides whether a bill is a money bill or not.**
2. **The Speaker of the Lok Sabha presides over the Joint Sitting** of the two houses of the Parliament, not the Chairman of the Rajya Sabha.

It must be noted that, though the Rajya Sabha does not elect its Chairman, **its Deputy Chairman is elected by from amongst its members. The Deputy Chairman of the Rajya Sabha acts as its Chairman** when the Chairman position is **vacant** or the Chairman is **absent** or the Chairman **is acting as the President of India.** If the Deputy Chairman wishes to resign, then he must write to the Chairman. The Rajya Sabha can remove the Deputy Chairman from his office **by passing a resolution** with regard to that. (Table 8.5 lists the Deputy Chairmen of the Rajya Sabha.)

The **salary of the presiding officer of a house is determined by the Parliament** and the same is charged **on the consolidate fund of India;** it is not subjected to vote in the Parliament.

SESSIONS OF THE PARLIAMENT

In the following, we have discussed about various sessions of the Parliament:

1. **Session:** It means a time period between the first meeting of a house and its ending. The maximum gap between the two sessions of the house should not be more than **six months.** In other words, the Parliament should meet at least **two times in a year.** There are three sessions of the Parliament in a year. They are as follows:

   (i) **Budget Session** (February–May). It is the **longest** session.

    (ii) **Monsoon session** (July–September).

    (iii) **Winter session** (November–December). It is the **shortest** session.

2. **Sitting:** It means a time period of each meeting in a day. There are two sittings in a day, that is, morning sitting (11 AM–1 PM) and post-lunch sitting (2 PM–6 PM).

3. **Summoning:** It means **starting a session** of the Parliament.

4. **Prorogation:** It means **terminating or ending a session** of the Parliament. **The President of India** summons and prorogues the Parliament.

5. **Recess:** It means a **time period between prorogation and reassembling or summoning** of a house.

6. **Adjournment:** It means the **suspension of work in a sitting of the Parliament for a specific period of time,** such as few minutes, hours, days and weeks by the presiding officer of a house.

7. **Adjournment sine die:** It means **ending a meeting of the Parliament by the presiding officer** of a house for **an indefinite time period,** that is, without clarifying about the day of its reassembly.

8. **Dissolution:** It means **terminating a term of the Lok Sabha by the President,** which **ends the life of the existing Lok Sabha** and leads to a fresh election of the Lok Sabha. **The Rajya Sabha is the permanent body, so it cannot be dissolved**. The President can dissolve the Lok Sabha, when **it completes its five-year term** and in **other situations like** when no party secures a majority in the house or no party or parties are willing to form a government.

9. **Quorum:** It means **the minimal number of members required to be present in a house to conduct its business.** The quorum of the Parliament is **one-tenth** of the total strength in each house. In the Lok Sabha, it is 55 and in the Rajya Sabha, it is 25.

10. **Lame-duck session:** It is the one when the existing Lok Sabha meets for the last time after electing the new Lok Sabha. The exiting MPs, those could not get re-elected to the new Lok Sabha, are called as **'Lame-ducks'**.

TOOLS OF PARLIAMENTARY PROCEEDINGS

The following are the tools of the Parliamentary proceedings, which are also the **act tools of the legislature to exercise control over the executive:**

1. **Question Hour:** The **first hour of each sitting** of the Parliament on each day is allocated for the Question Hour—usually, from 11 AM–12 PM. This is a formal device available for the MPs to ask questions for ministers and the latter must give answers to those questions. There are three kinds of questions:

    (i) **Starred Question** that contains a star mark and such a question is answered orally; thus, the supplementary questions are allowed.

    (ii) **Unstarred Question** that needs a written answer and, hence, supplementary questions are not allowed.

(iii) **Short-notice Question** that can be asked by members by giving a notice of less than 10 days and needs to be answered orally.

2. **Zero Hour:** It **starts just immediately after the Question Hour** (that is, usually at 12 noon) and **ends when the regular business of a house is getting started.** This is an **informal device** available for the MPs to ask questions to ministers, that is, the members simply raise questions usually on an urgent public matter without following any procedure like that in the question hour.

3. **Calling Attention Motion:** It is meant to attract the **'attention of a minister'** on an urgent public matter by the MPs.

    Both, the Zero Hour and the Calling Attention Motion **are Indian innovations** in the Parliamentary proceedings.

4. **Adjournment Motion:** It is meant to attract the **'attention of the house'** on an urgent public matter by its members. It must be held at least for two-and-half hours, and it disturbs the regular business of the house. **Adjournment Motion is not applicable to the Rajya Sabha.**

5. **No Confidence Motion:** It is used by the members of the Lok Sabha to ascertain, whether or not, the Council of Ministers enjoys the confidence (or majority) of the Lok Sabha. If it is passed by the Lok Sabha, then the entire **Council of Ministers, including the Prime Minister will lose their official positions.** This is because, as per the Article 75 of the Constitution, the Council of Ministers are **collectively responsible to the Lok Sabha.** Thus, the Council of Ministers held their offices so long as they enjoy the majority support or confidence of the Lok Sabha.

    Motion of Thanks: In this motion, the MPs make discussion about preceding and upcoming year's policies and programmes of the Government as mentioned by the President in his speech in the Parliament.

6. **Half-an-Hour Discussion:** It is used when any important public matter is already discussed sufficiently in the Parliament, but still there are some requirements of certain clarifications on a matter of facts.

7. **Short-duration Discussion:** It is also called a two-hour discussion as time allocated for the discussion in this session must not be more than two hours. The MPs can raise questions under this tool to discuss about on an urgent and important public matter. There is no formal motion or voting in the house for the Half-an-Hour and Short-duration discussions.

BUDGET OR ANNUAL FINANCIAL STATEMENT (ARTICLE 112)

Article 112 of the Constitution is about the **'Annual Financial Statement'** or **'Budget',** which is **estimated expenditure and receipts in a financial year of the Government**. It is also considered as the financial policy of the Government for the upcoming year. The time period of **the Indian financial year is** from **1 April to 31 March.** The Central government has **two budgets,** namely the General Budget and the Railway Budget.

The President lays down a budget before each house of the Parliament. Without the recommendation of the President, **no 'demand for the grant'** (means the Council of Ministers seeks the approval of the Lok Sabha to draw money from the Consolidated Fund of India for expenditure in the form of demand which are decided by vote) shall be made. **The Rajya Sabha has no power** to vote on demand for grants. Money can be withdrawn from the Consolidated Fund of India only according to the **appropriation law** made with regard to that. Only an authority of law **can levy taxes. The Parliament cannot increase a tax but can reduce or abolish it.** The word 'budget' has **not been mentioned in any part of the Constitution.**

FUNDS

Three kinds of funds are provided by the Constitution of India. They are as follows:

1. **Consolidated Fund of India** (Article 266): To this fund, all receipts and payments of the Government of India are credited and debited, respectively. Money from this fund can be used by the Government of India, only according to the law of the Parliament.
2. **Public Account of India** (Article 266): This is the fund to which all other money received by the Government of India, except money credited to the Consolidated Fund of India, is credited, such as deposits in banks, provident funds and courts and so on. This fund is managed by the executive, not by the Parliament.
3. **Contingency Fund of India** (Article 267): In order to meet the unforeseen expenditure, the Parliament contributes a certain amount of money to this fund from time to time. This fund is managed by the executive (the President), not by the Parliament. On behalf of the President, this fund is held by the Finance Secretary.

BILLS OF PARLIAMENT

A bill is a proposed law or a statute in the form of a draft before it becomes a law. A **bill becomes an act only if the President of India signs it.** There are three kinds of bills that are introduced in the Parliament. They are as follows:

1. **Ordinary bill:** These bills relate to any matter other than financial matters. They can be originated in any house of the Parliament and both the houses of the Parliament have equal say with respect to these bills. There is a provision for Joint Sitting of the two houses of the Parliament in case of the ordinary bill.
2. **Money bill** (Article 110): These bills are related to the financial matters, such as tax, public spending and so on. **A money bill can be introduced only in the Lok Sabha** (not in the Rajya Sabha) **with the prior recommendation**

of the President. Whether a bill is a money bill or not is **decided only by the Speaker** of the Lok Sabha. The Rajya Sabha must return a money bill to the Lok Sabha with or without recommendations within 14 days; the Lok Sabha is not bound to follow the recommendations of the Rajya Sabha in this regard. The President can give his assent or withhold a money bill, but **he cannot return it** to the Parliament for reconsideration. There is no provision of Joint Sitting of the two houses of the Parliament in case of money bills as the Lok Sabha has the final say in this regard.

3. **Finance bill:** These bills are also related to the financial or fiscal matters, that is, revenue and expenditure, but different from the money bill. All money bills are a kind of financial bills, but all financial bills are not money bills. A financial bill can be **introduced only in the Lok Sabha** (not in the Rajya Sabha) with the prior recommendations of the President. But the Rajya Sabha and the Lok Sabha have **equal say** with respect to the financial bill like in case of the ordinary bill. There is a provision for the Joint Sitting of the two houses of the Parliament in case of the financial bill.

JOINT SITTING OF THE TWO HOUSES OF THE PARLIAMENT

Both the houses of the Parliament must agree on a bill and pass it separately in their respective houses before it can be sent to the President for his assent. If one house agrees to a bill and another house disagrees, then it is considered as a **deadlock** between the two houses of the Parliament.

In order to resolve such a deadlock, **the President of India summons a Joint Sitting** of the two houses of the Parliament, in which members of the both houses sit together and decide upon a deadlock **by voting.** As the Lok Sabha has more strength in numbers than the Rajya Sabha, **its decision prevails** in Joint Sitting. The Joint Sitting of the two houses of the Parliament is **presided over by the Speaker of the Lok Sabha;** in his absence, the **Deputy Speaker** of the Lok Sabha. And if the Deputy Speaker of the Lok Sabha is absent, then the **Deputy Chairman** of the Rajya Sabha presides over the Joint Sitting. It must be noted that, **the Chairman of the Rajya Sabha (the Vice-President of India) never presides over the Joint Sitting** of the two houses of the Parliament. The Joint Sitting of the two houses of the Parliament is not applicable in case of the **Constitutional Amendment Bill and the Money Bill.**

LEADERS IN PARLIAMENT

There is a leader and a leader of opposition in each house of the Parliament, and they are recognized by the presiding officers of the respective houses. **The Leader of the Lok Sabha** is the Prime Minister or a minister nominated by the Prime Minister in case the Prime Minister is not a member of the Lok Sabha. **The Leader of the Raja Sabha** is a minister nominated by the Prime Minister.

The **Leader of Opposition** in either the Lok Sabha or the Rajya Sabha is a **leader of the largest opposition party which secured at least one-tenth seats** of the total strength of that respective house. The Leader of Opposition leads the opposition party in the house and his main function is to criticize the acts and policies of the Government in a healthy and positive manner and to provide an alternative government. In the USA, the Leader of the Opposition is known as the 'Minority Leader'.

In the present **16th Lok Sabha (2014–2019),** so far, the **position of the Leader of Opposition is vacant** as no opposition party has secured at least one-tenth seats (55 seats) of the total strength of the Lok Sabha. So the leader of the single largest opposition party in the Lok Sabha, that is, the Congress Party (which secured 48 seats) is considered for the position of the Leader of Opposition.

PRIVILEGES OF PARLIAMENT AND ITS MEMBERS

The Parliament and its members enjoy certain privileges or special rights; these are called the individual privileges and the collective privileges, respectively.

1. **Individual privileges:** An MP enjoys **immunity from arrest** in civil cases (not in criminal cases) before and after 40 days of a session of the Parliament and when a session of the Parliament is going on. A **court cannot summon any MP** to give evidence as a witness during a session of the Parliament. An MP is not liable to any courts with respect to his/her speech or vote in the Parliament as he/she enjoys **freedom of speech.**
2. **Collective privileges:** The Parliament can punish its members or outsiders for the breach of its privileges by reprimand, imprisonment, and in case of its members, it even can suspend and forcibly expel them; publish about its debates and proceedings; prevent strangers attending from its proceedings; hold secret meetings. No member or person can be arrested in any house of the Parliament.

PARLIAMENTARY COMMITTEES

To effectively and efficiently handle its complex works, the Parliament constitutes various committees in its both the houses. These committees are either elected by the house or appointed by the presiding officers of a house. They function under the direction of the presiding officers of their respective house and submit reports to them. Temporary committees are called **'Ad hoc Committees'** that are constituted for specific purpose like parliamentary investigation. Permanent committees are called **'Standing Committees'** that work continuously and are established from year to year. Important Standing Committees are as follows: **'the Public Account Committee',** which is headed by the Leader of Opposition and its main function is to examine the report of the Comptroller and Auditor General of India (CAG);

'the Estimates Committee', which is headed by a ruling party member, who is not a minister, and its main function is to examine estimations mentioned in the budget by the executive. Other important committees are: Departmental Standing Committees, Committee on Public Undertakings, Business Advisory Committee and so on.

TABLE 8.1

ALLOCATION OF SEATS TO THE STATES AND UTS IN THE PARLIAMENT

States/UTs	No. of Seats in the Lok Sabha	No. of Seats in the Rajya Sabha
Andaman and Nicobar Islands	1	–
Andhra Pradesh	25	11
Arunachal Pradesh	2	1
Assam	14	7
Bihar	40	16
Chandigarh	1	–
Chhattisgarh	11	5
Dadra and Nagar Haveli	1	–
Daman and Diu	1	–
NCT of Delhi	7	3
Goa	2	1
Gujarat	26	11
Haryana	10	5
Himachal Pradesh	4	3
Jammu & Kashmir	6	4
Jharkhand	14	6
Karnataka	28	12
Kerala	20	9
Lakshadweep	1	–
Madhya Pradesh	29	11
Maharashtra	48	19
Manipur	2	1
Meghalaya	2	1
Mizoram	1	1
Nagaland	1	1
Orissa	21	10
Puducherry	1	1
Punjab	13	7

(Table 8.1 Contd)

(Table 8.1 Contd)

States/UTs	No. of Seats in the Lok Sabha	No. of Seats in the Rajya Sabha
Rajasthan	25	10
Sikkim	1	1
Tamil Nadu	39	18
Telangana	17	7
Tripura	2	1
Uttarakhand	5	3
Uttar Pradesh	80	31
West Bengal	42	16
Total	**545**	**245**

TABLE 8.2
LIST OF THE SPEAKERS OF THE LOK SABHA

S. No.	Name of Speaker	Term	Lok Sabha
1	Ganesh Vasudev Mavalankar	1952–1956	1st
2	M. A. Ayyangar	1956–1957	
		1957–1962	2nd
3	Sardar Hukam Singh	1962–1967	3rd
4	Neelam Sanjiva Reddy	1967–1969	4th
5	Gurdial Singh Dhillon	1969–1971	
		1971–1975	5th
6	Bali Ram Bhagat	1976–1977	
(4)	Neelam Sanjiva Reddy	1977–1977	6th
7	K. S. Hegde	1977–1980	
8	Balram Jakhar	1980–1985	7th
		1985–1989	8th
9	Rabi Ray	1989–1991	9th
10	Shivraj Patil	1991–1996	10th
11	P. A. Sangma	1996–1998	11th
12	G. M. C. Balayogi	1998–1999	12th
		1999–2002	13th
13	Manohar Joshi	2002–2004	
14	Somnath Chatterjee	2004–2009	14th
15	Meira Kumar	2009–2014	15th
16	Sumitra Mahajan	2014–Present	16th

TABLE 8.3
LIST OF THE DEPUTY SPEAKERS OF THE LOK SABHA

S. No.	Name	Term
1.	M. A. Ayyangar	1952–1956
2.	Sardar Hukam Singh	1956–1962
3.	S. V. Krishnamoorthy Rao	1962–1968
4.	R. K. Khadilkar	1967–1969
5.	G. G. Swell	1970–1977
6.	Godey Murahari	1977–1979
7.	G. Lakshmanan	1980–1984
8.	M. Thambi Durai	1985–1989
9.	Shivraj Patil	1990–1991
10.	S. Mallikarjunaiah	1991–1996
11.	Suraj Bhan	1996–1997
12.	P. M. Sayeed	1998–2004
13.	Charanjit Singh Atwal	2004–2009
14.	Karia Munda	2009–2014
15.	M. Thambi Durai	2014–Present

TABLE 8.4
LIST OF THE CHAIRMEN OF THE RAJYA SABHA

S. No.	Name	Terms
1.	Dr Sarvepalli Radhakrishnan	13 May 1952–12 May 1957
		13 May 1957–12 May 1962
2.	Dr Zakir Husain	13 May 1962–12 May 1967
3.	Shri Varahagir Venkata Giri	13 May 1967–3 May 1969
4.	Shri Gopal Swarup Pathak	31 August 1969–30 August 1974
5.	Shri Basappa Danappa Jatti	31 August 1974–30 August 1979
6.	Shri M. Hidayatullah	31 August 1979–30 August 1984
7.	Shri R. Venkataraman	31 August 1984–24 July 1987
8.	Dr Shanker Dayal Sharma	3 September 1987–24 July 1992
9.	Shri K. R. Narayanan	21 August 1992–24 July 1997
10.	Shri Krishan Kant	21 August 1997–27 July 2002
11.	Shri Bhairon Singh Shekhawat	19 August 2002–21 July 2007
12.	Shri Mohammad Hamid Ansari	11 August 2007–Present

TABLE 8.5

LIST OF THE DEPUTY CHAIRMEN OF THE RAJYA SABHA

S. No.	Deputy Chairman	Term
1.	S. V. Krishnamoorthy Rao	31 March 1952–2 April 1956
	S. V. Krishnamoorthy Rao	25 April 1956–1 March 1962
2.	Violet Alva	19 April 1962–2 April 1966
	Violet Alva	7 April 1966–16 December 1969
3.	B. D. Khobragade	17 December 1969–2 April 1972
4.	Godey Murahari	4 April 1972–2 April 1974
	Godey Murahari	26 April 1974–20 March 1977
5.	Ram Niwas Mirdha	30 March 1977–4 April 1980
6.	Shyamlal Yadav	30 July 1980–4 April 1982
	Shyamlal Yadav	28 April 1982–29 December 1984
7.	Najma Heptulla	25 January 1985–20 January 1986
8.	M. M. Jacob	2 February 1986–22 October 1986
9.	Pratibha Patil	18 November 1986–5 November 1988
7.	Najma Heptulla	11 November 1988–4 July 1992
	Najma Heptulla	10 July 1992–4 July 1998
	Najma Heptulla	9 July 1998–10 June 2004
10.	K. Rehman Khan	24 July 2004–2 April 2012
11.	P. J. Kurien	21 August 2012–Present

CHAPTER

State Legislatures

INTRODUCTION

The state legislature is the legislative organ of the state governments and the union territories (UTs; only Delhi and Puducherry), which enacts laws in their respective states/UTs. The Constitution provides for the **'parliamentary form of government'** at the state-level too. **Articles 168–212 of Part VI** of the Constitution cover various aspects of the state legislature.

The structure of the state legislatures throughout the country is not uniform, as 22 states have unicameral legislature, which consists **the Governor, the Vidhan Sabha (or State Legislative Assembly, SLA);** only six states have bicameral legislature, which consists **the Governor, the Vidhan Sabha (or SLA) and the Vidhan Parishad (State Legislative Council, SLC);** those six states are Karnataka, Andhra Pradesh, Maharashtra, Jammu and Kashmir, Uttar Pradesh and Bihar. Thus, **the Governor is an integral part of the state legislature, though he is not a member of either the Vidhan Sabha or the Vidhan Parishad.**

Unlike the Vidhan Sabha (SLA), having the Vidhan Parishad (SLC) is not mandatory for any states. However, **the Parliament can only create or abolish a Vidhan Parishad** in any state by simple majority, **based on a resolution passed by the concerned state legislature** by special majority.

VIDHAN SABHA

The Vidhan Sabha or simply the Assembly is also known as **'the house of the people', 'the lower house', 'the popular house' and 'the First Chamber'.** The Vidhan Sabha **represents the people of a state as a whole at the state level**.

The maximum strength of the Vidhan Sabha is **500** and the minimum strength is **60,** as fixed by the Constitution. But the states such as Goa, Sikkim, Arunachal Pradesh and Mizoram have less than 60 members.

The people **directly elect the members of the Vidhan Sabha** from 'territorial constituency' from their respective States/UTs according to **'Universal Adult Franchise'. One member is nominated by the Governor** from the **Anglo-Indian community** to the Assembly. Here, the **proportional representation**

system is not adopted. There is **a reservation for the SC and ST people** in the election of Vidhan Sabha according to their population ratio.

The Vidhan Sabha is not a permanent body, but a temporary body as it is subjected to dissolution after the end of its term or in other cases. **The term of the Vidhan Sabha as well as the term of its members is five years.** In other words, after the end of the five-year term of the Vidhan Sabha, all the members of it will lose their membership, and they need to get the fresh mandate of the people through a General Election.

VIDHAN PARISHAD

The Vidhan Parishad, simply the Council, is also known as **'the upper house', 'the house of elders' and 'the Second Chamber'.** Generally, the Vidhan Parishad represents an intellectual section of the states.

The maximum strength of the Vidhan Parishad is **one-third of the total strength of the Vidhan Sabha and the minimum strength is 40** as fixed by the Constitution; out of this, **238** members represent the states and the UTs. The maximum strength of the Vidhan Parishad of Karnataka is 75.

The **members of the Vidhan Parishad are indirectly elected;** the mode of indirect election is as follows:

- **One-third** members are elected **by local bodies.**
- **One-third** members are elected **by the members of the Vidhan Sabha.**
- **One-twelfth** members are elected **by graduates** (minimum three-year degree).
- **One-twelfth** members are elected **by teachers** (secondary school and above).
- **One-sixth** members are **nominated by the Governor** who are eminent personalities in the field of **literature, arts, science, social service** and **cooperative** (LASSC) **movement.**

The election to the Vidhan Parishad is conducted according to the **'proportional representation system'** by means of **'single transferable vote'.**

It must be noted that, like the Rajya Sabha, **the Vidhan Parishad is also a permanent body,** that is, a **continuing chamber** and is **not subjected to dissolution.** But **one-third members of the Vidhan Parishad get retired after every second year;** a retired member is eligible to become a member again. **The term of a member of a Vidhan Parishad is six years, but there is no term for the Vidhan Parishad** itself.

QUALIFICATION TO BECOME MEMBER STATE LEGISLATURE

The members of the Vidhan Sabha are called the Members of Legislative Assembly (MLAs), and members of the Vidhan Parishad are called the Members of Legislative Council (MLCs). In order to become an MLA or MLC, one should:

1. Be **a citizen of India.**
2. Have completed **30 years** of age in case of **Vidhan Parishad** and **25 years** of age in case of **Vidhan Sabha.**
3. Have any other qualification as stipulated by the Parliament.
4. Be an elector in any constituency of the Vidhan Sabha of the concerned state.

DISQUALIFICATION OF A MEMBER OF THE STATE LEGISLATURE

An MLA or an MLC may lose his/her position if he/she

1. Holds any office of profit in the Union Government or in the state governments.
2. Voluntarily acquires the citizenship of any other nation.
3. Is an undercharged insolvent.
4. Is proved to be having an unsound mind by a court.
5. Gets the imprisonment of two or more years for any convicted offences; also, such a person will be barred to contest election for the next six years after the completion of his/her imprisonment.
6. Proved to be guilty of corruption or any other offences in an election.
7. Fails to provide details of election expense in a given time to the Election Commission of India.
8. Get convicted of encouraging enmity between different groups.

Under the above circumstances, **the Governor** decides about the disqualification of an MLA/MLC in consultation with the Election Commission of India and **his decision is final.**

The **Speaker of the Vidhan Sabha** or **the Chairman of the Vidhan Parishad** decides about the disqualification of their respective house members in case of **'Defection'** (under the **10th Schedule** of the Constitution), but this decision is **not final** and can be questioned in the court.

CONDITION WHEN AN MLA/MLC VACATES HIS/HER SEAT

An MLA/MLC vacates his/her seat in the state legislature under the following conditions:

1. If he/she gets **two memberships,** that is,

   (i) If he/she is elected to both the Vidhan Sabha and the Vidhan Parishad at a time, his/her seat in any one of them becomes vacant as per the laws of the concerned state.
   (ii) If he/she is elected to both the Parliament and the state legislature and does not vacate his/her seat in the state legislature within 14 days, then his/her seat in the Parliament gets vacant.

2. If he/she is **disqualified** under the anti-defection law of the 10th Schedule of the Constitution.
3. If he/she **resigns** voluntarily for his/her seat in the house.
4. If he/she **does not attend meetings** of the house for 60 days without the permission of the house.
5. If his/her election to the house is declared as void by the courts.

PRESIDING OFFICERS OF THE STATE LEGISLATURE

Speaker of the Vidhan Sabha

The presiding officer of the Vidhan Sabha is the Speaker. Generally, when the term of the existing Vidhan Sabha ends or it is dissolved, the Speaker does not lose his office and continues till just before the first meeting of the new Vidhan Sabha. When the newly elected Vidhan Sabha meets for the first time, then the Governor appoints the senior most member of that house as **'the Speaker Pro Tem'** just to **administer the oath ceremony of the newly elected members and to make arrangement for the election of a new Speaker.**

The Vidhan Sabha elects the Speaker (also the Deputy Speaker) from amongst its members. The Vidhan Sabha is the sole authority to remove the Speaker (also the Deputy Speaker) **by passing a resolution** by an absolute majority with regard to that; thus, the Speaker **enjoys the security of tenure.** The Speaker can resign by submitting his resignation to the Deputy Speaker and vice versa.

As the presiding officer of the Vidhan Sabha, the Speaker's decision with respect to the Vidhan Sabha affairs **is final** and cannot be questioned in the courts. He acts as the representative and chief spokesperson of the Vidhan Sabha and the protector of the power and privileges of its members. He has vested powers and responsibilities to smoothly conduct the business of the house. All the Chairmen of the Parliamentary Committees in the Vidhan Sabha are appointed by the Speaker and he directs their functions.

The **Deputy Speaker acts as the Speaker** and performs his duties when the Speaker's position is **vacant** or the Speaker is **absent.** In other times, the Deputy Speaker takes part in the business of the house as an ordinary member.

Chairman of the Vidhan Parishad

The presiding officer of the Vidhan Parishad is the Chairman. **The Vidhan Parishad elects the Chairman and the Deputy Chairman from amongst its members.** The Vidhan Parishad is the sole authority to remove them from their office **by passing a resolution** by an absolute majority with regard to that; thus, they **enjoy the security of tenure.** The Chairman can resign by submitting his resignation to the Deputy Chairman and vice versa.

The power and functions of the Chairman of the Vidhan Parishad are similar to those of the Speaker of the Vidhan Sabha. As the presiding officer of the Vidhan Parishad, the Chairman's decision with respect to the Vidhan Parishad affairs is final and cannot be questioned in the courts. He acts as the representative and chief spokesperson of the Vidhan Parishad and the protector of the powers and privileges of its members. He has vested powers and responsibilities to smoothly conduct the business of the house. All the Chairmen of the Parliamentary Committees in the Vidhan Parishad are appointed by the Chairman and he supervises their functions. But the Speaker of the Vidhan Sabha enjoys one special power that is not available to the Chairman of the Vidhan Parishad, that is, the Speaker of the Vidhan Sabha **decides whether a bill is a money bill or not.**

The **salary of the presiding officer of a house is determined by the state legislature,** and it is **charged on the Consolidate Fund State,** which is not subjected to vote in the state legislature. The **Deputy Chairman of the Vidhan Parishad acts as the Chairman of the Vidhan Parishad** and performs his duties when the Chairman position is **vacant** or the Chairman is **absent.** In other times, the Deputy Chairman takes part in the business of the house as an ordinary member.

NO JOINT SITTING OF THE HOUSES OF THE STATE LEGISLATURE

There is no deadlock situation between the Vidhan Sabha and the Vidhan Parishad (if it exists) with respect to any bill of the state legislature, as the decision of the Vidhan Sabha is final; with or without accepting the recommendations of the Vidhan Parishad, the Vidhan Sabha can pass any bill and send it for the assent of the Governor. Thus, the 'Joint Sitting' provision **is available only to the houses of the Parliament, not to the houses of the state legislature.**

LEADERS IN THE STATE LEGISLATURE

There is a leader and a leader of opposition in each house of the state legislature and they are recognized by the presiding officers of the respective houses. **The Leader of the Vidhan Sabha** is the Chief Minister or a minister nominated by the Chief Minister in case the Chief Minister is not a member of the Vidhan Sabha. **The Leader of the Vidhan Parishad** is a minister nominated by the Chief Minister.

The **Leader of Opposition** in either the Vidhan Sabha or the Vidhan Parishad is a **leader of the largest opposition party that secures at least one-tenth seats** of the total strength of that respective house. The Leader of Opposition leads the opposition party in the house and his main function is to criticize the acts and policies of the government in a positive manner and to provide an alternative government.

10

CHAPTER

The Electoral Process in India

One of the key factors in the success of democracy in India since last six decades is the Constitutional provision for strong election machinery to conduct free and fair elections across the country from time to time.

ELECTION COMMISSION OF INDIA

The Election Commission of India (ECI) is a **Constitutional body** as it is directly created by the Constitution to conduct free and fair elections by supervising the election process in India. It is also an **independent, permanent** and **all India body.** **Article 324 of Part XV** of the Constitution deals with the ECI. The ECI conducts elections for **the Parliament, the state legislature, the President of India and the Vice-President of India.**

Composition

According to the Constitution of India, the ECI is a **multimember body** as it must consists one Chief Election Commissioner (CEC) and as many numbers of Election Commissioners (ECs) as determined by the President from time to time. At present, the ECI is composed of **one CEC and two ECs;** all are **appointed by the President of India.** By consulting the ECI, the President also appoints the Regional Commissioners (RCs). (A list of all the Chief Election Commissioners of India till date has been provided in Table 10.1.)

Qualification

The Constitution of India **does not prescribe any qualification** to become the CEC or EC, but usually they are the Indian Administrative Services (IAS) officers.

Term, Independence and Removal

Although the Constitution of India does not specify about the term of the CEC or EC, their term is **six years or until they attain 65 years of age,** whichever is earlier, and it is determined by the President. The CEC enjoys the **security of tenure,** that is, **the President can remove the CEC** from his office on the grounds of proved **misbehaviour or incapacity; only after the Parliament passes a resolution** with the special majority with respect to it (just like the removal of a Judge of the Supreme Court or a High Court). The ECs or RCs can be removed by the President only on the recommendations of the CEC. The CEC or the ECs **submit their resignation to the President.** After their retirement, they are not prohibited to hold any office in the Government. The President determines their service condition and tenure of office. After the appointment of a member of the ECI, the service conditions cannot be changed to his advantage.

Powers and Functions

The ECI has **administrative, advisory and quasi-judicial** powers and functions. They are as follows:

1. It decides about the territorial constituency and performs the **delimitation** act after every 10 years on the basis of the new census report.
2. It prepares **electoral rolls.**
3. It **registers eligible voters** and issue **voters' identity cards.**
4. It **supervises** the election machinery for the Parliament, the state legislature, for the office of the President and the Vice-President.
5. It registers and recognizes **political parties,** categorizes them as a **national party or a regional party** on the basis of the number of seats secure by them in the Parliament and State legislature.
6. It allocates the **election symbol** to political parties.
7. For **settling disputes** regarding the recognition of a political party and the election symbol, it acts as a court.
8. It can order for an **inquiry** regarding election disputes, malpractice and so on.
9. It enforces **a code of conduct** during election time that needs to be followed by parties, candidates and the Government.
10. In certain cases, it **advises the President** to disqualify the members of the Parliament.
11. In certain cases, it **advises the Governor** to disqualify the members of the state legislature.
12. In case of any disturbance during election, such as booth capturing, violence and natural disaster, it can **cancel or post-pone** the election.

13. In the case of the **President Rule** or state emergency in the state, it decides the time of election and advises about the same to the President.

It must be noted that the **ECI does not conduct elections for the local bodies; the 'State Election Commission'** conducts free and fair elections for the **rural local governments (Panchayats), urban local government (Municipalities) and cooperative societies.**

THE ELECTORAL PROCESS IN INDIA

In India, **General Elections** are held, in which all the members of the Lok Sabha or the Vidhan Sabha are elected simultaneously after a specific period of time, as well as **by-election,** in which a member of a legislature (Parliament or state legislature) is elected to the vacant seat by a special election in an unspecific period of time. (Table 10.2 lists all the General Elections held in India till date.)

India is the most populous and largest democratic country in the world, hence General Elections here is considered as the biggest election in the world. In order to conduct proper and systematic elections in India, the ECI follows certain procedures. These procedures **involve seven steps as follows:**

1. **Notification and Model Code of Conduct:**
   The formal process for an election to a legislature starts with a notification, which calls for the electorate to elect members of a house. The ECI advises to issue the notification to the President and to the Governor for the elections of the Parliament and the state legislature, respectively. This notification gives a detailed provision of schedules of the election process, such as the nomination submission, withdrawal of candidature, polling day and so on.

   Usually, on the same day of notification, the ECI enforces the 'Model Code of Conduct', which prescribes certain guidelines for the conduct of political parties and election-contesting candidates during the election time, especially regarding the polling day, speeches, polling booths, election manifestos and general conduct. The Model Code of Conduct also imposes restrictions on certain activities of the Government like new recruitment, transfer of its employees, announcing the new scheme/project and so on.

2. **Filing the nomination paper:**
   An eligible and aspiring candidate should file his/her name for the election within the due date as fixed by the ECI. One person can contest in multiple constituencies by filing separate nomination paper in each constituency. A candidate's name should be proposed and seconded by voters of the related constituency. A candidate must give his/her true personal details, such as about the property, educational background, criminal background (if exists) in the nomination paper. If any candidate wishes to not to contest after filing the nomination, then such a person can withdraw his/her candidature within the due date as fixed by the ECI.

3. **Scrutiny of the nomination paper:**
   Finally, the nomination papers will be scrutinized (very close examination) by the ECI. If any nomination paper is found to be not in order, then it gets rejected by the ECI and the candidate becomes ineligible to contest the election.

4. **Election campaign:**
   In this stage, political parties and candidates request for votes to the people by various means, such as public speech, destitution of posters and pamphlet, visiting home, advertisement in newspapers, TV, Radio, social media and public places. During this time, many political parties offer unlawful activities and malpractices, such as giving money, alcohol and other gifts to the public, leading to crime or violence and so on. The ECI is responsible to prevent such unlawful activities and malpractices. **Before the 48 hours of the polling day, the election campaign must be stopped** by the political parties and candidates.

5. **Polling day:**
   This is the key stage of the election. On pre-fixed voting or polling day by the ECI, the voters visit the polling booth in between 7 AM and 6 PM and cast their vote for the preferred candidate in the electronic voting machine (EVM). If a voter does not prefer any candidate, then he/she can reject all candidates by pressing the **None of the Above (NOTA)** button in the EVM. Voting is held by a secret ballot. Each candidate's representative is allowed to sit inside the voting booth by the ECI. At the end of the polling day, all EVMs will be sealed and will be kept in highly secured rooms in the supervision of the ECI.

6. **Counting votes and declaration of results:**
   On this day, all the EVMs will be taken out of the high security room and will be opened in front of candidates or their representatives. Each candidate gets to know about the number of votes he/she has secured in the election. A candidate who secures the highest number of votes will be declared as a winner or elected by the ECI.

7. **Election dispute:**
   In any candidate thinks that the election was held improperly or has any objection to the election process or results, then he/she can appeal it in the concerned High Courts. If the allegation or objection is proved to be true in the court, then the court can set aside the result of that election and may order for a fresh election.

Many political scientists think that **election is the mother of all corruption** in India as the roots of the corruption can be traced to the election. Through election the people delegate their power to their representatives and elected representatives get the power to rule the people. Usually, many candidates in election use a lot of money, muscle and religion to wow the voter and buy their votes so that they can come to the power. Such a kind of politician exploits the worse conditions of the poor people and encourages greed of the rich people. If such a person is elected and even becomes a minister, he/she usually tries to re-take the money that he/she already spent on or invested in the election in a shortest period, so he/she opts for corruption. As a result, government servants, officers and so on working with him/her get involved in corruption and a chain of corruption is created. Thus, the cycle of corruption goes like this in the form of political business.

So, if we are able to politically educate the people and create awareness about the value of their vote in elections, guide them not to vote because of money, muscle, religion, caste, but for the development of the nation by electing a right person for the right place, it could be possible to significantly reduce the menace of corruption in India.

TABLE 10.1

LIST OF THE CHIEF ELECTION COMMISSIONERS OF INDIA

S. No.	Name of CEC	From	To
1.	Sukumar Sen	1950	1958
2.	Kalyan Sundaram	1958	1967
3.	S. P. Sen Verma	1967	1972
4.	Dr. Nagendra Singh	1972	1973
5.	T. Swaminathan	1973	1977
6.	S. L. Shakdhar	1977	1982
7.	R. K. Trivedi	1982	1986
8.	R. V. S. Peri Sastri	1986	1990
9.	V. S. Ramadevi	1990	1990
10.	T. N. Seshan	1990	1996
11.	M. S. Gill	1996	2002
12.	J. M. Lyngdoh	2002	2004
13.	T. S. Krishnamurthy	2004	2005
14.	B. B. Tandon	2005	2006
15.	N. Gopalaswami	2006	2009
16.	Navin Chawla	2009	2010
17.	S. Y. Quraishi	2010	2012
18.	V. S. Sampath	2012	2015
19.	Harishankar Brahma	2015	2015
20.	Nasim Zaidi	2015	Present

TABLE 10.2
GLANCE AT GENERAL ELECTIONS IN INDIA

Year	Election	Major Party (Its Seat)
1951–1952	1st Lok Sabha	INC (364)
1957	2nd Lok Sabha	INC (371)
1962	3rd Lok Sabha	INC (361)
1967	4th Lok Sabha	INC (283)
1971	5th Lok Sabha	INC (352)
1977	6th Lok Sabha	BLD (295)
1980	7th Lok Sabha	INC(I) (351)
1984	8th Lok Sabha	INC (404)
1989	9th Lok Sabha	INC (197)
1991	10th Lok Sabha	INC (232)
1996	11th Lok Sabha	BJP (161)
1998	12th Lok Sabha	BJP (182)
1999	13th Lok Sabha	BJP (181)
2004	14th Lok Sabha	INC (145)
2009	15th Lok Sabha	INC (206)
2014	16th Lok Sabha	BJP (282)

Section IV

Union Executive and State Executive

President

INTRODUCTION

The President, the Vice-President, the Prime Minister, the Council of Ministers and the Attorney General of India (AGI) are the parts of the Union Executive. Articles 52–78 of Part V cover various aspects of the Union Executive. The main function of the Union Executive is to implement the laws enacted by the Parliament.

The Constitution provides one of the highest order, prestige and dignity to the President in the Indian democratic political system. The President is the **first citizen** of India, **head of the Indian State** and represents the solidarity, unity and integrity of India. (A list of all the Presidents of India till date has been tabulated in Table 11.1.)

However, in accordance with the parliamentary form of government, the President is **nominal or titular or ceremonial head of the Indian State,** with the **real head** being the Prime Minister and his Council of Ministers. The position of the President in India is the same like that of the **King/Queen in the British Constitution;** both represent their respective states, but **do not rule** the country.

QUALIFICATION

In order to qualify for the election for the position of the President, one should:

1. Be a citizen of India.
2. Have completed **35 years of age.**
3. Be qualified to become a member of **the Lok Sabha.**
4. Not have any **office of profit** in the both the Centre and state governments.

Each Presidential candidature must have 50 electorates as proposers and 50 electorates as seconders and need to deposit ₹15,000 in the Reserve Bank of India.

ELECTION

The President of India is **indirectly elected by the people,** that is, **directly elected by an electoral college** consisting of:

1. Only the elected members of the Parliament (Lok Sabha and Rajya Sabha), not the nominated members.
2. Only the elected members of the Legislative Assemblies (Vidhan Sabha) of the state and UTs, not the nominated members.

It must be noted that, the members (nominated or elected) of the **Vidhan Parishad** (state legislative council) **do not participate** in the Presidential election.

According to Article 55(1), the election of the President is held according to the **'proportional representation system'** by means of **'single transferable vote'.** The voting takes place by a **secret ballot** system. Article 55(3) provides for uniformity in the scale of representation of different states as well as parity between the states as a whole and the Union in the election of the President. To practically impalement this provision, the following formula is used:

$$\text{Value of an MLA vote} = \frac{\text{Total population of states}}{\text{Total number of elected members in state legislative assemblies}} \times \frac{1}{1000}$$

$$\text{Value of an MP vote} = \frac{\text{Total values of votes of all MLAs of all states}}{\text{Total number of elected members of the Parliament}}$$

$$\text{Electroal quota} = \frac{\text{Total number of valid votes polled}}{1+1} + 1$$

Each MP and MLA while casting his/her vote indicates the order of preference to all Presidential candidatures such as 1, 2, 3, 4 and so on. In the first round of counting, only the first preference votes are counted, and if any candidate secures the required quota, he/she is declared as the winner. But if no one secures the required quota, then a candidate who secures the least number of the first preference is eliminated and his/her vote is transferred to the candidate to whom he/she has given his/her second preference vote and so on. This transfer of vote process continues till a candidate secures the required quota.

The Chief Justice of India and in his absence the senior most judge of the Supreme Court **administers the oath of the office of the President.**

All disputes regarding the election of the President should be **inquired and decided by the Supreme Court only;** its decision is final. If the Supreme Court decides any Presidential election as void, the acts done by the President before such a decision are not invalidated.

CONDITIONS

The Constitution puts certain conditions on the office of the President. Those are as follows:

1. He must **not be an MP or MLA/MLC;** if such a person is elected as the President, his seat in his concerned house is considered to be vacant.
2. He should not have any **office of profit.**
3. He can **use** the **Rashtrapati Bhavan** (his official residence) without paying rent.
4. He has some emoluments, allowance and privileges as **determined by the Parliament;** it cannot be decreased during his term of office.

At present, the salary of the President is 1.5 lakhs per month. The President enjoys **immunity from criminal proceedings in all court of laws even for personal acts,** but he does not enjoy immunity from civil proceedings in terms of personal acts. He **cannot be arrested or imprisoned during his term** of office, and he is **not answerable to any courts** for his use of powers and performance of duties, that is, he has **no legal liability** for his official acts.

TERM

The term of the President is **five years.** If his successor does not enter the office, then he can hold office beyond five years. He is also **eligible for re-election** as many times as he wishes; but the President of the USA can hold office only for two terms, not more than that. The President of India submits his **resignation to the Vice-President.**

IMPEACHMENT

The Parliament can remove the President from his office by impeachment before the completion of his term of five years only on the ground of **'violation of the Constitution'.** It is a **quasi-judicial** function of the Parliament.

The process of impeachment of the President goes like this:

1. At least one-fourth members, either in the Lok Sabha or in the Rajya Sabha can initiate impeachment charges against the President by giving him at least 14 days advance notice.
2. If that house passes the impeachment bill with a majority of not less than two-thirds of its total membership, it is sent to the other house, where the impeachment charges get investigated. The President can appear and represent before such an investigation.

3. If the other house also upholds the impeachment charges against the President and passes the impeachment bill with a majority of not less than two-thirds of its total membership, then the President stands impeached from his office.

VACANCY

The office of the President gets vacant when

(i) His term of five years expires.
(ii) He resigns.
(iii) He is impeached.
(iv) He dies.
(v) In other cases, such as declaring his election void by the Supreme Court.

A successor must be elected before the expiry of the five-year term of the existing President. In other cases, such as resignation, impeachment, death and otherwise, the vacant President Office must be filled by an election **within six months** from the date of occurrence of the vacancy. During this period, the Vice-President acts as the President, but **only for a maximum period of six months.** It also means that there must be a President of India at all times.

POWER AND FUNCTIONS

The power and functions of the President can be studied under the following subheads.

Legislative Powers

As an indispensable part of the Parliament, the President has the power to:

1. **Summon and prorogue** different sessions of the Parliament from time to time.
2. Summon a **Joint Sitting of both the houses of the Parliament** in case of a deadlock between them on an issue.
3. **Address the Parliament,** in its first session after each General Election and the first session of each year.
4. **Dissolve the Lok Sabha** after its end of term or in other cases.
5. **Veto a bill** of the Parliament.
6. To **send message to the Parliament** regarding a bill or otherwise.
7. **Appoints the presiding officer** in a house of the Parliament, when the position of the presiding officer of a house of the Parliament falls vacant.

8. **Nominate two members** from **the Anglo-Indian community** to the Lok Sabha and **12 members to the Rajya Sabha** who are eminent personalities in the fields of **literature, art, science, social service (LASS).**
9. Decide on the **disqualification of MPs** in consultation with the Election Commission of India in some cases.
10. Lays down **annual reports** of the CAG, the UPSC, the Finance Commission, the National Commission of SCs and the National Commission of STs and so on before the Parliament.
11. Lays down the **Annual Financial Statement or Budget** before the Parliament.
12. Issues **ordinance** when the Lok Sabha and/or the Rajya Sabha are not in session.
13. Gives his prior recommendation to introduce certain bills in the Parliament, such as

    a) A bill with regard to creating a new state, altering boundaries of state and so on.
    b) A money bill.
    c) A bill involving expenditure from the Consolidated Fund of India.
    d) State legislative bill that restricts the freedom of trade.

Veto Powers

The WordWeb dictionary defines veto as 'the power or right to prohibit or reject a proposed or intended act; especially the power of a chief executive to reject a bill passed by the legislature'.

A bill of the Parliament cannot become an Act without the assent or signature of the President. So the Parliament presents each bill after it is forwarded to the President for his assent. According to Article 111, the President has the following options with regard to a bill presented by the Parliament to him:

1. He may declare his assent to the bill or
2. He may use the veto power on the bill. There are three veto powers available to the President:

   (i) **Absolute veto:** He **withholds his assent** to the bill and the bill will not become an Act until he signs it.
   (ii) **Suspensive veto:** He may **return the bill** (other than the money bill) for the reconsideration of the Parliament. However, if that bill is passed again by the Parliament with or without changes or amendments and again presented to the President, he **must give his assent** to the bill as it is now obligatory for him. It means that, the Parliament can nullify the suspensive veto of the President.

(iii) **Pocket veto:** He may take **no action** on the bill, that is, he **does not reject or return the bill or give his assent to the bill and may keep it pending so long as he wishes.** It is described that, 'the pocket of the Indian President is bigger than that of the American President' because the Indian President can use the pocket veto on a bill for an indefinite period of time but the American President can use the pocket veto on a bill only for a maximum period of 10 days.

The President can give his assent or withhold **a money bill but he cannot return** it to the Parliament for reconsideration as it is introduced in the Parliament only after his prior recommendation. It must be noted that the President **does not have any veto power** with respect to **a Constitutional Amendment Bill;** he must give his assent to such a bill as it is obligatory for him. The Constitution conferred the veto powers in the hand of the President to prevent the Parliament from enacting hasty or unconstitutional acts.

Veto power of the president over a state bill

A bill of a state legislature cannot become an Act without the assent or signature of the President, if it is reserved for the consideration of the President by the Governor of that state. In this case, the President has the following options with regard to a bill presented by a state legislature to him.

1. He may declare his assent to the bill, or
2. He uses his veto power on the bill. There are three veto powers available to the President.

   (i) **Absolute veto:** He withholds his assent to the bill and the bill will not become an Act.

   (ii) **Suspensive veto:** He returns the bill (other than the money bill) for the reconsideration of the state legislature. However, if that bill is passed again by the state legislature with or without changes or amendments and again presented to the President, he **may not necessarily give assent to the bill as it is not obligatory for him.** It means that, **the state legislature cannot nullify the suspensive veto of the President;** only the Parliament can do it.

   (iii) **Pocket veto:** He takes no action on the bill, that is, he does not reject nor return the bill nor give his assent to the bill and keeps it pending so long as he wishes.

Ordinance-making Power

The prime duty of the legislature is to enact laws for the nation, but when it is not in session, the **executive can enact temporary laws. These temporary laws**

are called as 'ordinance'. An ordinance is a temporary law based on the executive decision to legally manage urgent public affairs. An ordinance **is equal to an Act of the legislature,** but it is only temporary.

   The most important legislative power of the President is the ordinance-making power. According to Article 123 of the Constitution, the President has the power of **promulgate or withdraw** an ordinance **at any period of time**—only if the Parliament is in recess, that is, **any one house or both the houses of the Parliament are not in session**—based on the **recommendation of the Council of Ministers.** The Parliament must approve or disapprove an ordinance **within six weeks** of its reassembly; if not, it will lapse. Without the approval of the Parliament, the **maximum life of an ordinance is six months and six weeks** (6 months is maximum gap between the two sessions of parliament and 6 week is the maximum period of the ordinance to expire after the reassembly of the Parliament).

Executive Powers

According to Article 53 of the Constitution, **'All the executive powers of the Union are vested in the President'.** But the President exercises his executive powers **only on the aid and advice of the Council of Ministers.**

   Important executive powers of the President are as follows:

1. The Government of India performs all its actions **in the name of the President.**
2. He **appoints all the ministers,** including the Prime Minister, and they hold the office **during his pleasure.**
3. The UTs are **directly administered** by the President through administrators appointed by him.
4. He **appoints the Governors** of states, the CAG, the Attorney General of India, all election commissioners, members and chairmen of the Union Public Service Commission, the Finance Commission and so on.
5. He appoints the **Inter-State Council** to encourage a good relationship between the different state governments and the Central government.
6. He can notify an area as the **Scheduled Area** and has administrative power over the Scheduled Area and Tribal Areas.
7. To assess the conditions of **SCs, STs and backward classes,** he can appoint an Investigation Commission.
8. He can get any **information** related to the **administrative or legislative proposal** of the Central government from the Prime Minister.
9. He can make rules to smoothly run the transaction of business of the Central government and distributing related business between ministers.
10. He acts as the **visitor of most Central Universities;** in this capacity, he **appoints the Vice-Chancellors** of the Central Universities and has the powers to direct inspection or enquiry into the affairs of the Central Universities.

Judicial Power

The important judicial powers of the President are as follows:

1. He **appoints the Chief Justice and other judges of the Supreme Court and the High Courts.**
2. He can **remove the Chief Justice and other judges of the Supreme Court and the High Courts** based on the address presented to him **by the Parliament** in this regard.
3. Under Article 143, he can **seek advice from the Supreme Court** related to a law or fact, but the Supreme Court's advice in this regard is **not binding** on him.
4. He can **grant a pardon** to a convicted and sentenced person by a court, **including martial courts** for any offence against a Central law.

Pardoning Power

To **nullify judicial errors,** the Constitution of India, under Article 72, conferred pardoning power to the President. He can grant a pardon to a convicted and sentenced person by a court of law, including **martial courts** for any offence **against a Central law.** This power is an executive action and independent from judiciary; so one cannot appeal for the President to pardon as a matter of right. There are total four pardoning powers available to the President. They are as follows:

1. **Pardon:** It **completely absolves an offender from all punishments, sentences and disqualifications.** The President is the **only authority to pardon a death sentence in India.** Even if a state law provides for death punishment for any offence, the power to grant pardon rests with the President, **not the Governor.**
2. **Commutation:** It means the **substitution or change of one kind of punishment to a lighter form** of punishment, such as seven years of rigorous imprisonment can be commuted to seven years of simple imprisonment.
3. **Remission:** It means the **reduction of sentence without changing its character,** such as seven years of rigorous imprisonment can be commuted to four years of rigorous imprisonment.
4. **Respite:** Due to special reasons, such as the pregnancy of a woman, a physically challenged person, **giving lesser punishment or a temporary relief** instead of originally given by a court.
5. **Reprieve:** It means, **staying execution of sentence or punishment for a temporary period,** such as the death punishment to a person may be stayed by the President for a temporary period.

Military Powers

The important military powers of the President are as follows:

1. He is **the Supreme Commander of Indian Defence Forces,** such as the Army, Navy and Air Force.
2. He **appoints the Chiefs** of the Army, Navy and Air Force.
3. He can **officially declare war or arrive at peace** based on the approval of the Parliament.

Financial Power

The important financial powers of the President are as follows:

1. He lays down the **budget** or annual financial statement before the Parliament.
2. His **prior recommendation** is needed to introduce the **money bill** in the Parliament.
3. **His sanction** must be required to use the money from **the Contingency Fund of India.**
4. Without his prior recommendations, **no demand for grant can be made** in the Parliament.
5. Under Article 280, he constitutes **the Finance Commission** after **every five years,** which decides on the **distribution of revenue between the Centre and states.**

Emergency Powers

The Constitution has vested extraordinary powers in the President to impose three kinds of emergencies. They are as follows:

1. National Emergency (Article 352)
2. President Rule or State Emergency (Articles 356 and 365)
3. Financial Emergency (Article 360)

Diplomatic Powers

As the **Head of the Indian state,** the President represents India in the international-level affairs and forums, and sends and receives diplomats, such as ambassadors, high commissioners and so on. The Government of India negotiates and concludes all international treaties and agreements on behalf of the President, but for this, they require the approval of the Parliament.

It must be noted here that the President is the **nominal head** in our parliamentary form of government. Most of the powers of the President discussed above are exercised by the President **only on the aid and advice of the Council of Ministers headed by the Prime Minister** who is the real executive. The act done by the President (except using his discretionary power), without the aid and advice of the Council of Ministers is **illegal or unconstitutional.** However, the President has the **power to ask the Council of Ministers to reconsider an aid and advice** given to him on a matter. However, after the reconsideration, if the Council of Ministers renders an aid and advice on the same matter **with or without any changes, the President has no option left except giving his assent** for that aid and advice, that is, he must give his assent on that matter. This also means that the President can ask the Council of Ministers to reconsider an aid and advice on a **matter only once,** not more than that.

Discretionary Power of the President

The discretionary power of the President means, the President can act on a matter **without any aid and advice of the Council of Ministers by using his discretion.** The President **does not have any Constitutional discretionary powers like the Governor,** but he has **situational discretion,** that is, the President can use his discretion to act without the help of the Council of Ministers in following situations:

1. To appoint a Prime Minister when **the Prime Minister dies suddenly** and there is no successor and **no political party enjoys a clear majority** in the Lok Sabha to form a government.
2. To **dismiss the Council of Ministers after it fails to prove the confidence of the Lok Sabha,** that is, he may or may not dismiss the Council of Ministers when it fails to win no confidence motion.
3. To **dissolve the Lok Sabha if the Council of Ministers lost its majority,** that is, he may or may not dissolve the Lok Sabha.

TABLE 11.1

LIST OF THE PRESIDENTS OF INDIA

S. No.	Name of President	Period
1.	Dr Rajendra Prasad[a]	26 January 1950–13 May 1962
2.	Sarvepalli Radhakrishnan	13 May 1962–13 May 1967
3.	Zakir Hussain	13 May 1967–3 May 1969
	Varahagiri Venkata Giri[b]	3 May1969–20 July 1969
	Muhammad Hidayatullah[b]	20 July 1969–24 August 1969
4.	Varahagiri Venkata Giri	24 August 1969–24 August 1974
5.	Fakhruddin Ali Ahmed	24 August 1974–11 February 1977
	Basappa Danappa Jatti[b]	11 February 1977–25 July 1977
6.	Neelam Sanjiva Reddy	25 July 1977–25 July 1982
7.	Giani Zail Singh	25 July 1982–25 July 1987
8.	Ramaswamy Venkataraman	25 July 1987–25 July 1992
9.	Shankar Dayal Sharma	25 July 1992–25 July 1997
10.	Kocheril Raman Narayanan	25 July 1997–25 July 2002
11.	A. P. J. Abdul Kalam	25 July 2002–25 July 2007
12.	Pratibha Patil	25 July 2007–25 July 2012
13.	Pranab Mukherjee	25 July 2012–Present

Notes: [a]So far, only Dr Rajendra Prasad became the President for two times.
      [b]Acting President of India.

Vice-President

Article 63 of the Constitution says that there shall be a Vice-President of India. In the Official Warrant of Precedence, the **second highest position** after the President is given to the Vice-President. The Vice -President is **the ex-officio** (by virtue of the position) **Chairman of the Rajya Sabha** (Table 12.1 tabulates the list of all the Vice-Presidents of India till the present time). India has barrowed the model of the office of the Vice-President **from the USA.**

QUALIFICATION

In order to qualify for election for the position of the Vice-President, one should:

1. Be a **citizen of India.**
2. Be **35 years of old.**
3. Be qualified to become a member of **the Rajya Sabha.**
4. **Not have any office of profit** in both the Centre and state governments.

Each Vice Presidential candidate must have 20 electorates as proposers and 20 electorates as seconders and need to deposit ₹15,000 in the Reserve Bank of India.

ELECTION

Like the President, the Vice-President of India is also **indirectly elected by the people,** that is, **directly elected by an electoral college,** consisting of **both the elected and nominated members of the Lok Sabha and the Rajya Sabha.** The Vice-President is elected by the members of both the houses of the Parliament in a **Joint Session** in accordance to the **'proportional representation system'** by means of **'single transferable vote'** by a secret ballot.

It must be noted that, **no members** (nominated or elected) of the **State Legislative Assemblies, UT's Legislative Assemblies and State Legislative**

Councils participate in the Vice Presidential election. In others words, the states and the UTs **have no role** to play in the election of the Vice-President of India.

All disputes regarding the election of the Vice-President should be inquired and decided by **the Supreme Court only,** and its decision is **final.** If the Supreme Court decides any Vice Presidential election as void, the acts done by the Vice-President before such a decision are invalidated. **The President** or a person appointed by him **administers the oath of office** to the Vice-President.

CONDITIONS

The Constitution puts certain conditions on the office of the Vice-President. Those are as follows:

1. He **must not be an MP or MLA/MLC;** if such a person is elected as the Vice-President, his seat in his concerned house is considered to be **vacant.**
2. He should **not have any office of profit.**
3. He has some emoluments, allowance and privileges as **determined by the Parliament;** it cannot be decreased during his term of office.

The Vice-President gets his salary in the capacity of the Chairman of the Rajya Sabha. At present, the salary of the Chairman of the Rajya Sabha is 1.25 lakh per month.

TERM

The term of the Vice-President is **five years.** If his successor does not enter the office, then he can hold office beyond five years. He is also **eligible for re-election as many times as he wishes**. The Vice-President **submits his resignation to the President.**

NO FORMAL IMPEACHMENT

The Parliament can remove the Vice-President from his office before the completion of his term of five years without any formal impeachment process, like in the case of the President. **Only if the Rajya Sabha (not the Lok Sabha) passes a resolution by an absolute majority** to remove the Vice-President from his office and the **Lok Sabha accord for it,** then the Vice-President stands impeached from his office. The Rajya Sabha can pass such a resolution by giving at least 14 days advance notice to the Vice-President. The Constitution **does not specify any grounds to remove** the Vice-President from his office.

VACANCY

The office of the Vice-President falls vacant when:

1. His term of five years expires.
2. He resigns.
3. He is impeached.
4. He dies.
5. In other cases, such as declaring his election void by the Supreme Court.

A successor must be elected **before the expiry of five-year** term of the existing Vice-President. In other cases, such as resignation, impeachment, death and otherwise, the vacant Vice-President office must be filled by an election **as soon as possible** from the date of occurrence of vacancy.

POWER AND FUNCTIONS

The Vice-President has two important powers and functions. Those are as follows:

1. He acts as the **ex-officio Chairman of the Rajya Sabha.** He is the presiding officer of the Rajya Sabha, but **he is not a member of the Rajya Sabha. He has no right** to vote in the Rajya Sabha.
2. He **acts as the President of India,** when

    (i) The office of the President **falls vacant** due to resignation, impeachment, death and in other cases. He acts as the President **only for the maximum period of six months** as the vacant President office must be filled within six months from the date of occurrence of the vacancy.
    (ii) The President **is absent,** suffering from illness or any other reason.

When the Vice-President is acting as the President or discharging the President duties

1. He assumes all the powers, functions and immunity of the President.
2. The Deputy Chairman of the Rajya Sabha acts as the Chairman of the Rajya Sabha.

TABLE 12.1
LIST OF THE VICE-PRESIDENT OF INDIA

S. No.	Name	Term
1.	Dr Sarvepalli Radhakrishnan	13 May 1952–12 May 1957
		13 May 1957–12 May 1962
2.	Dr Zakir Husain	13 May 1962–12 May 1967
3.	Shri Varahagir Venkata Giri	13 May 1967–3 May 1969
4.	Shri Gopal Swarup Pathak	31 August 1969–30 August 1974
5.	Shri Basappa Danappa Jatti	31 August 1974–30 August 1979
6.	Shri M Hidayatullah	31 August 1979–30 August 1984
7.	Shri R. Venkataraman	31 August 1984–24 July 1987
8.	Dr Shanker Dayal Sharma	3 September 1987–24 July 1992
9.	Shri K. R. Narayanan	21 August 1992–24 July 1997
10.	Shri Krishan Kant	21 August 1997–27 July 2002
11.	Shri Bhairon Singh Shekhawat	19 August 2002–21 July 2007
12.	Shri Mohammad Hamid Ansari	11 August 2007–Present

13
CHAPTER

Governor

The Governor, the Chief Minister, the Council of Ministers and the Attorney General of State (AGI) are the parts of the state executive. Articles 153–167 of Part VI cover various aspects of the state executive. The main function of the state executive is to implement the laws enacted by the state legislature, and in some case, laws of the Parliament too.

Article 153 says that, there shall be a Governor for each state. (The list of the Governor of the Karnataka state has been provided in Table 13.1.) The Constitution provides for one of the highest orders, prestige and dignity to the Governor at the state-level democratic political system. The Governor plays a **dual role** in a state, that is,

1. The Governor acts as the **'Chief Executive Head'** of the state. However, in accordance with the parliamentary form of government, like the President, he is also a constitutional or nominal or a titular head of a state, with the real head being the Chief Minister and the Council of Ministers.
2. The Governor acts as an **agent or a nominee of the Central government** in the state government.

QUALIFICATION

The Constitution prescribes **only two qualifications** to become a Governor of a state. They are as follows:

1. He should be **a citizen of India.**
2. He should **be minimum 35 years of age.**

Along with these, two non-strictly followed **conventions** are also there. They are as follows:

1. The Governor should be **from another state or UTs,** that is, one person shall not be appointed as a Governor of his own home state.

2. The President is required to **consult the Chief Minister** of the concerned state before appointing a Governor to that state.

APPOINTMENT

The Governor is not elected **but appointed by the President by warrant under his hand and seal.** But in the USA, the Governor of a state is directly elected by the people; thus, there he is not an agent or a nominee of the Federal government.

According to the original Constitution, there must be one Governor for each state; but the 7th Constitutional Amendment Act 1956 provided for the **appointment of one person as a Governor of two or more states** by the President. The **Chief Justice of the concerned High Court** and in his absence, the senior most judge of that High Court, **administers the oath of office** to the Governor.

CONDITIONS

The Constitution puts certain conditions on the office of the Governor. Those are as follows:

1. He must **not be an MP or MLA/MLC;** if such a person is elected as the Governor, his seat in his concerned house is considered to **be vacant.**
2. He should **not have any office** of profit.
3. He can **use Raj Bhavan** (his official residence) without paying rent.
4. He has some emoluments, allowance and privileges as **determined by the Parliament** (not by the state legislature); it cannot be decreased during his term of office.

At present, the salary of the Governor is 1.10 lakh per month. Like the President, the Governor also enjoys **immunity from criminal proceedings** in all court of laws **even for personal acts,** but **he does not enjoy immunity from civil proceedings** in terms of personal acts. **He cannot be arrested or imprisoned during his term** of office, and he is **not answerable to any courts** for his use of powers and performance of duties, that is, he has **no legal liability** for his official acts.

TERM

The term of the Governor is **five years.** But his term is **insecure** as he holds the office **during the pleasure of the President.** In other words, the **President can remove a Governor at any time.** The Constitution does **not specify any**

grounds to remove the Governor from his office. In case of resignation, the Governor **submits his resignation to the President.**

A Governor can be **transferred from one state to another state** for the remaining term. A Governor is **eligible for reappointed as many times as he may wish** in the same state or in other state.

In case of the sudden death of a Governor during his term, the President may **appoint the Chief Justice of the concerned High Court** or **a Governor of other state** to temporarily perform the duties of the Governor of that state.

POWER AND FUNCTIONS

Like the President, the Governor has legislative, executive, judiciary and financial powers. But the Governor **does not have any military, diplomatic and emergency powers.**

Legislative Powers

As an indispensable part of the state legislature, the Governor has the power to:

1. **Summon and prorogue** different sessions of the **state legislature** from time to time.
2. **Address the first session of the state legislature** after each General Election and the first session of each year.
3. **Dissolve the State Legislative Assembly** after its end of term or in other cases.
4. **Veto a bill** of the state legislature.
5. To **send message to the state legislature** regarding a bill or otherwise.
6. **Appoint the presiding officer** in a house of the state legislature, when both the offices of presiding officers (the Speaker/Deputy Speaker of the Vidhan Sabha or the Chairman/Deputy Chairman of the Vidhan Parishad) in a house of the state legislature fall vacant.
7. **Nominate 'one member' from the Anglo-Indian community t**o the State Legislative Assembly and **one-sixth members to the State Legislative Council** who are eminent personalities in the fields of literature, art, science, social service and cooperative movement.
8. Decide on the **disqualification of MLAs/MLCs** in consultation with the Election Commission of India in some cases.
9. Lay down the **annual reports of** the Karnataka Public Service Commission (KPSC), the State Finance Commission and so on before the state legislature.
10. Lay down **annual financial statement or budget** of the state government before the state legislature.
11. **Issue ordinance** when the state legislature is not in session.

Veto Powers

A bill of the state legislature cannot **become an Act without the assent or signature of the Governor** or **the President, in case that bill is sent to the President for consideration by the Governor.** So the state legislature presents each bill after it is passed by it to the Governor for his assent. The Governor has the following options with regard to a bill presented by the state legislature to him:

1. He may declare his **assent** to the bill.
2. He may **withhold** his assent to the bill **(absolute veto)** and the bill will not become an act.
3. He may **return** the bill (other than a money bill) for the reconsideration of the state legislature **(suspensive veto).** However, if that bill is passed again by the state legislature with or without changes or amendments and again presented to the Governor, he **must give his assent** to the bill as it is now obligatory for him. It means that the state legislature can **nullify the suspensive veto** of the Governor.
4. He may **reserve the bill for the consideration of the President** and the President will have the final say on that bill.

The Governor can give his assent or withhold **a money bill** but he **cannot return it** to the state legislature for reconsideration as it is introduced in the state legislature only after his prior recommendation.

Ordinance-making Power

The most important legislative power of the Governor is the ordinance-making power. According to Article 213 of the Constitution, the Governor has the power to **promulgate or withdraw an ordinance at any period of time, only if the state legislature is in recess**—that is, any one house or both the houses (if it is a bicameral legislature) of the state legislature are not in session—and on the basis of the **recommendation of the Council of Ministers.** The state legislature must approve or disapprove an ordinance **within six weeks** of its reassembly; if not, then it will lapse. Without the approval of the state legislature, the maximum life of an ordinance is **six months and six weeks.** In some cases, the Governor needs instruction from the President to promulgate an ordinance.

Executive Powers

According to Article 154 of the Constitution, **'All the executive powers of the state are vested in the Governor'.** But the Governor exercises his executive powers (except discretionary powers) **only on the aid and advice of the Council of Ministers headed by the Chief Minister.**

The important executive powers of the Governor are as follows:

1. He is the **constitutional head of the state.**
2. The government of a state performs all its action **in the name** of the Governor.
3. He **appoints all the ministers,** including the Chief Minister, and they hold the office **during his pleasure.**
4. He **appoints the** Attorney General of State, the State Election Commissioners, members and Chairmen of the State Public Service Commissions, the State Finance Commission and so on.
5. He can **recommend the President to impose the President rule** in a state; during the President rule, **he exercises executive powers on behalf of the President.**
6. He can get any **administrative or legislative** proposal-related information of the state government from the Chief Minister.
7. He acts as **the Chancellor of State Universities;** in this capacity, he **appoints the Vice-Chancellors of State Universities** and has the powers to direct inspection or enquiry into the affairs of the State Universities.
8. He can make rules to smoothly run the transaction of business of the state government and distributing-related business between ministers.

Judicial Power

The important judicial powers of the Governor are as follows:

1. While appointing the Chief Justice and other judges of the concerned High Courts, **the President consults him.**
2. He **appoints the judges of courts below the High Court** by taking the opinion of the High Court.
3. He can **grant a pardon** to convicted and sentenced person by a court against **a state law.**

Pardoning Power

To nullify judicial errors, the Constitution of India, conferred pardoning power to the Governor. He can grant a pardon, commute, remit, reprieve and respite to a convicted and sentenced person by a court against a state law. This power is an executive action and independent from judiciary. So, one cannot appeal for the Governor to pardon as a matter of right. **The Governor has no power to pardon a death punishment, but he can suspend, remit or commute it.** Even if a state law provides for death punishment for any offence, **the power to grant pardon death punishment rests with the President,** not the Governor. **The**

Governor has no power over court martial punishments to grant any kind of pardon.

Financial Power

Important financial powers of the Governor are as follows:

1. He lays down **the budget** or annual financial statement before the state legislature.
2. His **prior recommendation** is needed to introduce a **money bill** in the state legislature.
3. **His sanction** is a must to use the money from **the Contingency Fund of State.**
4. Without his prior recommendation, **no demand for grant** can be made in the state legislature.
5. He constitutes **the State Finance Commission** after **every five years**, which decides on the **distribution of revenue between the state government and the local governments.**

It must be noted here that the Governor **is the nominal head** in our parliamentary form of government. Most of the powers of the Governor discussed above are exercised by him **only on the aid and advice of the Council of Ministers** headed by the Chief Minister who is the real executive. The act done by the Governor (except using his discretionary power) without the aid and advice of the Council of Ministers is **illegal or unconstitutional. However, like the President, the Governor is not bound to the advice of the State Council of Ministers.**

DISCRETIONARY POWER OF THE GOVERNOR

The discretionary powers of the Governor means that the Governor can act on a matter without any aid and advice of the Council of Ministers by using his discretion. The Governor's decision is final with respect to whether or not a matter falls under his discretion. The Governor has the **Constitutional discretionary** and **situational discretionary** powers.

The Governor uses his Constitutional discretionary powers in the following matters:

1. Recommendations to the President **to impose President's rule** in the state.
2. **Reserving a bill for the consideration of the President.**
3. In case of discharging his function as the administrator of an **adjourning UT**, he has the power to get any administrative or legislative proposal-related information of the state government from the Chief Minister.

The Governor uses his situational discretionary powers in the following matters:

1. To appoint a Chief Minister when **the Chief Minister dies suddenly** and there is no successor and **no political party enjoys a clear majority** in the Vidhan Sabha to form a government.
2. To **dismiss the State Council of Ministers after it fails to prove the confidence of the Vidhan Sabha,** that is, he may or may not dismiss the Council of Ministers when it fails to win no confidence motion.
3. To **dissolve the Vidhan Sabha if the Council of Ministers lost its majority,** that is, he may or may not dissolve the Vidhan Sabha.

Apart from these Discretionary powers, the Governor has important powers and functions in those areas, which got special status, for example, in the Hyderabad–Karnataka region.

TABLE 13.1
LIST OF THE GOVERNOR OF THE STATE OF KARNATAKA

S. No.	Name of Governor	Term of Office
1.	Jayachamarajendra Wadiyar	1 November 1956–4 May 1964
2.	S M Srinagesh	4 May 1964–2 April 1965
3.	V. V. Giri	2 April 1965–13 May 1967
4.	Gopal Swarup Pathak	13 May 1967–30 August 1969
5.	Dharma Vira	23 October 1969–1 February 1972
6.	Mohanlal Sukhadia	1 February 1972–10 January 1976
7.	Uma Shankar Dikshit	10 January 1976–2 August 1977
8.	Govind Narain	2 August 1977–15 April 1983
9.	Ashoknath Banerji	16 April 1983–25 February 1988
10.	Pendekanti Venkatasubbaiah	26 February 1988–5 February 1990
11.	Bhanu Pratap Singh	8 May 1990–6 January 1991
12.	Khurshed Alam Khan	6 January 1991–2 December 1999
13.	V. S. Ramadevi	2 December 1999–20 August 2002
14.	T. N. Chaturvedi	21 August 2002–20 August 2007
15.	Rameshwar Thakur	21 August 2007–24 June 2009
16.	Hans Raj Bhardwaj	24 June 2009–29 June 2014
17.	Konijeti Rosaiah	29 June 2014–31 August 2014
18.	Vajubhai Rudabhai Vala	1 September 2014–Incumbent

14

CHAPTER

Prime Minister

In accordance with the parliamentary form of government, the Prime Minister (PM) of India is the *de facto* **or real executive authority or the head of the Union Government,** with the nominal or titular or ceremonial head being the President of India. The President is the symbol of India and the Prime Minister is the **supreme political leader** of India. (A list of the Prime Ministers of India has been provided in Table 14.1.)

APPOINTMENT OF THE PRIME MINISTER

The Constitution **does not give** detailed explanation of the **manner of selection and appointment** of the PM. Article 75 says, 'The **PM shall be appointed by the President and he holds the office during the pleasure of the President.'** It does not at all mean that the President can appoint or remove the PM according to his whims and fancies.

According to the conventions of the parliamentary form of government, the President **appoints the leader of the majority party in the Lok Sabha as the PM** and then **asks him to win a 'vote of confidence' of the Lok Sabha within a month.** Here, the majority party means a party or coalition which has 272 or more seats in the Lok Sabha and the 'vote of confidence' means through which 272 members of the Lok Sabha **express and confirm their support to the PM.**

In case no party gets the clear majority in the Lok Sabha, then the President appoints the **leader of the largest party or coalition parties** in the Lok Sabha as the PM by using his discretionary powers. After that, if the appointed PM fails to win a 'vote of confidence' in the Lok Sabha within a month, as per the call of the President, he discontinues to act as the PM. That is why, Charan Singh (in 1979), A. B. Vajpayee (in 1996) and some others served as the PM for a very short time. If the PM dies suddenly during his term in the office, then also the President uses his discretionary powers to appoint a new PM.

According to the Constitution, the **PM may be a member of either the Lok Sabha or the Rajya Sabha.** The former PM, Dr Manmohan Singh was a member of the Rajya Sabha. A person can **become the PM without being a member of the Parliament only for a maximum period of six months.** A non-member of the Parliament can be appointed as the PM by the President if the majority party in the Lok Sabha supports him, **but such a person must become a member of the Parliament within six months** or he will be removed from the position of the PM. **The President** administers the **oath of the office** and secrecy to the PM.

TERM AND REMOVAL

According to the Constitution, **there is no fixed term for the PM.** The term of the Lok Sabha is five years, so a PM cannot hold his office for more than five years. Hence, it can be inferred that the PM can remain in the office for the maximum period of five years; after that, he must get a fresh mandate of the newly elected Lok Sabha to continue in his office.

The PM holds office during the pleasure of the President, but **so long as he enjoys the majority support in the Lok Sabha, the President cannot remove him.** If the PM **loses the confidence of the Lok Sabha,** he should resign or else the President can dismiss him. The PM is eligible for **re-appointment as many times as he may wish.** In case of resignation, the PM submits his resignation to the President.

The **Parliament decides** on the salary and allowances of the PM. At present, the salary of the PM is 1.6 lakh per month. Like the President and the Governors, the **PM does not have any Constitutional immunity** against criminal and civil proceedings.

POWERS AND FUNCTIONS

The PM has the following powers and functions:

1. He recommends a person to the President to be **appointed and removed as a minister.**
2. He is the **head of Union Council of Ministers.** In this capacity, he has the power to supervise, guide, control, direct and co-ordinate the Council of Ministers.
3. He **presides over the Council of Minister's meetings** and plays a key role in its all decision-making.
4. He **allocates and reshuffles** various departments among ministers.
5. He may **ask the resignation of a minister** at any time in case of difference or advise the President to dismiss him as a minister.
6. When the PM dies or resigns, the **Council of Ministers is automatically dissolved;** hence, all the ministers lose their powers and positions.
7. He is the **principal line of communication** between the President and the Council of Ministers.

8. The President exercises all his powers (except discretionary power) **only according to the aid and advice** rendered by the Council of Ministers headed by the PM.
9. He is the **leader of the Lok Sabha.** In this capacity, he advises the President to summon, prorogue and dissolve the house from time to time.
10. He is the Chairman of the National Institution for Transforming India Ayog **(NITI Ayog),** the National Integration Council, the National Development Council, the Inter-State Council and the National Water Resources Council.
11. He plays a very important role in **formulating our nation's overall developmental policies, including the foreign policy.**
12. He is the political chief **of crisis manager at the national level** and **chief spokesperson of the Central government.**

The PM is the leader of our nation. He is the most powerful person in our politico-administrative system. That is why the parliamentary form of government is also called as **'prime ministerial government'.**

The PM has been described as:

– 'The Government is the master of the country and the PM is the master of the Government', by H.R.G. Greaves
– 'A moon among lesser stars', by Sir William Vernor Harcourt
– 'The key stone of the Cabinet arch', by Lord Morely
– 'The key stone of the Constitution'
– 'He is like a Sun, around which the Planets revolve', by Jennings
– 'The PM is central to formation, life and death of Council of Ministers'

TABLE 14.1
LIST OF THE PRIME MINISTERS OF INDIA

S. No.	Name	Period	Political Party	Total Period
1.	Jawahar Lal Nehru	15 August 1947–27 May 1964	INC	16 years, 286 days
	Gulzarilal Nanda*	27 May 1964–9 June 1964	INC	13 days
2.	Lal Bahadur Shastri	9 June 1964–11 January1966	INC	1 year, 216 days
	Gulzarilal Nanda*	11 January 1966–24 January 1966	INC	13 days
3.	Indira Gandhi	24 January 1966–24 March 1977	INC	11 years, 59 days
4.	Morarji Desai	24 March 1977–28 July 1979	Janata Party	2 years, 126 days
5.	Charan Singh	28 July 1979–14 January 1980	Janata Party	170 days
3.	Indira Gandhi	14 January 1980–31 October 1984	INC	4 years, 291 days
6.	Rajiv Gandhi	31 October 1984–2 December 1989	INC	5 year, 32 days

(Table 14.1 Contd)

(Table 14.1 Contd)

S. No.	Name	Period	Political Party	Total Period
7.	V. P. Singh	2 December 1989–10 November 1990	Janata Dal	342 days
8.	Chandra Shekhar	10 November 1990–21 June 1991	Samajwadi Janata Party	223 days
9.	P. V. Narasimha Rao	21 June 1991–16 May 1996	INC	4 years, 330 days
10.	Atal Bihari Vajpayee	16 May 1996–1 June 1996	BJP	13 days
11.	H. D. Deve Gowda	1 June 1996–21 April 1997	Janata Dal	324 days
12.	I. K. Gujral	21 April 1997–19 March 1998	Janata Party	332 days
10.	Atal Bihari Vajpayee	19 March 1998–22 May 2004	BJP	6 years, 64 days
13.	Dr Manmohan Singh	22 May 2004–26 May 2014	INC	10 years, 4 days
14.	Narendra Modi	26 May 2014–Incumbent	BJP	

Chief Minister

In accordance with the parliamentary form of government, the Chief Minister (CM) of a state is the *de facto* **or real executive authority or the head of the state government,** with the nominal or titular or ceremonial head being the Governor. The Governor is the symbol of the state and the Chief Minister is the supreme political leader at the state level. (A list of the Chief Ministers of Karnataka has been provided in Table 15.1.)

APPOINTMENT OF THE CHIEF MINISTER

The Constitution does not give detailed explanation of the manner of selection and appointment of the CM. Article 164 says, **'The CM shall be appointed by the Governor and he holds the office during the pleasure of the Governor.'** It does not at all mean that the Governor can appoint or remove the CM according to his whims and fancy.

According to the conventions of the parliamentary form of government, **the Governor appoints the leader of the majority party in the Vidhan Sabha as the CM** and then asks him to **win a 'vote of confidence' of the Vidhan Sabha within a month.**

In case no party gets the clear majority in the Vidhan Sabha, then the Governor appoints the **leader of the largest party or coalition parties in the Vidhan Sabha** as the CM by using his discretionary powers. After that, if the appointed CM fails to win a 'vote of confidence' in the Vidhan Sabha within a month, as per the call of the Governor, he will be discontinued as a CM. If the CM dies suddenly during his term, then also the Governor uses his discretionary powers to appoint a new CM.

According to the Constitution, the CM may be a member of **either the Vidhan Sabha or the Vidhan Parishad.** A person can **become the CM without being a member of the state legislature only for a maximum period of six months.** A non-member of the state legislature can be appointed as the CM by the Governor if the majority party in the Vidhan Sabha supports him, but such a **person must become a member of the state legislature within six months** or he will be discontinued as a CM. The **Governor** administers the **oath of office** and secrecy to the CM.

TERM AND REMOVAL

According to the Constitution, **there is no fixed term for the CM.** The term of the Vidhan Sabha is five years, so it cannot support any one CM for more than five years; hence, it can be inferred that the CM can remain in the office for the maximum period of five years and after that he must get a fresh mandate of the newly elected Vidhan Sabha to continue in his office.

The CM holds office **during the pleasure of the Governor,** but **so long as he enjoys the majority support in the Vidhan Sabha, the Governor cannot remove him.** If the CM loses the confidence of the Vidhan Sabha, he should resign or else the Governor can dismiss him. The CM is eligible for **reappointment as many times as he may wish.** In case of resignation, the CM submits his resignation to the Governor.

The respective state legislature decides on the salary and allowances of the CM. At present, the salary of the CM varies from the state to state ranging from ₹1 lakh to ₹12 lakhs per annum. Like the President and the Governors, **the CM does not have any Constitutional immunity** against criminal and civil proceedings.

POWERS AND FUNCTIONS

The CM has the following powers and functions:

1. He recommends a person to the Governor to be **appointed and removed as a minister.**
2. He is the **head of the State Council of Ministers.** In this capacity, he has the power to supervise, guide, control, direct and coordinate with the Council of Ministers.
3. He **presides over the Council of Minister's meetings** and plays a key role in its all decision-making.
4. He **allocates and reshuffles** various departments among ministers.
5. He may **ask the resignation of a minister** at any time in case of difference or advise the Governor to dismiss him as a minister.
6. When the CM dies or resigns, other ministers and the council of ministers **are automatically dissolved;** hence, all the ministers lose their powers and positions.
7. He is the **principal line of communication** between the Governor and the Council of Ministers.
8. The Governor exercises all his powers (except discretionary power) **only according to aid and advice** rendered by the Council of Minister headed by the CM.
9. He is the **Chairman of the State Planning Board.**
10. He is **a member** of the **NITI Ayog,** the **National Integration Council,** the **National Development Council** and the **Inter-State Council,** which are **all chaired by the Prime Minister.**

11. On rotation basis, he **acts as a Vice-Chairman** of the concerned **Zonal Council** for a period of one year.
12. He is the **leader of the Vidhan Sabha.** In this capacity, he advises the Governor to summon, prorogue and dissolve the house from time to time.
13. He plays a very important role in **formulating state's overall developmental policies.**
14. He is the political **chief of crisis manager** at the state level and the **chief spokesperson** of the state government.

The CM is the leader of the respective state. He is the most powerful person in the state-level politico-administrative system.

TABLE 15.1
LIST OF THE CHIEF MINISTERS OF KARNATAKA

S. No.	Name	Term	Tenure Period	Party
1.	K. Chengalaraya Reddy	1947–1952	4 years, 157 days	
2.	K. Hanumanthaiah	1952–1956	4 years, 142 days	
3.	Kadidal Manjappa	1956–1956	73 days	
4.	S. Nijalingappa (the first CM after renaming Mysore State as Karnataka)	1956–1958	1 year, 197 days	INC
5.	B. D. Jatti	1958–1962	3 years, 297 days	
6.	S. R. Kanthi	1962–1962	98 days	
(4)	S. Nijalingappa	1962–1968	5 years, 342 days	
7.	Veerendra Patil	1968–1971	2 years, 293 days	
–	Vacant[a]	1971–1972	1 year, 1 day	—
8.	D. Devaraj Urs	1972–1977	5 years, 286 days	INC
–	Vacant[a]	1977–1978	59 days	—
(8)	D. Devaraj Urs	1978–1980	1 year, 313 days	INC
9.	R. Gundu Rao	1980–1983	2 years, 359 days	
10.	Ramakrishna Hegde	1983–1984	1 year, 354 days	Janata Party
		1985–1986	342 days	
		1986–1988	2 years, 176 days	
11.	S. R. Bommai	1988–1989	281 days	
–	Vacant[a]	1989–1989	193 days	—
(7)	Veerendra Patil	1989–1990	314 days	INC
–	Vacant[a]	1990–1990	7 days	—

(Table 15.1 Contd)

(Table 15.1 Contd)

S. No.	Name	Term	Tenure Period	Party
12.	S. Bangarappa	1990–1992	2 years, 33 days	INC
13.	M. Veerappa Moily	1992–1994	2 years, 22 days	
14.	H. D. Deve Gowda	1994–1996	1 year, 172 days	Janata Dal
15.	J. H. Patel	1996–1999	3 years, 129 days	
16.	S. M. Krishna	1999–2004	4 years, 230 days	INC
17.	Dharam Singh	2004–2006	1 year, 245 days	
18.	H. D. Kumaraswamy	2006–2007	1 year, 253 days	JDS
–	Vacant	2007–2007	33 days	—
19.	B. S. Yeddyurappa	12 September 2007–19 September 2007	7 days	BJP
–	Vacant[a]	20 September 2007–27 May 2008	189 days	—
(19)	B. S. Yeddyurappa	30 May 2008–31 July 2011	3 years, 62 days	BJP
20.	D. V. Sadananda Gowda	4 August 2011–12 July 2012	343 days	
21.	Jagadish Shettar	12 July 2012–12 May 2013	304 days	
22.	Siddaramaiah	13 May 2013–Present	2 years, 95 days	INC

Note: [a]Vacant because of the imposition of the President rule.

16
CHAPTER

Union Council of Ministers

In accordance with the parliamentary form of government, the Union Council of Ministers headed by the Prime Minister is the **real executive authority,** with the nominal or titular head being the President. The Central Council of Ministers is **a Constitutional body** consisting of **all the ministers including the Prime Minister** in the Central government.

Article 74 says,

There shall be a Council of Ministers with the Prime Minister at the head to aid and advise the President, who shall, in the exercise of his functions, act in accordance with such advice. The advice tendered by Ministers to the President shall not be inquired into in any court.

In other words, although the Constitution vested all the executive powers of the Union Government in the President, in reality all these powers are exercised by the Council of Ministers headed by the Prime Minister in his name. The Council of Ministers are **collectively responsible to the Lok Sabha,** not the Rajya Sabha.

APPOINTMENT OF THE COUNCIL OF MINISTERS

Articles 74 and 75 of the Constitution deal with the various aspects of the Union Council of Ministers. According to Article 75, 'The Prime Minister shall be appointed by the President and other **ministers shall be appointed by the President on the advice of the Prime Minister.'** It means that, those who are **recommended by the Prime Minister should be appointed as ministers** by the President.

The total strength of the Council of Ministers including the Prime Minister **should not be more than 15 per cent of the total strength of the Lok Sabha.** So, the number of ministers in the Central government should be around 80.

According to the Constitution, a Council of Minister may be a **member of either the Lok Sabha or the Rajya Sabha,** but he is **only responsible to the Lok Sabha.** A person can become a minister **without being a member of the Parliament only for a maximum period of six months.** A non-member of the Parliament can be appointed as a minister by the President on the basis of the recommendation of the Prime Minister, but such a person **must become a member of the Parliament within six months** or he discontinues being a minister. A member of a house in the Parliament as a minister can participate in the other house with the **right to speak and without the right to vote.**

The **President administers the oath of the office** and secrecy to the Council of Ministers. According to the Constitution, **there is no fixed term for the Council of Ministers.** The Council of Ministers holds the office **during the pleasure of the President.** A minister submits his/her **resignation to the President.** The **Parliament decides** on the salary and allowances of the Council of Ministers.

RESPONSIBILITY OF THE COUNCIL OF MINISTER

The Council of Ministers has two kinds of responsibilities. They are as follows:

1. **Collective responsibility:**
   Article 75 says that the Union Council of Ministers is **collectively responsible to the Lok Sabha.** This is the **very foundation of our Parliamentary form of government,** in which **the executive is responsible to the legislature**. The Council of Ministers are the one which **enjoys the majority** support or confidence of the Lok Sabha; so for all its acts, the Council of Ministers is collectively responsible to the Lok Sabha, irrespective of the fact whether they belong to the Rajya Sabha or the Lok Sabha. The **No Confidence Motion** is the tool of the Lok Sabha to ascertain its confidence in the Council of Ministers.

   The collective responsibility implies that

   (i) It is the **joint responsibility of all ministers,** under which each minister takes the responsibility of other minister's acts, whether he likes or dislikes those acts. One minister must support and defend the other minister's acts.

   (ii) All ministers **work as a team or one unit**. All ministers **swim and sink together.** It means that they stay in the office or lose office together. If the Lok Sabha passes **No Confidence Motion** against the Council of Ministers, **all ministers, including the Prime Minister, must resign,** and the PM advises the President to dissolve the Lok Sabha.

2. **Individual responsibility:**
   According to Article 75, the minister holds the office during the pleasure of the President. In case, one minister fails to tolerate difference with the other ministers, **he may resign or the Prime Minister may advise the President to dismiss him.** It means that the President can remove a minister even when the Council of Ministers enjoys the confidence of the Lok Sabha based on the advice of the PM. In this way, the Prime Minister ensures the collective responsibility of the Council of Ministers to the Lok Sabha.

COUNCIL OF MINISTERS' AID AND ADVICE TO THE PRESIDENT

According to the Constitution, the President **must act only according to the aid and advice rendered by the Union Council of Ministers** headed by the Prime Minister. The act done by the President (except using his discretionary power), without the aid and advice of the Council of Ministers is **illegal or unconstitutional.** However, the President has the power to ask the Council of Ministers to **reconsider an aid and advice given to him on a matter.** But after the reconsideration, if the Council of Ministers renders the aid and advice on the same matter with or without any changes, **the President has no option left except giving his assent** for that aid and advice, that is, he **must give his assent** on that matter. This also means that the President can ask the Council of Ministers to reconsider the aid and advice on a matter **only once,** not more than that.

COMPOSITION OF COUNCIL OF MINISTERS

All Central ministers are not of the same type. Based on their ranks, powers and significance of ministerial positions, the Council of Ministers is divided into three categories. They are as follows:

1. **Cabinet ministers:** These ministers **head one or more important ministries,** such as home, finance, agriculture and defence and so on in the Central government. They constitute the **cabinet** and attend its meetings.
2. **Ministers of state:** These ministers **may independently head the ministries/departments or they may be attached to cabinet ministers,** such as they may be given the charge of departments or specific work within ministries headed by the cabinet ministers. These ministers **are not the members of cabinet** and do not attend its meeting without an invitation.
3. **Deputy ministers:** These ministers **have no separate charge of ministries/ departments.** They are **attached to cabinet ministers or ministry of states to assist them** in administrative and parliamentary functions. These ministers are **not members of cabinet** and do not attend its meetings.

The **'Parliamentary Secretaries'** are the last category of the Council of Ministers. They **do not head** any departments but assist the senior ministers in their **parliamentary functions. However, since 1967, no parliamentary secretaries have been appointed** except in the Rajiv Gandhi government.

The **Deputy Prime Minister** is part of the Cabinet and he is mostly appointed for political compulsions. He does not have any special powers or Constitutional position like that of the Prime Minister. The first Deputy Prime Minister of India was Sardar Vallabhbhai Patel. The Prime Minister stands above all these ministers and heads the Council of Ministers.

UNION CABINET

The Union Cabinet is composed of **all the cabinet rank ministers including the Prime Minister** of the Central government. **It is headed by the Prime Minister.** It is **the Constitutional body** as Article 352 defines it. Usually, it consists of around 15–20 members. It is the most **powerful, highest decision-making, policy-making and supreme executive authority** in our politico-administrative system. Their advice to the President is **binding on the President.** The Cabinet plays a key role in **managing an emergency situation** as it is the prime crisis manager of our country. It decides on the **highest level of appointments** in the Government and of the Constitutional bodies. The Central government administration is **co-ordinated by it.** The cabinet has various committees to smoothly and effectively handle its functions, such as Ad-hoc Committees, Standing Committees like Political Affairs Committee, Economic Affairs Committee and so on.

KITCHEN CABINET

It is the **extra-constitutional and informal body** consisting of the **Prime Minister and his 2–4 influential colleagues, friends, family members and relatives** who are very close to the Prime Minister and enjoy his **confidence and faith.** These people give advice and assist the Prime Minister to perform his duties.

SHADOW CABINET

The Shadow Cabinet does **not exist in India.** It exists in Britain. In the Shadow Cabinet system, **each minister has a corresponding 'shadow minister' belonging to the opposition party.** The Shadow Cabinet provides an alternative to the Cabinet. A shadow minister of the opposition party becomes the cabinet minister when his party forms the government.

17

CHAPTER

State Council of Ministers

In accordance with the parliamentary form of government, at the state level, the State Council of Ministers headed by the Chief Minister is the **real executive authority,** with the nominal or titular head being the Governor. The State Council of Ministers means, it is the **Constitutional body** consisting of **all the ministers including the Chief Minister** in the state government.

Article 163 says,

There shall be a Council of Ministers with the Chief Minister at the head to aid and advise the Governor, who shall, in the exercise of his functions (except his discretionary powers), act in accordance with such advice. The advice tendered by Ministers to the Governor shall not be inquired into in any court.

In other words, although the Constitution has vested all the executive powers of the state in the Governor, in reality all these powers are exercised by the Council of Ministers headed by the Chief Minister in his name. The Council of Ministers is **collectively responsible to the Vidhan Sabha,** not the Vidhan Parishad.

APPOINTMENT OF THE COUNCIL OF MINISTERS

Articles 163 and 164 of the Constitution deal with the various aspects of the State Council of Ministers. According to Article 164- 'The Chief Minister shall be appointed by the Governor and other **ministers shall be appointed by the Governor on the advice of the Chief Minister.'** It means that those who are **recommended by the Chief Minister should be appointed as ministers** by the Governor.

The total strength of the Council of Ministers including the Chief Minister **should not be more than 15 per cent of the total strength of the Vidhan Sabha.**

According to the Constitution, a Council of Minister may be **a member of either the Vidhan Sabha or the Vidhan Parishad.** But he is **only responsible to the Vidhan Sabha.** A person can become a minister **without being a member of the state legislature only for a maximum period of six**

months. A non-member of the state legislature can be appointed as a minister by the Governor on the basis of the recommendation of the Chief Minister. But **such a person must become a member of the state legislature within six months** or he discontinues as a minister. A member of a house in the state legislature as a minister can participate in the other house with the **right to speak and without the right to vote.**

The **Governor administers the oath of the office** and secrecy to the Council of Ministers. According to the Constitution, **there is no fixed term for the Council of Ministers.** The Council of Ministers holds office **during the pleasure of the Governor.** A minister submits his/her **resignation to the Governor.** The **state legislature** decides on the salary and allowances of the Council of Ministers.

RESPONSIBILITY OF THE COUNCIL OF MINISTERS

The Council of Ministers has two kinds of responsibilities:

1. **Collective responsibility:**
   Article 164 says that the State Council of Ministers is **collectively responsible to the Vidhan Sabha.** The State Council of Ministers is the one which enjoys the **majority support or confidence** of the Vidhan Sabha; so for all its acts, the Council of Ministers is collectively responsible to the Vidhan Sabha, whether they belong to the Vidhan Parishad or the Vidhan Sabha. The **No Confidence Motion** is the tool of the Vidhan Sabha to ascertain its confidence in the Council of Ministers.

   The collective responsibility implies that

   (i) It is the **joint responsibility of all ministers,** under which each minister takes the responsibility of other minister's acts, whether he likes or dislikes that. One minister must support and defend the other minister's acts.

   (ii) All ministers work as **a team or one unit**. All ministers **swim and sink together.** It means that they stay together in the office or lose office. If the Vidhan Sabha passes No Confidence Motion against the Council of Ministers, all ministers, including the Chief Minister, must resign and the CM advises the Governor to dissolve the Vidhan Sabha.

2. **Individual responsibility:**
   According to Article 164, the minister holds the office during the pleasure of the Governor. In case, one minister fails to tolerate difference with the other ministers, he may **resign or the Chief Minister advises the Governor to dismiss him.** It means that the Governor can remove a minister even when the Council of Ministers enjoys the confidence of the Vidhan Sabha based on the advice of the Chief Minister. In this way, the Chief Minister ensures the collective responsibility of the Council of Ministers to the Vidhan Sabha.

COUNCIL OF MINISTERS' AID AND ADVICE TO THE GOVERNOR

According to the Constitution, the Governor shall act (except in using his discretion) **only according to the aid and advice rendered by the State Council of Ministers** headed by the Chief Minister. The act done by the Governor (except using his discretionary power), without the aid and advice of the Council of Ministers is **illegal or unconstitutional. However, like the President, the Governor is not bound to the advice of the State Council of Ministers.**

COMPOSITION OF COUNCIL OF MINISTERS

All ministers of a state government are not one of the same type, based on their ranks, powers and significance of ministerial positions, the State Council of Ministers are divided into three categories. They are as follows:

1. **Cabinet ministers:** These ministers **head one or more important ministries,** such as home, finance, agriculture, defence and so on in the state government. They **constitute the cabinet** and attend its meetings.
2. **Ministry of state:** These ministers **may independently head the ministries/departments or they may be attached to state cabinet ministers**, such as they may be given the **charge of departments or specific work** within ministries headed by the cabinet ministers. These ministers **are not the members of the cabinet** and do not attend its meeting without an invitation.
3. **Deputy ministers:** These ministers have **no separate charge of ministries/departments.** They are **attached to the cabinet ministers or the ministry of states to assist** them in administrative and state legislature functions. These ministers are **not the members of the cabinet** and do not attend its meetings.

The Deputy Chief Minister is part of the state cabinet and he is mostly appointed for political compulsions. He does not have any special powers or Constitutional position like that of the Chief Minister. The Chief Minister stands above all these ministers and heads the Council of Ministers.

STATE CABINET

The State Cabinet is composed of the **all cabinet-rank ministers including the Chief Minister** of the state government. **It is headed by the Chief Minister.** The cabinet is the **most powerful, highest decision-making, policy-making and supreme executive authority in the state level** politico-administrative system. Its advices to the Governor are **non-binding** on the Governor. The State cabinet plays a key role in managing the emergency situation as it is the prime crisis manager of the State. It decides on the highest level of appointments in the state government and some Constitutional bodies in the concerned states. The state government administration is coordinated by it. The state cabinet has various committees to smoothly and effectively handle its functions, such as the Ad-hoc Committees and Standing Committees.

18
CHAPTER

Attorney General of India and Advocate General of the State

ATTORNEY GENERAL OF INDIA

The Attorney General of India (AGI) **is the highest-rank law officer** in India. He is **appointed by the President** under Article 76 (1) of the Constitution of India. He **holds the office during the pleasure of the President.** He must be **qualified to be appointed as a Judge of the Supreme Court.** In other words, the qualification of the AGI and that of the Judges of the Supreme Court should be the same.

He has **no fixed term** and can be **removed by the President** at **any point of time.** The AGI submits his resignation to the President. Usually, he resigns **when the government changes** as he is appointed by its advice. His remuneration and other conditions are fixed **by the President.**

Without being a Member of Parliament, **he is the only person to take part in the proceedings of the Parliament or its Joint Sitting or any Parliamentary Committee without a right to vote.** The AGI is entitled to **all the privileges and immunities** as those of a Member of Parliament. He has the **right of audience in all courts** in the territory of India.

The AGI is **not a Cabinet Minister.** A separate minister of Law and Justice handles the legal matters of the Government of India. The AGI is not considered as a servant of the Government of India, so **he is not prohibited from private legal practice.**

Important Duties and Functions of the AGI

The AGI is the **chief law officer of the Government of India.** Generally speaking, the AGI is like an advocate or a **legal advisor** to the Government of India. He has the following duties and functions to exercise:

1. He gives necessary **legal advice** to the Government of India on any matters **referred by the President** to him.

2. He is the **primary lawyer** of the Government of India in **the Supreme Court.** He is the **primary lawyer** of the Government of India; so he appears on behalf of the Government of India in its all concerned cases in the Supreme Court as well as High Courts.
3. He performs any other legal duties given to him by the President.
4. He represents the Government of India when the **President seeks advice of the Supreme Court** under Article 143.
5. He is prohibited from **advising against** the Government of India.

To assist the AGI to perform his duties, there are two Solicitor Generals and four Additional Solicitor Generals. However, these positions are not mentioned in the Constitution.

ADVOCATE GENERAL OF THE STATE

The Advocate General of the State (AGS) **is the highest-rank law officer in a state.** He is **appointed by the Governor** under Article 165. He **holds the office during the pleasure of the Governor.** He must be **qualified to be appointed as a Judge of a High Court.** In other words, the qualification of the AGS and that of a Judge of a High Court should be the same.

He has **no fixed term** and can be **removed by the Governor** at any point of time. The AGS submits his resignation letter to the Governor. Usually, he resigns when concerned state government changes as he is appointed by its advice. His remuneration and other conditions are fixed by the Governor.

Without being a member of the state legislature, he is the **only person** to take part in the proceedings of the state legislature or any of its committees without a right to vote. The AGS is entitled to all the privileges and immunities as those of a member of state legislature. He has the right of audience in all courts in the territory of the concerned state.

The AGS is not a Cabinet Minister. A separate minister of law handles the legal matters of the state government. The AGS is not considered as a servant of the state government, so he is not prohibited from private legal practice.

Important Duties and Functions of the AGS

The AGS is the **chief law office of the state government.** Generally speaking, the AGS is like an advocate or a **legal advisor** of the state government. He has the following duties and functions to exercise:

1. He gives necessary **legal advice** to the state government on any matters referred by the Governor to him.
2. He performs any other legal duties given to him by the Governor.

3. He is the primary layer of the state government. So he appears on behalf of the state government in all its concerned cases in the respective High Court.
4. He appears on behalf of the state government in all its concerned cases in the respective High Court.
5. He is prohibited from advising against the state government.

Section V

Supreme Court and High Courts

19

Supreme Court

India has an **integrated and independent** judicial system—integrated because it has a **single system of courts,** that is, all the courts, such as lower level courts, the High Courts (HC) and the Supreme Court (SC) are hierarchically arranged, which enforces both the Central laws and the state laws—and independent as it is not dependent on the legislature or the executive organs of the Government. The USA has a double system of courts, in which the Central laws are enforced by the Federal Court and the state laws by the state-level courts.

The present SC replaced the erstwhile Federal Court of India, which was created by the British Government through the Government of India act 1935. Articles 124–147 of Part V of the Constitution are about the various aspects of the SC. The SC is **the final interpreter** and **guardian** of the Constitution. It is also the **guarantor of the FRs** of the people. The SC is the **highest court of appeal** in our land.

Originally, there were a total of **eight judges** in the SC. At present, there are a total of **31 judges,** including the **Chief Justice of India (CJI).** (Table 19.1 lists all the Chief Justices of India.) The SC is located in **New Delhi.**

QUALIFICATIONS OF THE JUDGES OF THE SC

The qualifications of a person to be appointed as a judge of the SC are as follows:

1. He must be **a citizen of India.**
2. He should have been a **judge of the High Court/s for five years**
   Or
   He should have been an **advocate of the High Court/s for 10 years**
   Or
   In the **opinion of the President**, he must be a **distinguished jurist.**

Except these qualifications, the Constitution does not prescribe any other qualifications, such as education, age limit and so on.

APPOINTMENT OF JUDGES

The **President of India appoints the judges of the SC including the CJI** on the **advice of the Union Cabinet.** The SC laid down the '**Collegium System**' to appoint the judges of the SC and the HCs in its three judgements, which are together known as the 'three judges cases' (1982, 1993 and 1998).

In the matter of the appointment of **the CJI, the President** shall consult such **judges of the SC and the HCs** as he may deem necessary. According to the judgement of the SC in second judges case (1993) and convention, **only the senior most judge of the SC is appointed as the CJI.**

In the matter of the appointment of **other Judges of the SC,** the **President must consult the CJI** and also he shall consult such **judges of the SC** (usually four senior most judges) and **judges of the HCs** as he may deem necessary.

The President or a person appointed by him **administers the oath of office** to all the judges of the SC. The Constitution does **not provide for the fixed tenure** of the judges of the SC. However, they hold the office till the age of **65 years**. They **submit their resignations to the President.**

The salaries, pension and other facilities of the judges of the SC are **determined by the Parliament** and after their appointment, they cannot be changed for their disadvantage. The salary of the CJI is ₹1 lakh per month and other judges is ₹90,000 per month.

REMOVAL OF JUDGES

The only ground to remove or impeach the judges of the SC **is proved misbehaviour or incapacity.** On the **recommendation of the Parliament, the President can remove a judge of the SC** from his office. The impeachment process is discussed in the following paragraph.

A removal motion to remove a judge of the SC can be initiated by, at least, either 100 members of the Lok Sabha or 50 members of the Rajya Sabha in their respective house; the Speaker/Chairman may or may not admit this motion. In case it is admitted, a committee of three members consisting of the CJI or a judge of the SC, a Chief Justice of the High Court and an eminent jurist will be created by the Speaker/Chairman to inquire into the allegation/charge on the concerned judge of the SC. If the committee finds the judge incapable or of misbehaving nature, the Parliament shall consider the removal motion. The Parliament, after passing the removal motion in its each house, by special majority shall present an address to the President for the removal of the judge. At last, the President removes the judge by issuing an order with effect to that. So far no judge of the SC has been impeached by the Parliament. Although the Parliament, for the first time in independent India, initiated impeachment proceedings against V. Ramaswami, a former judge of the SC in 1993, it was not passed by the Lok Sabha as the Congress Party MPs walked out of the house.

JURISDICTION AND POWERS

The Constitution vests more powers and broad jurisdiction in the SC. Alladi Krishnaswamy Ayyar pointed out, 'The Supreme Court of India has more powers than any other Supreme Court in any part of the world.' The SC has the following powers and jurisdictions:

1. **Original jurisdiction:** It means the power of hearing and deciding a dispute in the first instance, not by appeal, such as a dispute between the Union Government and one or more state governments, one or more state governments (like interstate water dispute), violation of FRs (this power is concurrent with the High Court) and the dispute related to the election of the President and the Vice-President.

2. **Appellate jurisdiction:** It means the power to review a judgement of a lower court or granting a fresh trial. The SC is the **highest court of appeal** in India. The SC's appellate jurisdiction includes matters related to the Constitution, civil, criminal and special leave. A case involving substantial question of law can be referred by a High Court to the SC. A **special leave** is allowed by the SC at its discretion to appeal from any judgement related to an issue by any court or tribunal in India except the military tribunal and court martial.

3. **Writ jurisdiction:** As the Constitution entrusted the task of the SC to act as a **guarantor of the FRs** of the people, it empowered it to issue writs under Article 32, such as Habeas Corpus, Mandamus, Prohibition, Quo Warranto and Certiorari to defend and enforce the FRs of the aggrieved people.

4. **A court of record:** It means two things: first, the proceedings, acts and decisions of the SC are recorded or documented, are considered as highly authentic and can be used as evidence when needed; and second, the SC has the power to punish for not only its contempt but also all other courts in India.

5. **Advisory jurisdiction:** It means power to give **advice to the President** of India when he seeks under Article 143 on a law related to public importance or any pre-constitutional issue.

6. **Judicial review:** It means the SC has power to **examine the Constitutionality validity** by reviewing the **acts of legislatures and the orders of executives of both the Central and state governments.** The SC can declare such acts or orders as **unconstitutional (*Ultra-vires*), illegal and invalid** if they are found to be violative of the Constitution. As a result, they do not come to force. The word judicial review has not been mentioned in any part of the Indian Constitution, though. For instance, Section 66A of the Information Technology Act 2000, an act of the Parliament, empowered the police to arrest the one who makes objectionable comment on social media such as Facebook, Twitter and so on. In May 2015, the SC declared Section 66A of this act as unconstitutional because it violated the FRs (right to speech and expression) of the people and, hence, the SC upheld the supremacy of the Constitution.

7. **Other powers:** The decisions of the SC are bounded on all the courts in India, **but the SC itself is not bound to its own decisions** as Article 137 gave the power to the SC to review its own judgement. The SC can transfer cases pending before a High Court to itself or another High Court. The SC can recommend the President for the **removal of the Chairman and members of the UPSC** based on inquiry conducted by it; its recommendation is **binding on** the President in this regard. The SC exercises control over all the courts and tribunals in India. The SC is the ultimate interpreter of the Constitution of India.

INDEPENDENCE OF THE SC

To provide a conducive environment for the SC to exercise its vast power and functions without any influence, the Constitution provided much independence to it from the legislature and the executive, such as the judge of the SC is appointed on the recommendation of the Union Cabinet and can be removed on the recommendation of the Parliament to the President. Hence, they **enjoy the security of tenure.** Their service conditions including salary are fixed by the **Parliament** and cannot be changed to their disadvantage after appointment. Their expenses are **charged on the Consolidated Fund of India;** hence, it is not subjected to vote in the Parliament. It is **prohibited** for retired judges of the SC to work in any court so that to prevent them from favouring any person in their judgement for personal gain in the future. The legislatures of the Centre and the states are prohibited from discussing the conduct of the judges of the SC. The SC has the power to appoint its own staff and determine their service conditions. The Parliament **cannot curtail** the jurisdiction of the SC, though it can extend it.

NATIONAL JUDICIAL APPOINTMENT COMMISSION

As the 'Collegium System' to appoint judges of the higher judiciary lacks accountability, the Government of India **replaced the 'Collegium System'** by **establishing the 'National Judicial Appointment Commission (NJAC)'** on 13 April 2015 **to appoint and transfer the judges of the SC and the HCs.** For this, it enacted the **99th Constitutional Amendment Act 2014.** This act **added three new Articles** to the Constitution of India. They are as follows:

1. **Article 124-A:** The President shall appoint the judges of the SC and HCs **on the recommendation of the NJAC.**
2. **Article 124-B:** It is the **duty of the NJAC** to recommend such a person's name for the appointment as the judges of the SC and HCs who are **able to perform their duties.**
3. **Article 124-C:** States about the **Parliament's power** to make laws related to the **manner of selection and appointments** of the judges of the SC and HCs.

The NJAC is composed of:

1. The Chief Justice of India as its Chairman.
2. Two senior most judges of the Supreme Court.
3. The Union Minister of Law and Justice as ex-office members.
4. Two eminent personalities as nominated members, nominated by a committee consisting of the CJI, the Prime Minister and the Leader of Opposition in the Lok Sabha. Out of these, the two eminent personalities, one person should be a woman or should belong to the SCs, STs, OBCs or minority community. These nominated members hold the office for a period of three years and shall not be eligible for re-nomination.

THE PROCEDURE FOR THE APPOINTMENT OF JUDGES

In the matter of appointing the CJI, the NJAC recommends the name of the senior most judges of the SC to the President. For this, it considers the knowledge and fitness of a judge than merely his age. In the matter of appointing the other judges of the SC, the NJAC recommends a person on the basis of his ability, merit and other criteria specified in the regulations.

In the matter of appointing the CJHC, the NJAC recommends the name of a judge of an HC based on the seniority across the HCs to the President. For this, it considers ability, merit and other criteria specified in the regulations. In the matter of appointing the other judges of an HC, the NJAC considers the opinion of the concerned CJHC, the Governor and the Chief Minister.

However, the Constitutional validity of the NAJC has been challenged in the SC by a few lawyers. The Constitutional bench of the SC is examining this issue.

TABLE 19.1
LIST OF THE CHIEF JUSTICES OF INDIA

S. No.	Name	Period
1.	H. J. Kania	26 January 1950–6 November 1951
2.	M. Patanjali Sastri	7 November 1951–3 January 1954
3.	Mehr Chand Mahajan	4 January 1954–22 December 1954
4.	Bijan Kumar Mukherjea	23 December 1954–31 January 1956
5.	Sudhi Ranjan Das	1 February 1956–30 September 1959
6.	B.P. Sinha	1 October 1959–31 January 1964
7.	P. B. Gajendragadkar	1 February 1964–15 March 1966
8.	Amal Kumar Sarkar	16 March 1966–29 June 1966
9.	Koka Subba Rao	30 June 1966–11 April 1967

(Table 19.1 Contd)

(Table 19.1 Contd)

S. No.	Name	Period
10.	Kailas Nath Wanchoo	12 April 1967–24 February 1968
11.	Mohammad Hidayatullah	25 February 1968–16 December 1970
12.	Jayantilal Chhotalal Shah	17 December 1970–21 January 1971
13.	Sarv Mittra Sikri	22 Jan 1971–25 April 1973
14.	Ajit Nath Ray	26 April 1973–27 January 1977
15.	Mirza Hameedullah Beg	28 January 1977–21 February 1978
16.	Y. V. Chandrachud	22 February 1978–11 July 1985
17.	P. N. Bhagwati	12 July 1985–20 December 1986
18.	R. S. Pathak	21 December 1986–18 June 1989
19.	E. S. Venkataramiah	19 June 1989–17 December 1989
20.	Sabyasachi Mukharji	18 December 1989–25 September 1990
21.	Ranganath Misra	26 September 1990–24 November 1991
22.	Kamal Narain Singh	25 November 1991–12 December 1991
23.	Madhukar Hiralal Kania	13 December 1991–17 November 1992
24.	Lalit Mohan Sharma	18 November 1992–11 February 1993
25.	M. N. R. Venkatachaliah	12 February 1993–24 October 1994
26.	Aziz Mushabber Ahmadi	25 October 1994–24 March 1997
27.	Jagdish Sharan Verma	25 March 1997–17 January 1998
28.	Madan Mohan Punchhi	18 January 1998–9 October 1998
29.	Adarsh Sein Anand	10 October 1998–11 January 2001
30.	Sam Piroj Bharucha	11 January 2001–6 May 2002
31.	Bhupinder Nath Kirpal	6 May 2002–8 November 2002
32.	Gopal Ballav Pattanaik	8 November 2002–19 December 2002
33.	V. N. Khare	19 Dec 2002–2 May 2004
34.	S. Rajendra Babu	2 May 2004–1 June 2004
35.	Ramesh C. Lahoti	1 June 2004–1 November 2005
36.	Yogesh Sabharwal	1 November 2005–13 January 2007
37.	K. G. Balakrishnan	13 January 2007–11 May 2010
38.	S. H. Kapadia	12 May 2010–28 September 2012
39.	Altamas Kabir	29 September 2012–18 July 2013
40.	P. Sathasivam	19 July 2013–26 April 2014
41.	Rajendra Mal Lodha	27 April 2014–27 September 2014
42.	H. L. Dattu	28 September 2014–Incumbent

20
CHAPTER

High Courts

In the state judiciary system, the High Courts (HCs) are at the top position. The HCs work below the SC and above the lower level courts. The oldest HC in India is the Calcutta High Court, which was established in 1862. Later in the same year, the High Courts of Bombay and Madras were established by the British Government.

Articles 214–231 of Part VI of the Constitution of India are about various aspects of the High Courts in India. According to the Constitution, there must be one HC for each state, but it has authorized the Parliament to establish **a common HC for one or more states and/or a union territory.** At present, there **are total 24 HCs in India.**[1] There are **three common HCs.** Except **Delhi,** no UT has its own HC.

Each HC consists of one Chief Justice and judges. Their number varies from state to state. The strength of each HC is determined by the President. The seat of each HC is usually located in the capital city of the respective state. However, an HC can have **one or more bench within its jurisdiction.** For example, the permanent bench of the High Court of Karnataka is in Bangalore; however, it has its additional benches at Dharwad and Kalaburagi.

QUALIFICATIONS OF JUDGES

Qualifications of a person to be appointed as a judge of the HC are as follows:

1. He must be **a citizen of India.**
2. He should have been an **advocate of the high court/s for 10 years.**
   Or
   He must have held a **judicial office for 10 years in India.**

Except these qualifications, the Constitution does not prescribe any other qualifications, such as education, age limit and so on.

---

[1] With creation of High Courts for Tripura, Meghalaya and Manipur in 2013.

APPOINTMENT OF JUDGES

The **President of India appoints the judges of a HC including the Chief Justice of the HC (CJHC)** on the **advice of the Union Cabinet.** Like in the case of the SC, here too the **'Collegium System'** is there to appoint the judges of the HCs.

In the matter of **appointing the CJHC, the President** shall consult the CJI and the Governor of the concerned state. In the matter of the appointment of **other judges of an HC, the President** shall consult the CJI, the Governor and the CJHC of the concerned state. In the case of the appointment of a judge of an HC, the CJI must consult the collegium of two senior most judges of the SC before giving his opinion to the President; the CJI's sole opinion is not valid.

The Governor of the concerned state or a person appointed by him **administers the oath of office** to all the judges of the HC. The Constitution does not provide a fixed tenure of the judges of the HC. However, they hold office till the age of **62 years.** The judges of the HC submit their **resignations to the President.**

A judge of an HC can be **transferred from one HC to another by the President** after consulting the CJI. In this case, the CJI must consult the collegium of four senior most judges of the SC and two CJHC of the concerned states before giving his opinion to the President; the CJI's sole opinion is not valid.

The salaries, pension and other facilities of the judges of the HCs are **determined by the Parliament.** After their appointment, it cannot be changed for their disadvantage. The salary of the CJHC is ₹90,000 per month and those of the other judges are ₹80,000 per month.

REMOVAL OF JUDGES

The only ground to remove or impeach a judge of an HC **is proved misbehaviour or incapability.** On the **recommendation of the Parliament, the President can remove a judge of an HC** from his office. Thus, grounds for the removal and process of impeachment for the judges of the SC and the HC are the same. The impeachment process of judges of HC is given in the following paragraph.

A removal motion to remove a judge of HC can be initiated by, at least, either 100 members of the Lok Sabha or 50 members of the Rajya Sabha in their respective houses; the Speaker/Chairman may or may not admit this motion. In case it is admitted, a committee of three members, consisting of the CJI or a judge of the SC, a Chief Justice of the High Court and an eminent jurist will be created by the Speaker/Chairman to inquire into the allegation/charge on the concerned judge of the HC. If the committee finds the judge of misbehaving nature and incapable, the Parliament shall consider the removal motion. The Parliament, after passing the removal motion in its each house by a special majority, shall present an address to the President for the removal of the judge. At last, the President removes the judge of the HC by issuing an order with effect to that.

So far no judge of the HC has been impeached by the Parliament. The Rajya Sabha, for the first time in the independent India, impeached Mr Soumitra Sen, a former judge of the Calcutta HC in 2011. After this, he resigned from his position, so the Lok Sabha dropped his impeachment motion.

JURISDICTION AND POWERS

The Constitution vested more powers and broad jurisdiction in the HCs. They are as follows:

1. **Original jurisdiction:** It means, the power of hearing and deciding a dispute in the first instance, not by appeal, such as disputes related to the election of an MP, MLA and MLC; violation of FRs of the people; revenue matters; legal will, marriage, divorce, contempt of courts and company law and so on.
2. **Appellate jurisdiction:** It means, the power to review a judgement of a lower court or granting a fresh trial. The HCs are **primarily a court of appeal.** The HCs appellate jurisdiction includes matters related to civil and criminal cases.
3. **Writ jurisdiction:** As the Constitution entrusted the task for the SC and HCs to act as a guarantor of the FRs of the people, it **empowered the HCs to issue writs** under **Article 226,** such as Habeas Corpus, Mandamus, Prohibition, Quo Warranto and Certiorari, to defend and enforce the FRs of the aggrieved people. **The HCs have wider writ jurisdiction than that of the SC** because the SC can issue writs only in cases related to the violation of FRs, whereas the HCs can issue writs not only in cases related to the violation of fundamental rights but also in other cases.
4. **A court of record:** It implies three things. First, the proceedings, acts and decisions of an HC are recorded or documented, are considered highly authentic and can be used as evidence when needed. Secondly, an HC has the power to punish for its contempt. Finally, an HC is not bound by its own decision and can review and correct it.
5. **Judicial review:** It means that the HCs have power to examine the **Constitutional validity by reviewing the acts of legislatures and orders of executives of both the Central and state governments** under Articles 13 and 226. An HC can declare such acts or orders **unconstitutional (*Ultra-vires*), illegal and invalid** if they are found to be violative of the Constitution. As a result, they do not come to force. The word judicial review has not been mentioned in any part of the Indian Constitution, though.
6. **Other powers:** An HC can transfer cases pending before a lower court to itself. It exercises control over and supervises subordinate courts and tribunals in its respective states.

Section VI

Local Governments and Cooperative Societies

21

CHAPTER

Local Governments in India: Panchayats and Municipalities

INTRODUCTION

The local government is a form of the administrative system at the local level. In India, the local government is **third-level** governments, with the first and second levels being the Centre and the state, respectively. The local governments are **democratic units at the basic level.** They are very proximate to the people.

The local governments in India have an ancient origin, but the British paved the way for modern local governments. **'Rippon's Resolution of 1881 and 1882'** is considered as **'Magna Carta of the local government in India'** and **Lord Ripon** is regarded as **'the father of local self-government in India'.** At present, there are around 6,45,000 local governments in India. There are two kinds of local governments: **panchayats for rural areas** and **municipalities for urban areas.**

The **73rd and 74th Constitutional Amendment Acts of 1992** imposed the **Constitution obligation** on all the state governments to establish panchayats and municipalities. Now, neither the creation nor the election nor the power and functions of the panchayats and municipalities are under the control of the state government as the Constitution itself decides on these issues and the state government must follow it. This Act not only strengthened **grass-roots level democracy,** but also transferred it into participatory democracy. This Act is a revolutionary concept and a significant milestone in the evolution of grass-roots level democracy in India.

THE PANCHAYATI RAJ INSTITUTIONS

The terms 'Panchayat' or 'Panchayati Raj' implies 'self-governing institutions in **rural areas** in India'. After the Independence, the Government was trying to empower the Panchayati Raj Institutions (PRIs) with innovative approaches, such as launching the Community Development Programme in 1952 and the National Extension Scheme in 1954, but these were unsuccessful.

Before 1991, PRIs in India had no uniformity in structure and they did not have enough power as they were under the control of the state governments. But the

73rd Constitutional Amendment Act 1992, which came into force on 24 April 1993, gave **the Constitutional status** to the PRIs by making it **mandatory for all the state governments to establish the PRIs.** In India, **April 24** is celebrated as **'National Panchayati Raj Day'.**

This Act gave a pragmatic shape to one of the **DPSPs** (also the **Gandhian principle),** under **Article 40** which says, 'The state shall take steps to organise village Panchayats and endow them with such powers and authority as may be necessary to enable them to function as units of self-government.' This is related to the **Swaraj concept of Gandhi,** and he said on this thought, 'My Idea of Village Swaraj is that it is a complete republic, independent of its neighbours for its own vital wants....'

The 73rd Constitutional Amendment Act 1992 **added new Part IX,** with the **title 'Panchayat'** and **new Articles 243–243 (O)** to the Constitution of India. It also added **new '11th Schedule'** to the Constitution, which consists of **29 functional items** of the panchayats.

IMPORTANT PROVISIONS OF THE 73RD CONSTITUTIONAL AMENDMENT ACT 1992

The important provisions of the 73rd Constitutional Amendment Act 1932 are as follows:

1. **Gram Sabha**
   Gram Sabha means a body consisting of people registered on the electoral lists of a village comprised within the area of Panchayat at the village level. It is **the lowest unit of a panchayat.**

2. **Constitution of a Three-tier System**
   This Act brought **uniformity in the structure of PRIs** in India, that is, it provided the Constitution of a three-tier system of Panchayati Raj in all the states, that is, a panchayat at the

   (i) **Village level,** comprising one or more villages, namely 'Gram Panchayat' or 'Village Panchayat'

   (ii) **Intermediate level,** at the Taluk level, namely 'Taluk (Janapad or Block) Panchayat'

   (iii) **District level,** at the district level, namely 'District Panchayat'.

3. **Composition and Election**
   The people directly elect the members of all the three levels of panchayats through periodic elections. A separate election is conducted for each level of panchayat. The **Chairpersons of all three levels of panchayats are indirectly elected,** that is, the Chairpersons are elected by and from amongst the elected members of a panchayat. The Chairperson enjoys the **right to vote** at the meetings. The state legislature may provide for the representation of **MPs and MLAs** of concerned constituency in panchayats. At Village Panchayats, the official election **is not fought on party lines.**

4. **Reservation of Seats**

This Act provides for the reservation of seats in each panchayat election for **SCs and STs in proportion to their population** in that panchayat area; minimum **one-third** of these shall be reserved for **women** belonging to SCs/STs. Also, it provides the **reservation for women of minimum one-third of the total number of seats** for the members and Chairpersons in each panchayat (including those reserved for SC/ST women). The state legislature may provide reservations for the **OBC** people, but it is not mandatory.

5. **Duration**

The term of each panchayat is **five years.** It can be **dissolved** before the completion of its term. After dissolution, the election should be conducted **within six months.** In case of the expiry of five-year terms, the election should be held before the expiration of its duration.

6. **Disqualification of Members**

A person should have completed minimum **21 years of age** to become a member of a panchayat. A person disqualified to become a member of the state legislature is also disqualified to become a member of a panchayat (except 25 years age condition). The state legislature may provide an authority and manner of removal of panchayat members.

7. **Powers and Authority**

The state legislature may endow the panchayats with such powers and authority that enable them to function as an institution of self-governments, to prepare and implement **social and economic plans** and to implement such schemes as may be entrusted in 29 functional items.

8. **Finances**

The state legislature may also establish funds for crediting or withdrawing all money of panchayats. There are three main financial sources of the panchayats. They are as follows:

(i)   The state legislature may **authorize panchayats** to levy, collect and appropriate taxes, duties, tolls and fees.

(ii) The state government may **assign** the taxes, duties, tolls and fees levied and collected by it to the panchayats.

(iii) The state government may provide **grant-in-aid** to the panchayats from the Consolidated Fund of the State.

9. **Audit of Accounts**

The state legislatures make provisions with respect to the maintenance of accounts by panchayats and their auditing.

10. **Application to Union Territories**

The President of India directs about the application of this Act to the Union Territories by a notification.

11. **Bar on Interference by Courts**

This Act bars the interference by courts in the electoral matters of panchayats, such as delimitation of constituencies or the allotment of seats to such constituencies. Also, the state legislatures make provisions for an authority and a manner in which election petitions are to be presented.

THE MUNICIPALITIES

'The municipalities' or 'the urban local governments (ULGs)' implies 'self-governing institutions in **urban areas** in India'. The ULGs have a very long history in India. In modern India, the British set up **the first 'municipal corporation' at Madras in 1687.** In 1726, municipal corporations were set up in Bombay and Calcutta.

Before 1991, ULGs in India had no uniformity in structure and they did not have enough power as they were under the control of the state governments. But the **74th Constitutional Amendment Act 1992,** which came into force on 1 June 1993, gave **Constitutional status** to the ULGs by making it **mandatory for all the state governments to establish ULGs.**

The 74th Constitutional Amendment Act 1992 **added new Part IX-A,** with the **title 'the municipalities'** and the **new Articles 243 (P)–243 (ZG)** to the Constitution of India. It also added **the new '12th Schedule'** to the Constitution, which consists of **18 functional items** of the municipalities.

There are eight types of ULGs in India. They are: Municipal Corporation, Municipality, Notified Area Committee, Town, Area Committee, Cantonment Board, Township, Port Trust and Special Purpose Agency.

IMPORTANT PROVISIONS OF THE 74TH CONSTITUTIONAL AMENDMENT ACT 1992

The following are the important provisions of the 74th Constitutional Amendment Act 1992:

1. **Constitution of Three Types of Municipalities**
   This Act brought **uniformity in the structure of ULGs** in India, that is, it provided for the Constitution of three types of municipalities in all the states, that is,

   (i) **Nagar Panchayat** or by whatever name called, for the transition area, that is, an area in transition from the rural area to an urban area.
   (ii) **Municipal Council,** for smaller urban areas.
   (iii) **Municipal Corporation,** for larger urban areas.

2. **Composition and Election**
   The people directly elect the members of all three types of municipalities through periodic elections. A separate election is conducted for each level of municipality. For this purpose, municipal areas in each municipality are divided into territorial constituencies or **wards**. The **chairpersons of all the three types of municipalities are indirectly elected,** that is,

the Chairpersons are elected by and from amongst the elected members of a municipality. The chairperson enjoys the **right to vote** in the meetings. The state legislature may provide the provision for the representation of **MPs and MLAs** of the concerned constituency and persons having special knowledge/experience in municipal administration in municipalities.

3. **Reservation of Seats**

   This Act provides the provision for the reservation of seats in each municipality election for **SCs and STs in proportion to their population** in that municipality area; minimum **one-third** of these shall be reserved for women belonging to SCs/STs. Also, it provides the provision for the **reservation for women of minimum one-third of the total number of seats** for the members and chairpersons in each municipality (including those reserved for SC/ST women). The state legislature may provide the reservation for **OBC** people, but it is not mandatory.

4. **Duration**

   The term of each municipality is **five years.** It can be **dissolved** before the completion of its term; after dissolution, the election should be held **within six months.** In case of expiry of five-year terms, the election should be held before the expiration of its duration.

5. **Disqualification of Members**

   A person should have completed **21 years of age** to become a member of a municipality. A person disqualified to become a member of the state legislature is also disqualified to become a member of the municipality (except 25 years age condition). The state legislature may provide for an authority and a manner in which the municipality members can be removed.

6. **Powers and Authority**

   The state legislature may endow municipalities with such powers and authority that enable them to function as an institution of self-governments, to prepare and implement social and economic plans and to implement such schemes as may be entrusted in 18 functional items.

7. **Finances**

   The state legislature may also establish funds for crediting or withdrawing all money of municipalities. There are the three main financial sources of the municipalities. They are as follows:

   (i)   The state legislature may **authorize municipalities** to levy, collect and appropriate taxes, duties, tolls and fees.

   (ii) The state government may **assign** the taxes, duties, tolls and fees levied and collected by it to the municipalities.

   (iii) The state government may provide **grant-in-aid** to municipalities from the Consolidated Fund of the State.

8. **Audit of Accounts**

   The state legislatures make provisions with respect to the maintenance of accounts by the municipality and their auditing.

9. **Application to Union Territories**

The President of India directs on the application of this Act to the Union Territories by a notification.

10. **Bar on Interference by Courts**

This Act bars the interference by courts in the electoral matters of municipality, such as delimitation of constituencies or the allotment of seats to such constituencies. Also, the state legislatures make provisions for an authority and manner to present election petitions.

IMPORTANT INSTITUTIONS RELATED TO THE LOCAL GOVERNMENTS

STATE ELECTION COMMISSION

Articles 243 (K) and 243 (ZA) provide the provision for the establishment of the **State Election Commission (SEC)** to supervise, direct, control and conduct all elections of all levels of **panchayats, municipalities and cooperative societies.** The SEC is headed by the **State Election Commissioner** and he is **appointed by the Governor.** His conditions of tenure and services are determined by the Governor. The SEC can be removed from his office in the same manner and on the same grounds like a **judge of a High Court.** In other words, although the SEC is appointed by the Governor, he can be removed by the **Parliament** only.

STATE FINANCE COMMISSION

Articles 243 (I) and 243 (Y) provide the provision for the establishment of the **State Finance Commission (SFC)** for every **five years by the Governor** to review the **financial position of all levels of panchayats and municipalities.** The state legislature provides the provisions for its composition, powers, qualifications and so on. The SFC recommends to the Governor about the following things:

1. Principles of governing the distribution of the net proceed of the taxes, duties, tolls and fees levied by the state between the state and the municipalities/panchayats.
2. Determine taxes, duties, tolls and fees that may be assigned to or appropriated by the municipalities and the panchayats.
3. Providing **grant-in-aid** to municipalities and panchayats from the Consolidated Fund of the State by the states.
4. Measures needed to improve the financial position of municipalities and panchayats.
5. Any other financial matters referred by the Governor.

DISTRICT PLANNING COMMITTEES

Article 243 (ZD) provides the provision for the establishment of the 'District Planning Committee (DPC)' in every district to **consolidate plans prepared by panchayats and municipalities in the district** and prepare a draft development plan for the entire district as a whole. The chairperson of the DPC forwards such plans to the state government. The state legislatures make provisions with respect to composition, power and functions of the DPC. Four-fifths of members of the DPC are elected by and amongst the elected members of the panchayat at the district level and of the municipalities in the district in proportion to the rural and urban population ratio in the district.

METROPOLITAN PLANNING COMMITTEES

Article 243 (ZE) provides the provision for the establishment of the 'Metropolitan Planning Committee (MPC)' in every metropolitan area to prepare a draft development plan as whole. The chairperson of the MPC forwards such plans to the state government. The state legislatures make provisions with respect to composition, power and functions of the MPC. Two-thirds of the members of the MPC are elected by and amongst the elected members of the municipalities and chairpersons of the panchayats in the metropolitan areas in proportion to the rural and urban population ratio in the metropolitan areas.

11TH SCHEDULE OF THE CONSTITUTION

The 29 functional items under this schedule are as follows:

1. Agriculture, including agricultural extension
2. Animal husbandry, dairying and poultry
3. Fisheries
4. Social forestry and farm forestry
5. Minor forest produce
6. Public distribution system
7. Maintenance of community assets
8. Khadi, village and cottage industries
9. Rural housing
10. Drinking water
11. Fuel and fodder
12. Adult and non-formal education
13. Libraries
14. Cultural activities
15. Markets and fairs

16. Family welfare
17. Women and child development
18. Non-conventional energy sources
19. Health and sanitation, including hospitals, primary health centres and dispensaries
20. Poverty alleviation programme
21. Small-scale industries, including food-processing industries
22. Rural electrification, including the distribution of electricity
23. Education, including primary and secondary schools
24. Technical training and vocational education
25. Minor irrigation, water management and watershed development
26. Roads, culverts, bridges, ferries, waterways and other means of communication
27. Social welfare, including the welfare of the handicapped and mentally retarded
28. Welfare of the weaker sections, and, in particular, of the Scheduled Castes and the Scheduled Tribes
29. Land improvement, implementation of land reforms, land consolidation and soil conservation.

12TH SCHEDULES OF THE CONSTITUTION

The 18 functional items under the 12th Schedule are as follows:

1. Urban planning including town planning
2. Regulation of land use and construction of buildings
3. Planning for economic and social developments
4. Roads and bridges
5. Water supply for domestic, industrial and commercial purposes
6. Public health, sanitation conservancy and solid waste management
7. Fire services
8. Urban forestry, protection of the environment and promotion of ecological aspects
9. Safeguarding the interests of weaker sections of society (including handi-capped and mentally retarded)
10. Slum improvement and upgradation
11. Urban poverty alleviation
12. Provision of urban amenities and facilities, such as parks, gardens, playgrounds
13. Promotion of cultural, educational and aesthetic aspects
14. Burials and burial grounds; cremations, cremation grounds and electric crematoriums
15. Cattle pounds; prevention of cruelty to animals
16. Vital statistics including the registration of births and deaths
17. Public amenities including street lighting, parking lots, bus stops and public conveniences
18. Regulation of slaughter houses and tanneries

22
CHAPTER _____

Cooperative Societies

INTRODUCTION

The word 'Cooperation' came from Latin word *'co-operari'*, which means 'to work with'. The 'cooperative societies' are **autonomous associations** of persons joined voluntarily to meet their **mutual benefits** (economic, social, cultural and so on) through **collectively owned** and **democratically governed** enterprises.

The cooperation is an ideal way to lead collective life. **'All for one and one for all'** is the underlying concept of cooperative societies. Achieving individual development as well as collective development through unity is the main theme of cooperative societies. In the modern world, the idea of cooperative societies was originated in England. The British sociologist **'Robert Owen'** is regarded as the **'father of cooperation or cooperative movement** in the world'.

FORMATION

In India, cooperative societies came into existence at the end of the nineteenth century and the British laid down the legal framework for these by enacting **'Indian Cooperative Societies Act in 1904',** with the main objective to eradicate poverty and increase agricultural and industrial production. After this Act, India's first cooperative society 'Urban Cooperative Credit Society' was established in Kanjivaram in the Madras Presidency in October 1904.

The state of **Karnataka** is regarded as the **'cradle of cooperative movement in India'.** Shri **Siddana Gowda Sannaraman Patil** is regarded as the **'father of cooperation or cooperative movement in India'** as he established India's first successful cooperative society **'Primary Agricultural Cooperative Credit Society'** in May 1905 in **the Kannaginhalla village** of **Gadag** district in Karnataka.[1]

_____

[1] A. C. Diwakar, *Cooperative Movement in Karnataka*, pp. 2–3. Available at http://www.atimysore. gov.in/trg_ppt/2014-15/resource/2nd%20Week%20Sep/CFC/12-9/Co-operative%20Movement%20 in%20Karnataka%20updated.pdf. Although some people regard Frederic Nicholson as the 'father of co-operative movement in India', it is controversial.

The **97th Constitutional Amendment Act 2011** strengthened the cooperative societies by making certain changes in the Constitution, such as:

1. It made the formation of cooperative societies as a **'fundamental right'** of the people.
2. In Part IV (DPSPs), it added **new Article 43 (B),** which says, 'The state shall endeavour to promote the voluntary formation, autonomous functioning, democratic control and professional management of the cooperative societies.'
3. Added **new Part IX-B** after Part IX-A which specified the Centre and the state duties with respect to the cooperative societies.
4. It provided fixed term of **five years** to elected members and other officials of cooperative societies and uniformity in the tenure of the Board of Directors.
5. It restricted the number of Board of Directors to **21.**
6. It provided the provision for the suspension of a member of board for a maximum period of six months.
7. It provided the provision for the reservation of **two seats for women** in Board of Directors in each cooperative society.
8. It provided the **'right to information'** for all members to know all the activities of the cooperative society.
9. It provided for the independent professional audit.
10. The **State Election Commission conducts elections for the cooperative societies,** but this Act gave power to set agencies to oversee the elections of cooperative societies by the state law.
11. It provided the provision for the **penalty** for offences relating to cooperative societies.

The cooperative societies are well organized in India. Although all cooperative societies do not have uniformity in their organizational structures, the general organizational structure of a cooperative society is as follows:

1. Primary cooperative societies at the rural level, for example, primary credit cooperative society.
2. Block or Taluk- level cooperative societies at the Taluk level, for example, Taluk credit cooperative society.
3. District cooperative societies at the district level, for example, district credit cooperative society.
4. State cooperative societies at the state level, for example, state credit cooperative union/federation.
5. National cooperative societies at the national level, for example, the National Federation of State Cooperative Banks Ltd (NAFSCOB).
6. International cooperative societies at the international level.

In order to understand the cooperative societies, it is very necessary to know the important principles or characteristics of cooperative societies. They are as follows:

1. **Voluntary and open membership:** One can join or not join any cooperative society according to his/her will. Anyone having similar interests in a cooperative society can join it voluntarily, irrespective of his/her religion, caste, race, gender and so on.

2. **Democratic control:** All the members of a cooperative society have **only one vote, irrespective of one's amount of investment.** All members of a cooperative society elect a committee or board of directors to look after its management affairs, but the 'General Body of Members' enjoys the supreme power, which consists of all the members. It means that all the members have **equal voice or opportunity** to participate in its management affairs. In other words, here a person is treated as just a human being, not rich or poor, educated or uneducated and so on. This is not possible in private companies.

3. **Equal distribution of profits:** Profits earned by a cooperative society are distributed among all the members according to **their proportion of investment.** Hence, here the profit is shared equally. Usually, in a private company, the rich person makes investments and keeps all profits, but pays money to other members of the company as salary.

4. **The principle of equity:** The cooperative society was born as a response to an unjust and exploitative business practice. Hence, it tries to maintain equality between its members and customers,. that is, it pays fair salaries to its employees and does not charge excessive fees from its customer for its products and services.

5. **Political and religious neutrality:** Essentially, the cooperative societies are economic enterprises for social welfare, so these are secular and apolitical.

6. **Service motive:** In a private company, the main purpose is to make profit. However, the cooperative society's main purpose is to **serve the people** and not to make profits. That is why the cooperative societies seek for eliminating middleman from their businesses to provide their products and services to the people at low price.

7. **Social ownership:** Unlike a private company, a cooperative society is not owned by individuals or fewer persons, but by all its members. It is also called as **co-ownership.** Any member of a society can become an owner of a cooperative society by joining it.

8. **Self-help through the mutual help:** The people having similar interests help each other to fulfil their interests in a cooperative society. Hence, they do not compete with each other here as everyone's interest is the same.

9. **Limited interest on capital:** A private company or a capitalist organization tries to make as much as possible on its capital, even at the cost of

exploiting the poor by keeping high interest rates. But a cooperative society keeps low interests of its capital as it has a non-profit and service motive. For example, many agricultural cooperative credit societies provide loan just at 2–4% interest rate.

10. **Cooperative education:** Each cooperative society seeks to provide knowledge and training to its members to educate them about cooperative principles, affairs and their rights and duties. As knowledge is power, the cooperative society seeks to achieve their goals by empowering its members by providing knowledge.

11. **Cooperation among cooperatives:** Two or more companies manufacturing a similar product compete with each other to make profits, but two or more cooperative societies working on the same product or service field cooperate with each other to serve the people at the local, state, national and international levels for mutual benefits.

12. **Social or community concern:** Most cooperative societies provide help to the people in critical situations, such as earthquakes, cloudbursts, floods and so on, and they also organize certain social functions, such as group marriages, free medical services and so on because they have social or community concerns.

TYPES OF COOPERATIVE SOCIETIES

Based on the functions of cooperative societies, they can mainly be divided into the following eight categories:

1. **Cooperative credit societies:** These societies provide financial support to the needy people at low interest rates and with flexible rules. For example, Agricultural Cooperative Credit Societies and Gramin Banks.

2. **Consumer cooperative societies:** These societies are owned and democratically controlled by consumers; its main purpose is to make consumer products available to the people at affordable prices and protect the interest of consumers. They follow the concept of the public distribution system in their functions. These societies do not entertain middleman and supply products to the consumers at a lower price than the market price; for example, KSRTC Consumers Cooperative Society. The National Cooperative Consumer Federation is the apex body in India for consumer cooperative societies.

3. **Producers cooperative societies:** These societies are owned and democratically controlled by producers. Its main purpose is to protect the interest of producers, such as raw material procurement, business affairs and so on and make their products available to the people at affordable prices with good quality. These societies do not entertain middleman and supply products to the consumers at a lower price than the market price; for example, Milk Producer Cooperative Societies.

4. **Industrial cooperative societies:** These societies are owned and democratically controlled by industrial labours. Its main purpose is to protect the interest

of industrial labours particularly from exploitative owners or management of industries and to provide opportunities for the development of small-scale industries and their members; for example, Handloom Cooperative Societies and Handicraft Cooperative Societies.

5. **Service cooperative societies:** These societies are owned and democratically controlled by the people getting some particular services, such as credit, agricultural equipment, clothes and so on. These kinds of societies are mainly located in rural areas, and its main purpose is to provide all necessary services or products for the overall development of a village.

6. **Processing and marketing cooperative societies:** These societies mainly deal with storage, preservation, processing and marketing of agricultural products. These societies work to give fair price for agricultural produce and eliminate the middlemen.

7. **Farming cooperative societies:** These societies are owned and democratically controlled by small agricultural land holders. Its main purpose is to encourage the small land holders in collective farming, thereby increasing the net agricultural productivity and income of all the members, as small land decreases the agricultural produce.

8. **Housing cooperative societies:** The main purpose of these societies is to provide shelters for homeless people and facilitate house construction by providing things, such as land, credit, cement and so on.

BENEFITS OF COOPERATIVE SOCIETIES

Important benefits of cooperative societies are as follows:

1. They are very beneficial for isolated individuals as they bring them together or organize them to work collectively for the benefit of each other.
2. They **eliminate the middlemen** from the business cycle, thereby preventing the exploitative practice in business.
3. They provide services and products at low cost compared to the market price, and also maintaining good quality.
4. They stress to supply products and services that are in the nature of basic human needs, such as food, cloth, housing and so on and do not give importance to luxury items.
5. They equally distribute the earned wealth among the members according to their proportion of investment. Thus, they prevent the wealth from getting accumulated into the hands of fewer people, and thus contribute to establish social and economic equality.
6. They significantly contribute to the upliftment of the weaker sections of the society, such as women, children, SCs, STs and OBCs.
7. They control the monopoly tendencies of a private businessman by supplying the best products and services at low costs.

8. They follow fair business policies, so they eliminate fraudulent activities in businesses, such as adulteration, weight reduction and so on.
9. They give fair treatment to labours, so like in a private business organization, it is hard to find management–labours conflicts in cooperative societies.

WEAKNESSES OF COOPERATIVE SOCIETIES

The main weaknesses of cooperative societies in India are as follows:

1. Unlike in the Western countries, in India, they are not developed as a people's movement, but as a government's movement.
2. They are suffering from financial problems due to the lack of good and efficient sources.
3. They expect too much help from the government rather than putting their own efforts in their organizational development.
4. Many of them concentrating only on the supply of loan, not in investment, service and so on. Also, much of the loan is supplied for the production-related activities only.
5. They are becoming weak to face money lenders because of the lack of financial sources.
6. Nowadays, in management affairs of cooperative societies, the political inter-ference is increasing day by day and also the rich men and upper caste people are influencing its functions.
7. They do not have well-trained staff as there is no better system to train them.
8. Due to unsound financial management, they are suffering from an overdue of loans.
9. They lack effective and efficient administrative system. As a result, corruption, despotism and so on are increasing in these organizations, too.

ACHIEVEMENTS

Despite the above weaknesses, the achievements of cooperative societies in India have been phenomenal and remarkable. For example, they gave relief to the public from exploitative money lenders and provided loan at very low costs. They have also immensely contributed to increase the production. Today, India is the largest producer of milk products in the world, this happened only because of the success of milk producer's cooperative societies such as Amul. The cooperative societies provide loans for production activity at the right time; they provide fair price for agricultural produce; supply essential products to the people at low cost and have immensely contributed to the upliftment of the weaker sections by increasing their net earnings and so on. Owing to all this, the cooperative societies have been playing a very sig-nificant role in the overall development of our nation.

Section VII

Amendment of the Constitution and Emergency Provisions

Amendment of the Constitution and Important Amendments (42nd, 44th, 74th, 76th, 86th and 91st)

AMENDMENT OF THE CONSTITUTION

The Constitution of India is a living document and it is capable of adjusting itself according to time, situations and needs. **Article 368 of Part XX** in the Constitution exclusively deals with the various provisions of the amendments of the Constitution. **The Parliament can only amend the Constitution,** but not the state legislatures. Article 368 states, 'The Parliament may, in the exercise of its constituent power, amend by way of addition, variation or repeal any provision of the Constitution in accordance with the procedure laid down for the purpose.'

The Supreme Court in the **Kesavananda Bharati Case 1973** ruled, 'The Parliament can amend any provisions of the Constitution **without disturbing the "Basic Structure"** of the Constitution.'

The Constitutions of modern democratic countries are classified into rigid and flexible based on the procedure of amendment of the Constitution. A **Rigid Constitution** is the one to which making any amendment or change is very difficult as it requires a special procedure, for example the USA Constitution. A **Flexible Constitution** is the one to which making any amendment or change is easy as it requires a simple procedure, for example the British Constitution. **The Indian Constitution is neither rigid nor flexible, but a blend of both,** this is because some provisions of the Constitution can be amended by following a simple procedure and some others by following a special procedure. Article 368 deals with the amendment of the Constitution by following a special procedure.

There are three ways to amend the Constitution of India by the Parliament. They are as follows:

1. **By a simple majority:** Some provisions of the Constitution can be amended by the Parliament by a 'simple majority', that is, by the support of a majority or **more than 50 per cent** members of the House **present and their voting.** Examples of these provisions are: the abolition or creation of a State Legislative

Council in a state, creation of new states, citizenship, election to the Parliament and state legislature and so on.

2. **By a special majority:** Many provisions of the Constitution can be amended by the Parliament by a 'special majority', that is, the majority or support of **more than 50 per cent of the total membership of the House and a majority or support of two-thirds of members of the House present and their voting.** Examples of these provisions are: the FRs, the DPSPs and any other matter that does not come under the first and third categories.

3. **By a special majority and with the consent of half of the state legislatures:** The provisions of the Constitution related to the federal structure of India can be amended, not only by a 'special majority' of the Parliament but also with the consent of the half of the state legislatures by a simple majority. Examples of these provisions are: the election of the President, CJI of the Supreme Court and CJHC of High Courts; the distribution of legislative powers between the states and the Centre; seventh schedule; states representation in the Parliament and Article 368 itself (the Parliament power to amend the Constitution).

PROCEDURE TO AMEND THE CONSTITUTION UNDER ARTICLE 368

The procedure to amend the Constitution under Article 368 is as follows:

1. A process of amending the Constitution can be initiated only after the introduction of a 'Constitutional Amendment Bill' in **either the Lok Sabha or in the Rajya Sabha**, **not in the state legislatures.**

2. The Constitutional Amendment Bill **does not require a prior permission of the President** for its introduction in the Parliament.

3. The Constitutional Amendment Bill can be introduced in the Parliament by **a minister or by a private member** (a member who does not act on behalf of the Government or in his/her party).

4. The Constitutional Amendment Bill must be **passed separately by each house** of the Parliament with **the special majority;** in case of disagreement between the two houses, there is **no provision for the 'Join Sitting** of the two houses of the Parliament' to resolve the deadlock.

5. If the Constitutional Amendment Bill is related to the amendment of **any federal structure** of the Constitution, it must be supported by **half of the total state legislatures by a simple majority.**

6. If the Constitutional Amendment Bill is passed by the Parliament and it is consented by state legislatures (in the necessary case) as mentioned above, it will be presented to the President for his assent.

7. The President **cannot Veto** the Constitutional Amendment Bill, that is, he can neither withhold his assent to the bill nor he can return it for the reconsideration of the Parliament, but **he must give his assent to the bill.**

8. After the assent of the President, the Constitutional Amendment Bill becomes the **Constitutional Amendment Act.** It implies that the Constitution amendment process is complete and the executive may implement the new Act.

IMPORTANT CONSTITUTIONAL AMENDMENT ACTS

From 1950 to June 2015, so far total **100 Constitutional** amendments have been made to the Constitution of India. Out of them, some important Constitutional Amendment Acts, as per the syllabus, are as follows:

1. **42nd Constitutional Amendment Act of 1976**
   This Constitutional Amendment Act is known as **'Mini-Constitution'** as it almost rewrote most of the provisions of the Constitution during the National Emergency period (1975–1977) by the Congress Party headed by Indira Gandhi. Its important provisions are as follows:

   (i)   It added three new words, that is, **Socialist, Secular and Integrity in the Preamble.**
   (ii)   It added the **Fundamental Duties** by inserting **Part IV-A and Article 51-A.**
   (iii)   It provided for the creation of the **All India Judicial Service.**
   (iv)   It made the President **bound by the advice of the Cabinet.**
   (v)   It increased the term of the Lok Sabha and Vidhan Sabha from five years to six years.
   (vi)   It kept the Constitutional amendment outside the scope of judicial review.
   (vii)   It restricted the judicial review and Writ powers of the Supreme Court and the High Courts.
   (viii) It transferred five subjects from the state list to the concurrent list, namely, **weigh and measures, education, forestry, administration of justice in lower level courts and protection of wild animals and birds.**
   (ix)   It added **three new** DPSPs, namely, equal justice and free legal aid; workers' participation in the management of industries and protection of environment, forest and wildlife.
   (x)   It provided for the establishment of **administrative tribunals.**
   (xi)   It gave up the Quorum requirement in the Parliament and the state legislatures.
   (xii)   It empowered the Parliament to deal with anti-national elements by giving more law-making power that affects the FRs.
   (xiii) It provided for the imposition of national emergency in a part of the country.

(xiv) It extended the one-time duration of the President rule in a state from six months to one year.

(xv) It empowered the Centre to deploy its armed forces in any state to manage worse law-and-order situations.

2. **44th Constitutional Amendment Act of 1976**

This Constitutional Amendment Act was mainly enacted to repeal the errors of 42nd Constitutional Amendment Act by the Janata Government headed by Morarji Desai in 1976. Its important provisions are as follows:

(i) It restored the Quorum requirement in the Parliament and the state legislatures.

(ii) It restored the original terms of the Lok Sabha and Vidhan Sabha to five years.

(iii) It made clear that Articles 20 and 21 (FRs) **cannot be suspended** during the national emergency period.

(iv) It made clear that the President can declare a national emergency only **on the written recommendation of the Cabinet.**

(v) It replaced the term 'internal disturbance' by 'armed rebellion' with regard to national emergencies.

(vi) It gave the power to the President to **send back once** the advice of the Cabinet for its reconsideration and made reconsidered advice binding on him.

(vii) It deleted the **Right to Property** as the FR and made it just a legal right.

(viii) It added certain safeguards with respect to national emergencies and the President rule.

(ix) It restored some judicial review and writ powers of the Supreme Court and High Courts.

(x) It gave the Constitutional safeguards for newspapers to publish true reports of the Parliament and the state legislatures.

3. **73rd Constitutional Amendment Act of 1992**

This Act provided **the Constitutional status** and safeguards to the **Panchayati Raj Institutions** or rural local governments. It added a **new Part IX and a new 11th Schedule** to the Constitution, which gave **29 functional items** to panchayats.

4. **74th Constitutional Amendment Act of 1992**

This Act provided **the Constitutional status** and safeguards to **the urban local governments**. It added a new **Part IX-A and a new 12th Schedule** to the Constitution, which gave **18 functional items** to municipalities.

5. **76th Constitutional Amendment Act of 1994**

This Act amended the 9th Schedule of the Constitution by including Tamil Nadu Reservation Act (provided total 69 per cent of reservation in education institutions and state government jobs) to the 9th Schedule to **protect the**

reservation provision from the judicial review. But the Supreme Court said that the total reservation **should not be more than 50 per cent.**

6. **86th Constitutional Amendment Act of 2002**

This Act is one of the **milestones** in the Indian education system. This Act was enacted by the National Democratic Alliance (NDA) Government headed by Atal Bihari Vajpayee in 2002. Its important provisions are as follows:

(i) It added **new Article 21-A** to the Constitution, which gave the **'Right to Education'** for children. It made **elementary education of all children of the ages of 6–14 years as the FR.**

(ii) It also made the state to provide **'free and compulsory'** education to all children of the ages of 6–14 years.

(iii) It added a **new FDs,** that is, it made the FD of all Indian parents or guardian to provide opportunity for elementary education for their children or ward between the ages of 6 and 14 years.

7. **91st Constitutional Amendment Act of 2003**

Some of the important provisions of these acts are as follows:

(i) It restricted the total strength of the Union Council of Ministers including the Prime Minister to **not more than 15 per cent of the total strength of the Lok Sabha.**

(ii) It restricted the total strength of the State Council of Ministers including the Chief Minister to **not more than 15 per cent of the total strength of the Vidhan Sabha.**

(iii) It made clear that, if an MP belonging to any political party in the Parliament is disqualified on the ground of **defection,** he/she is also disqualified to be appointed as a minister and to hold any remunerative political post.

(iv) It made clear that, if an MLA or MLC belonging to any political party in the state legislature is disqualified on the ground **of defection**, he/she is also disqualified to be appointed as a minister and to hold any remunerative political post.

24

CHAPTER

Emergency Provisions

The Emergency Provisions are the special provisions provided by the Constitution of India to enable the Government to effectively handle any abnormal situations that threaten India's democracy, unity, integrity, sovereignty, security and the Constitution. **Part XVIII and from Articles 352 to 360** of the Constitution deal with the various aspects of Emergency Provisions.

One of the most unique features of the Indian Constitution is that, during an emergency period, it **automatically transforms itself to the 'unitary system of government'** from the 'federal system of government'. In other words, during an emergency period, the Central government becomes **more powerful** and takes the control over the state governments.

The Constitution provided **three kinds of emergencies.** They are as follows:

1. National Emergency (Article 352)
2. President Rule (Article 356)
3. Financial Emergency (Article 360)

NATIONAL EMERGENCY

Article 352 is about the National Emergency. There are two kinds of National Emergencies. If a National Emergency is imposed on the grounds of **'war' or 'external aggression'**, it is called **'External Emergency'.** If a National Emergency is imposed on the grounds of **'armed rebellion'**, it is called **'Internal Emergency'.** The term 'armed rebellion' was introduced by the **44th** Constitutional Amendment Act of 1976, by replacing the original term **'internal disturbance'.**

The President of India can proclaim a National Emergency on the grounds of war, external aggression and armed rebellion in the entire country or in any part of it. He can declare a National Emergency even if he is satisfied that there is a threat of war, external aggression and armed rebellion in the near future.

The President must proclaim a National Emergency **only based on the written recommendation of the Union Cabinet.** Even the PM's advice is not enough, a National Emergency must be approved **by both the houses of the Parliament**

by a special majority within one month from the date of its proclamation. After the approval of the Parliament, a National Emergency **continues for the next six months,** and it can be extended to **any number of times** based on an approval of the Parliament every six months.

The President can revoke a National Emergency **at any period of time** without the Parliament approval. If **the Lok Sabha** (not the Rajya Sabha) passes a resolution to revoke a National Emergency by a simple majority, then the President must revoke that National Emergency.

So far, National Emergency has been imposed in India **three times.** They are described below:

1. First time, in 1962, because of Chinese aggression. It was an External Emergency. It was revoked in 1968.
2. Second time, in 1971, because of the attack of Pakistan on India. It was also an External Emergency. It was revoked in 1977.
3. Third time, in 1975, because of 'internal disturbances'. It was an Internal Emergency. It was also revoked in 1977 along with the second one. It was the most controversial National Emergency. The then Prime Minister, Indira Gandhi, recommended to President Fakhruddin Ali Ahmed to proclaim an Internal Emergency without consulting the Cabinet. Many politicians believe that she did so to continue in her office, as the Allahabad High Court found her guilty of election malpractices.

Consequences of a National Emergency

If a National Emergency is declared, it will have significant impacts on the political system. Important consequences of a National Emergency are as follows:

1. The five-year term of the Lok Sabha and Vidhan Sabha can be **extended to one more year** at a time for any number of times by the Parliament.
2. **Article 19** (six FRs) is **automatically suspended** during the External Emergency (not during the Internal Emergency) time.
3. The President may suspend the **right to move any court** for the enforcement of any FRs **except FRs given under Articles 20 and 21** for a specific period of time.
4. The Central Government **can give directions to any state** government on any matter. Thus, the state governments will come under the control of the Central Government.
5. The **Parliament can enact laws on any subject mentioned in the state list.** However, the state legislatures are not suspended during this time.
6. The **President can issue ordinances for the state governments** when the Parliament is not in session.
7. The President can modify (reduce, increase or cancel) the distribution of revenue between the Centre and the states.

THE PRESIDENT RULE

The relationship between the Centre and the state in India is like that of a mother and a child. It is the duty of the Centre to make sure that the all states work according to the Constitutional provisions. In case of failure of the Constitutional machinery in a state, the Centre takes over the state government under Article 356. This is known as the **'President Rule'**, or **'Constitutional Emergency'** or **'State Emergency'**.

The President Rule is also imposed in case of a **Hung Assembly,** that is, when no political party or parties in a State Legislative Assembly get the absolute majority and no political party in a State Legislative Assembly is able or not interested to form a government and there is a grave law-and-order problem in a state, or when some other situations are considered as a failure of the Constitutional machinery in a state.

The President imposes the President Rule in a state on **two grounds** as follows:

1. If he is satisfied that the government of a state **cannot run according to the Constitution under a situation** (Article 356). The President can impose a President Rule in a state **with or without the recommendation of the Governor** of the concerned state. In this regard, the President is **not bound** (that is, he may accept or reject) to the Governor's recommendation.
2. If the government of a state **fails to comply with or to give effect to a direction** of the Central Government, the President may impose the President Rule in that state (Article 365).

A President Rule in a state must be approved by **both the houses of the Parliament** by **a simple majority within two months** from the date of its proclamation. After the approval of the Parliament, a President Rule in a state is continued for the **next six months**, and it can be **extended up to the maximum period of three years** based on an **approval of the Parliament for every six months**. In other words, the maximum time period of the President Rule in a state is **three years.** The President can **revoke** a President Rule in a state **at any period of time** without the Parliament's approval. The Supreme Court in its landmark verdict in the Bommai Case 1994 held that the President's satisfaction with respect to the imposition of the 'President Rule' in a state **is subjected to judicial review.**

Consequences of the President Rule

If the President Rule is imposed in a state, it will give extra-ordinary powers to the President. The **executive powers of the state are transferred to the Governor (on behalf of the President)** and **the legislative powers to the Parliament.** The President Rule will have the following consequences when it is imposed in a state:

1. The President **dismisses the State Council of Ministers,** including the Chief Minister.

2. On behalf of the **President, the Governor looks after the state administration** with the help of advisors appointed by the President and the Chief Secretary of that State.
3. The **Parliament** passes state legislative **bills and the state budget.**
4. The President may **suspend or dissolve** the State Legislative Assembly. In either case, **the Parliament** may empower the President to enact laws or **issue ordinance** for the governance of that state. Such laws are known as **'President's Act'.**
5. The President Rule does not have any kind of consequences on the High Court of the state.

FINANCIAL EMERGENCY

Under **Article 360, the President of India** can proclaim the Financial Emergency if he is satisfied that there is a **threat to the financial stability or credit** of India or any part of it under a given situation. In this case too, the satisfaction of the President comes under **judicial review.**

A Financial Emergency must be approved by **both the houses of the Parliament by a simple majority** within **two months** from the date of its proclamation. After the approval of the Parliament, it will continue from **an indefinite period of time till it is revoked by the President.** In other words, there is no requirement of the Parliament from time to time for its continuations and there **is no maximum time limit** for its operation. The President can **revoke** a Financial Emergency **at any period of time** without the Parliament's approval.

Consequences of Financial Emergency

During a Financial Emergency period, the Centre takes full control over the state's financial matters. Important consequences of Financial Emergencies are as follows:

1. The **President can give directions to the states** to observe the canons of financial propriety.
2. The President may ask that all money bills and other financial bills passed by the state legislature be **reserved for his consideration.**
3. The President may direct for the **reduction of salaries and allowances** of all or any person serving in the Union and the state governments, including the judges of the Supreme Court and High Courts.

So far, no Financial Emergency has been imposed in India. Although India faced very difficult financial conditions in 1991, the President did not proclaim Financial Emergency at that time.

Section VIII

Constitutional Provision for the Weaker Section of Society

25
CHAPTER

Special Provision for SCs, STs, OBCs, Women and Children

The Indian society is suffering from inequality, mainly because of historical mistakes. The weaker sections of the society, such as women, children, STs, SCs, OBCs, women and children have been subjected to injustice, exploitation, inequality. They have not enjoyed the human life with dignity for a long period of time. The Constitution of India intended to end the sufferings of the weaker sections of the society by protecting their interest and by allowing the Government to make positive discrimination between the people to provide opportunities for these weaker sections of the society.

CONSTITUTIONAL PROVISION FOR SCs AND STs

The ancient Indian society was based on the 'Varna System' that divided people into four classes: Brahmins, Kshatriyas, Vaishyas and Shudras based on their *Karma* (work or actions). But later, the upper class people started to practise the Varna System based on *Janma* (Birth) in hierarchy, instead of *Karma*. Because of this, Shudras have not only remained as low-level people but they have also been subjected to exploitation and socio-economic injustice for thousands of years.

The Constitution of India refers to the Shudras as **Scheduled Casts (SCs); Gandhi called them as 'Harijans'** and in the literature, they are referred to as **Dalits**. Also, In India, there are some communities having their **own distinct culture and religion** and living in their own **traditional social structure;** these communities are called Scheduled Tribes (STs) in the Constitution. These communities are called **Scheduled Tribes (STs)** in the Constitution. Like the SCs, the STs have also been marginalized for thousands of years and they still remain underdeveloped. According to the 2011 Census, the SCs constitute **16.6 per cent** and the **STs constitute 8.6 per cent** of India's population.

The mother law of the nation provided certain special provisions for the SCs and STs to protect them from further exploitation by the upper class people and give them equal opportunity for development. Those provisions are as follows:

1. Under Articles 341 and 342, it (the Constitution of India) gave the power to the **President** to prepare the first lists of the SCs and STs across India in

consultation with the Governors. **The Parliament is the only authority to add or remove or modify** these lists.

2. It provided a few **exceptions to Article 15,** which prohibits the state from making a discrimination between the people based on caste, religion, creed, gender, place of birth and so on for the development of the SCs and STs.

3. It provided a few **exceptions to Article 16** (equality of opportunity in the matter of public employment) by providing the **reservations for SCs and STs in government jobs.**

4. By the 85th Constitutional Amendment Act of 2001, it provided the provision for the **reservation** for SCs and STs **for promotion** in the government jobs.

5. It prohibited the **practice of untouchability** (Article 17) and made such a practice a punishable offence.

6. It provided a **few limitations in Article 19,** that is, restricted right to movement and right of residence in the **STs area** to protect their distinct culture and traditions.

7. Under Article 46, it directed the State to protect the **educational interests of** the SCs and STs, along with other weaker sections of the society.

8. Under Article 164, it provided for **Minister in Charge of Tribal Welfare** in the states of Bihar, Madhya Pradesh, Jharkhand, Odisha and so on to look after the welfare of the SCs.

9. Under the **5th and 6th Schedules** (Article 244), it gave **special provisions for the administration** and welfare of the Scheduled Areas and the STs.

10. Under Article 275 (1), it authorized the Government of India to **provide grants to the state governments** to implement the welfare schemes of the Scheduled Areas and the STs.

11. Under Articles 330, 332 and 334, it provided the **reservation of seats for SCs and STs** in **the Parliament and the State Legislative Assemblies** according to their population.

12. Under Article 335, it made the State to consider the **claim of the SCs/STs** for making a reservation in service with keeping in mind about the efficiency of administration.

13. Under Article 339, it gave the power to the President to **appoint a Commission** to report on the administration of the Scheduled Areas and the welfare of SCs after 10 years of its commencement. It also empowered the Government of India to **issue directions** to the state governments for the welfare of the SCs and STs.

14. Under Articles 338 and 338-A, it provided for the establishment of the **National Commission of Scheduled Castes and the National Commission of Scheduled Tribes,** respectively.

Besides, the Parliament enacted **'The Protection of Civil Rights Act 1955'** and **'The SCs and the STs (Prevention of Atrocities) Act 1989'.** Besides, the Parliament enacted **'the Protection of Civil Rights Act-1955'** and **'the SCs and the STs (Prevention of Atrocities) Act, 1989',** with the purpose to, – strengthen the SCs and STs Protection Cell and Special Police Stations Special Courts were established to speed up the delivery of justice and to provide relief and rehabilitation for victims of atrocity. Also, efforts were made to create awareness among the people and encourage inter-caste marriage.

The National Commission for Scheduled Castes and the National Commission for Scheduled Tribes

The 89th Constitutional Amendment Act 2003 bifurcated the erstwhile National Commission for SCs and STs into two separate bodies, namely, **the National Commission of Scheduled Castes (Article 338)** and **the National Commission of Scheduled Tribes (Article 338-A).** Both the Commissions are **Constitutional bodies** (directly created by the Constitution itself).

Each commission is composed of **a chairperson, a vice-chairperson and three members**. All of them are **appointed by the President of India by warrant under his hand and seal.** Their service conditions and tenures are also determined by the President of India.[1]

Both the Commissions have the duties to investigate, monitor and evaluate all matters related to Constitutional and legal safeguards provided for the SCs and STs in the Constitution; to facilitate inquiry into complaints related to the rights and safeguards of the SCs and STs; to participate and to advise on the planning process of the development (socio-economic) of the SCs and STs; and to recommend suitable measures for the effective implementation of these safeguards and for the protection, welfare and advancement of the SCs and STs. Both the Commissions submit their **annual reports to the President** who lays down them before the Parliament.

Both the Commissions have the power of a **civil court** while investigating complaints. Both the Centre and states are needed to consult these Commissions while formulating policies that affect the SCs and STs. The National Commission for SCs have similar powers and discharge similar functions **with respect to OBCs and the Anglo-Indian Community.**

CONSTITUTIONAL PROVISION FOR OTHER BACKWARD CLASSES (OBCs)

The 'Other Backward Classes (OBCs)' is a collective term used by the Constitution of India for the **socially and economically deprived or backward castes** (other than SCs and STs). According to the 2001 Census, **the OBCs constitute 52 per cent of India's population.** As they fall under the marginalized section of the society, the Constitution provided certain special provisions for their upliftment **(excluding Creamy Layer).** They are as follows:

1. The Preamble of the Constitution seeks to secure to its citizen, 'Justice (social, economic and political) and Equality' of status and opportunity.

---

[1] Usually, they hold the office for three years under the rules.

2. It provided a certain **exception to a few FRs,** such as Articles 14, 15 and 19 for the protection and development of the OBCs.

3. It provided for an exception to Article 16, under which the Government provides **27 per cent reservation in educational institutions and public employment for the OBCs; this is based on the recommendation of Mandal Commission in 1979.** But there is **no reservation for the OBCs for promotion** in public employment.

4. Under Article 340, it authorized the President to **appoint a Commission** to investigate the conditions of the OBCs and the President lays down the report of this Commission before the Parliament.

5. Under Article 338, it provided for the **National Commission for the SCs** to also look into the interest of the OBCs.

Besides, the Government established **'The National Commission for Backward Classes'** as a permanent **'Statutory Body'** (a body created by a statute or an act of the Parliament) **in 1993**, which is under the Ministry of Social Justice and Empowerment. So it is a **Non-Constitutional body.** It consists of **five members**, including the **chairperson** (usually the present or a retired Judge of the Supreme Court or High Courts). All of them are **nominated by the Central government** and they hold the office for a period of **three years.** It considers the **inclusion or exclusion** of any caste in the OBC lists and renders advice to the Government on the issues related to them.

Creamy Layer

The term 'Creamy Layer' is being used to indicate the well-educated, wealthier and better developed people **within the OBC group**. The Creamy Layer is **excluded from availing reservation in education and government employment,** and some other facilities meant for the OBCs. In other words, the people belonging to the Creamy Layer are treated as the general category people and **do not get the 27 per cent quota benefit** that is meant for the OBC people.

The 'Children' of the following persons constitute the Creamy Layer:

1. Persons having a gross **annual income of more than 6 lakhs** or having the wealth above the exemption limits.

2. Persons holding Constitutional positions, such as the President, Vice-President, Governor and so on.

3. Persons having Group A or Class I and Group B or Class II posts in the All India, Central and state services, Public Sector Undertakings, banks and so on, and also in private employment.

4. Persons practising professions, such as lawyers, engineers, doctors, authors and so on.

5. Persons involved in trade, business and industry.

6. Persons holding agricultural land, vacant land, buildings in urban places above the limit.
7. The person who holds the rank of Colonel and above in the army and equivalent posts in other Armed Forces.

CONSTITUTIONAL PROVISION FOR WOMEN AND CHILDREN

The status of women in India has been changing with time. In the ancient period, women enjoyed equal status with men, but in the medieval period women were pushed to a very low status and were deprived of social, political, educational and economical freedom. In modern India, women are on the way to get equal status with men. The main driving force behind this is the Constitution of India. Along with women, children are also considered as a weaker section of the society as they are not strong enough (mentally and physically) to protect their interests and have been subjected to exploitation from mischiefs. Society thinks that women are not equal to men, but the Constitution **gave equal status to men and women,** and it **upholds the principle of gender equality.**

The Constitution not only protects women and children from further exploitation and injustice, but also provides enough provisions for their development. The important Constitutional provisions for women and children are as follows:

1. Under Article 14, it provided for **equality for all before the law,** including women and children.
2. Under Article 15, it provided for a few **exceptions to Article 15,** which prohibits the State from making a discrimination between the people based on gender, for the development of women and children.
3. Under Article 15, it gave **equal opportunity to women in public employment.**[2]
4. Under **Article 21A**, it made availing **elementary education a FR** (Right to Education) for all children in the age group of 6–14 years and made it mandatory for the state to provide free and compulsory elementary education for all children falling within that age group.
5. Under Article 23A, it **prohibited the Traffic in human beings** and beggar and other similar forms of forced labour.
6. Under Article 23A, it **prohibited the employment of children** below the age of 14 in any factory or mines or in any other hazardous places.
7. Under Article 39A, it directed the State to secure opportunity for the **healthy development of children.**
8. Under Articles 39(a) and 39(d), it directed the State to equally secure the right to an adequate means of **livelihood for both women and men** and **equal pay for equal work** for both women and men.

---

[2] But in some Armed Forces, women candidates still not allowed.

9. Under Article 39A, it directed the State to promote justice on the basis of equality and provide free legal aid by suitable means to ensure that no citizen shall be denied opportunity for securing justice for reasons of economic and other disabilities.

10. Under Article 42, it directed the State to make the provision for just and **humane conditions** for work and for **maternity relief.**

11. Under Article 45, it directed the State to provide **early childhood care** and education for all children until they complete the age of 6 years.

12. Under Article 46, it directed the State to promote the **educational and economic interests** of the weaker sections of the people with special care and to protect them from social injustice and all forms of exploitations.

13. Under Article 47, it directed the State to **raise the level of nutrition and the standard of living** of its people.

14. Under Article 51A, it assigned a **fundamental duty** for the citizen, who is a parent or a guardian, to provide **education to his/her child** or, as the case may be, ward between the age of 6 and 14.

15. Under Article 51A (e), it assigned a fundamental duty for the citizens to promote harmony and the spirit of common brotherhood amongst all the people of India and to **renounce practices derogatory to the dignity of women.**

16. Under Articles 234D and 234T, it provided the **reservation of one-third of seats and one-third of chairperson positions for women** (including SCs/STs women) in the elections of each **panchayat and municipality.**

Besides these Constitutional provisions, the Parliament also provided some special provisions for women and children. They are as follows:

1. The National Commission for Women (NCW) was established in January 1992 (NOT in 1993) under the National Commission for Women Act, 1990, as a **statutory body** to look after the Constitutional and legal safeguards of women, to facilitate the redressal of grievances and to advise the Government on all policy matters affecting women and remedial legislative measures. It is a national forum for women to express their concerns, issues and represent their rights.

2. The Parliament established the '**National Commission for Protection of Child Rights** (NCPCR)' in 2007, under the 'Commission for Protection of Child Rights Act 2005', as a **statutory body** to protect the rights of children by ensuring that all laws, rules, policies, programmes and schemes are in accordance with the provisions of the Constitution and the UN Convention on the Rights of the Children. It considers **0 and 18 years of age** as the age bracket for anyone to be called or considered a child.

Section IX

Human Rights

26
CHAPTER _____

Human Rights: Meaning, Definitions and Specific Themes

MEANING AND DEFINITIONS

The word 'Human' implies 'any living or extinct member of the *Homo sapiens* species characterized by superior consciousness, intelligence, intellect and articulate speech; a person, a man, a woman or a child.' The word 'Right' implies 'freedom that is guaranteed or things to which one is entitled or allowed.' So **'Human Rights'** implies 'rights of a person simply because of **being a human.'** Human rights are based on the principle of respect for the individual.

Human rights are **inalienable FRs** (fundamental rights in this SECTION. It does not necessarily carry the same meaning as in Chapter 5.) to all persons because of being a human. The most **basic FRs** needed to **live with dignity** for a human are called human rights. Human rights are **moral norms or principles** that describe the **standard of human life or behaviour.** A person exclusively enjoys or entitled to human rights for just being a human; other things such as citizenship, men, women or gender, religion, nationality, race, residence and so on are inclusive or secondary. According to the United Nations Human Rights Council (UNHRC),

All human rights are **indivisible,** whether they are **civil and political rights,** such as the right to life, equality before the law and freedom of expression; **economic, social and cultural rights,** such as the rights to work, social security and education, or collective rights, such as the rights to development and self-determination, are indivisible, interrelated and interdependent.

As humans belong to one family, the human rights have **universal applicability** anywhere and at any time. Human rights should be taken away only in specific situations and that too **according to the due process of law;** for example, right to speak may be restricted in order to protect peace and tranquillity in the society according to the law in force.

The WordWeb Dictionary defines human rights as follows:

Human Right is any basic right or freedom to which all human beings are entitled and in whose exercise a government may not

interfere (including rights to life and liberty as well as freedom of thought and expression and equality before the law).

According to the **UNHRC:**

Human rights are rights inherent to all human beings, whatever our nationality, place of residence, sex, national or ethnic origin, colour, religion, language, or any other status. We are all equally entitled to our human rights without discrimination. These rights are all interrelated, interdependent and indivisible.[1]

Human rights are **inalienable,** as one cannot lose these rights any more than cease to be a human being; **indivisible,** as one cannot be denied a right because it is more important or very essential and **interdependent,** as all human rights are part of a complementary framework or it is part of other rights, such as political, moral, economic and so on.

According to Amnesty International, a **non-governmental organization** (NGO):

Human Rights include **civil and political rights,** such as the right to life, liberty and freedom of expression; and social, cultural and economic rights, including the right to participate in culture, the right to food, and the right to work and receive an education.

Human rights are protected and upheld by the national and international laws and treaties. After the terrific experience of the Holocaust and World War-II, the **United Nations Generally Assembly,** declared 'the **Universal Declaration of Human Rights (UDHR)'** on **10 December 1948**. The UDHR laid down the solid **foundation of the international system of protection for human rights.** This day, that is, **10 December** of every year is celebrated as **'International Human Rights Day'.**

There are three dimensions to the promotion of human rights through education. First, by **knowledge** by providing information about human rights and the mechanisms that exist to protect those rights. Second, by **values, beliefs and attitudes** by promoting a human rights culture through the development of these processes. Third, **by actions** by encouraging people to defend human rights and prevent human rights abuses.

SPECIFIC THEME IN HUMAN RIGHTS

According to the UNHRC, there are **six cross-cutting themes** in the UDHR. They are as follows:

1. **Dignity and Justice:** It is one of the main components of the UDHR. According to it, the concept of dignity lies in the heart of human rights, and it

---

[1] http://www.ohchr.org/en/hrbodies/hrc/pages/hrcindex.aspx

means treating each other with respect, esteem, tolerance and understanding, and the governments must make the same provisions in law as well as in practice, for the individuals, communities, societies and nations. But the concept of dignity is the most difficult right to express and put into a tangible form. The core values of non-discrimination and equality are ultimately a commitment to universal justice and recognition of inherent human dignity.

2. **Development:** Muhammad Yunus noted, 'Poverty is the absence of all human rights.' Poverty is a key factor that undercuts the realization of the full potential of human beings and societies. Development is the best answer for the poverty. The human rights seek to provide 'equal opportunity to grow and develop in freedom and equality in all aspects and to the fullness of their potential to all human beings'.

3. **Environment:** The UDHR never specifically mentioned about the environment, but it is an inclusive part of human rights. One human cannot live a dignified life in a polluted area as it affects human health, peace, happiness, money and so on, for others' mistakes. Hence, human rights seek to, not only prevent and protect environmental pollution, but also to encourage people, communities and nations to develop the better environment on the earth.

4. **Culture:** The UDHR says, 'Every human being has the right freely to participate in the cultural life of the community and by implication, this also means that no-one has the right to dominate, direct or eradicate that culture or impose theirs upon us.' The concept of culture of any society forms its identity; taking away means taking away their culture that has grown over hundreds of years. Hence, trying to destroy other's culture is a violation of human rights.

5. **Gender:** Any inappropriate discrimination between the gender of human beings, like men and women, amounts to a violation of human rights. The UDHR acknowledges that men and women are not the same, but insists on their rights to be equal before the law and treated without discrimination. It is evident that the human rights of women have been widely violated in the form of female infanticide, sexual slavery, rape, practice of dowry, exclusion from education and health, and the right to compete equally for jobs. Human rights seek to deliver justice to women and ensure '**Gender** equality', which is not a 'women's issue', but refers to the equal rights, responsibilities and opportunities of women and men.

6. **Participation:** Denying a human being from participating in his/her community is not in line with the principle of human rights. It is one's basic right to take a full part in the life of his/her community. Active, free and meaningful **participation** of a person gives experience and enjoyment of the range of rights and freedoms and opportunity to express his/her view of improving lives. For instance, the British Government in India was violating the human rights of Indian women by not allowing them to participate in elections, but the Indian Constitution gave voting right for both men and women.

27
CHAPTER

Human Rights: Legislation and National Human Rights Commission

LEGISLATIONS ON HUMAN RIGHTS IN INDIA

Human rights in India are as old as Indian civilization. Jawaharlal Nehru said, 'An unbroken continuity between the most ancient and the most modern phases of Hindu thought extending over three thousand years.' The concepts of human rights are very much inclusive in ancient India's scripture, mythologies, religions, culture and traditions. The Indian thought shows that, an individual, the society, the world and the Universe is an organic whole, so it believes in the universal applicability of human rights. The concept of *'Vasudev Kutumbakam'* (the world is a one family) illustrates this stand of India.

In modern India, the **Constitution of India endorses the principle of human rights,** particularly in **Preamble, Fundamental Rights, Directive Principles and Fundamental Duties.** Part III of the Constitution that covers the FRs is nothing but a form of human rights. For instance, the provisions of the FRs in the Indian Constitution and the UDHC are similar. Also, many provisions of the Directive Principles overlap with the UDHC. The Indian Constitution elaborated in detail about human rights in the form of FRs and Directive Principles, and it guarantees these and has also authorized the higher courts with strong powers to protect these rights of the people.

India is also signatory for the **'Universal Declaration of Human Rights'**, the **'International Covenant on Civil and Political Rights'** and the **'International Covenant on Economic, Social and Cultural Rights'**, also known as the **'International Bill of Rights'**.

THE PROTECTION OF HUMAN RIGHTS ACT OF 1993

The Parliament enacted **'The Protection of Human Rights Act (TPHRA)' in 1993** to provide **exclusive and effective legal framework for human rights issues** in India. Important provisions of the TPHRA are as follows:

1. It provided a detailed **definition** of human rights.

2. It provided for the **establishment of the National Human Rights Commission (NHRC)** at the national level and the **State Human Rights Commission** at the state level. It also provided these Commissions, composition, powers, functions, duties, procedures and so on in detail.
3. It provided for the **establishment of 'Human Rights Courts'** in the states to speed up the trials of offences involving human rights violation.
4. It provided for the **allocation of grants** to these Commissions by the Central and state governments and to **audit** these Commissions by the Comptroller and Auditor General of India (CAG).

Some other laws related to the protection and promotion of human rights in India are as follows:

1. The Protection of Civil Rights Act, 1955
2. Suppression of Immoral Traffic in Women and Girls Act, 1956
3. Maternity Benefit Act, 1961
4. Dowry Prohibition Act, 1961
5. Equal Remuneration Act, 1976
6. Bonded Labour (Abolition) Act
7. 1976 Employment of Children Act
8. 1938 (Amended in 1985)
9. Juvenile Justice Act, 1986
10. Sati (Prevention) Act, 1987
11. The Mental Health Act, 1993
12. The Child Labour (Prohibition and Regulation) Act, 1986
13. Indecent Representation of Women (Prohibition) Act, 1986
14. The Scheduled Castes and the Scheduled Tribes (Prevention of Atrocities) Act, 1989
15. The National Commission for Women Act, 1990
16. The National Commission for Minorities Act, 1992
17. The National Commission for Safai Karamcharis Act, 1993
18. The National Commission for Backward Classes Act, 1993
19. The Persons with Disabilities (Equal Opportunities, Protection of Rights and Full Participation) Act, 1995

NATIONAL HUMAN RIGHTS COMMISSION

The NHRC was established **in 1993 as a statutory body (not a Constitutional body)** by the Government under **TPHRA.** The NHRC **acts as a watchdog of human rights** in India. The **definition** of human rights according to the TPHRA is, 'Rights relating to life, liberty, equality and dignity of the individual guaranteed by the Constitution or embodied in the International Covenants (only that is justifiable in India).' The TPHRA has given compositions, objectives, functions, procedures, powers and so on for the smooth functioning of the NHRC.

The **main objectives** of the NHRC is to strengthen the institutional framework to deal with human rights issues, to conduct an independent inquiry into the allegation of human rights violation, to underline the commitment of the Government to protect human rights and to support and strengthen the efforts that have already made in this direction.

Composition

The NHRC is a **multi-member body.** It is composed of **a Chairman, four full-time members and four ex-office members:**

1. **A Chairman:** He should be **a retired Chief Justice of India** (CJI).
2. **Four members** (full time):

   (i) One member should be serving or a retired **judge of the Supreme Court.**
   (ii) One member should be serving or a retired **Chief Justice of a High Court.**
   (iii) **Two members** should be persons having **knowledge and experience of Human rights.**

3. **Four ex-office members:**

   (i) The Chairman of the National Commission for **SCs.**
   (ii) The Chairman of the National Commission for **STs.**
   (iii) The Chairman of the National Commission for **Women.**
   (iv) The Chairman of the National Commission for **Minorities.**

Appointment

The Chairman and all four full-time members are **appointed by the President by warrant under his hand and seal, only on the recommendation of a Committee** consisting of:

1. The **Prime Minister** as the Committee **head.**
2. The **Home Minister,** Government of India.
3. The **Speaker** of the Lok Sabha.
4. The **Deputy Chairman** of the Rajya Sabha.
5. The **Leaders of the Oppositions,** both in the Rajya Sabha and the Lok Sabha.

In case of the appointment of the serving judge of the Supreme Court or the serving Chief Justice of a High Court as members, this Committee should consult the Chief Justice of India.

Terms and Conditions

The term of both the Chairman and members is **five years or until they attain the age of 70 years.** After the end of their term, they **are not eligible to get any government employment.** The members are **eligible for re-appointment** for another term of five years. The Central government decides on the salaries, allowances and other conditions of the Chairman and members, but it cannot be changed after their appointment to their disadvantage. At the time of resignation, they submit their **resignations to the President.**

Removal

The President can remove the Chairman and the members before the expiry of their terms under any one of the following situations:

1. If he is adjudged as **an insolvent.**
2. If he is unfit to continue in his office by the reason of **infirmity of mind or body.**
3. If a competent court declared that he has an **unsound mind.**
4. During his term, if he is involved in **paid employment** outside the duties of his office.
5. If he is **convicted and sentenced** to imprisonment for an offence by a court.
6. If his **misbehaviour or incapability is proved.** But in this case, the President should refer such a matter to the Supreme Court for an inquiry and based on the Supreme Court's inquiry report, he can act further on this issue.

Functions

According to the TPHRA, the followings are the functions of the NHRC:

1. On **a petition** by a victim or on *'suo motu'* (on its own initiative, without a complaint or request) or on **an order** of a court, **inquiry into** violations of human rights or negligence in the prevention of such violation **by a public servant.**
2. To **intervene in a court's proceedings** relating to the allegation of the violation of human rights.
3. To **visit jails, detention places or other institutions,** to study the living conditions of the inmates and make necessary recommendations.
4. To **review the safeguards** provided by the Constitution or any law for the protection of human rights and recommend measures for their effective implementations.

5. To **review the factors,** including acts of terrorism that inhibit or suppress the enjoyment of human rights and recommend appropriate remedial measures.
6. To **study treaties and other international instruments** on human rights and make recommendations for their effective implementation.
7. To undertake and promote **research** in the field of human rights.
8. To engage in the **spread of human rights education or literacy** among the people and promote the awareness of the safeguards available for the protection of these rights.
9. To encourage the **efforts of NGOs** working in the field of human rights.
10. To undertake such other functions as it may consider necessary for the protection and promotion of human rights.

Working of the NHRC

The headquarter of the NHRC is in **New Delhi.** The NHRC is equivalent to a **civil court** as it has all the powers of a civil court. It has the **power to get information or report** from the Central and state governments or its subordinate authorities. It has the power to **regulate** its own procedure, and its proceedings have a **judicial character.** The NHRC has good coordination and cooperation with the NGOs to get direct information about the violation of human rights.

For conducting inquiry into complaints of human rights violations, the NHRC has its **own investigative staff.** Besides, for this purpose, it has the power to **utilize any investigation agency** or officers of the Central government and any state government. However, the NHRC can inquire into the violation of human rights allegations **only within one year of its occurrence;** after expiry of one year, it has no power to initiate such inquiries.

The NHRC, during or after the completion of an inquiry, may take any of the following actions:

1. It may **recommend** the concerned governments or authority

    (i) To **compensate or pay for damages** to the victim.
    (ii) To take **actions against the guilty** of public servant.
    (iii) To provide **grants for immediate interim relief** to the victim.

2. It may **approach the Supreme Court or the concerned High Court** for necessary orders, directions and writs.

It must be noted that the recommendations of the NHRC are **not binding** on the concerned government or authority; they **may accept or reject** its recommendations by giving information about the same within one month. So the functions of the NHRC are mainly **recommendatory or advisory in nature.** It neither has the **power to punish** the guilty nor any power to give any **kind of relief** including monetary relief to the victim. Its role is limited with respect to the violation of human rights by the Armed Forces.

The NHRC submits its **annual report** to the Central government or to the concerned state government; they laid it down before their respective legislatures along with a memorandum of action taken on the recommendations of the NHRC, including the reason for the non-acceptance of any recommendations.

SIGNIFICANCE OF HUMAN RIGHTS

Human rights are a very complicated and sensitive issue in India because India is a democratic, secular and republic country. Also, it is a very big and diverse nation and one of the fastest developing countries in the world. Also, human rights are interpreted differently by different people; their definitions are not static as they change with the time. But they have tremendous significance for the well-being of humans. The following quotes/phrases illustrate this:

'To deny people their human rights is to challenge their very humanity.' — Nelson Mandela

'Freedom is not worth having, if it does not include the freedom to make err. It passes my comprehension how human beings, be they ever so experienced and able, can delight in depriving other human beings of that precious right.' — Mahatma Gandhi

'Human rights are of universal interest because it is the inherent nature of all human beings to yearn for freedom, equality and dignity, and they have the right to achieve it.' — The Fourteenth Dalai Lama

'All human beings are born free and equal in dignity and rights.' — Article 1 of the UDHR

'I am in favour of animal rights as well as human rights. That is the way of a whole human being.' — Abraham Lincoln

'Women Rights are human rights and human rights are women's rights.' — Hillary Clinton

'Give to every human being every right that you claim for yourself.' — Robert Ingersoll

'Human rights are universal standard. It is a component of every religion and every civilization.' — Shirin Ebadi

Section X

Engineering Ethics

28

CHAPTER

Scope and Aims of Engineering Ethics

BACKGROUND

In the modern world, technology has become an integral part of humanity. It is a main component in the evolution of human civilization. It is imperative to make sure that all the technologies would be used for the goodness of human, environment and wildlife. It is highly impossible to achieve this without inculcating the high standard of ethics and morality among persons working in the technological field.

Albert Camus rightly said, 'A man without ethics is a wild beast loosed upon this world.' The human race has the greatest threat of the unethical use of technology; for instances, the unethical use of ultrasound technology to determine the gender of foetus is leading to a large number of female infanticide in India; one cannot imagine the catastrophic damage if the nuclear technology, biological weapon and other key technologies fall in the hands of terrorists. One of the best ways to counter this threat is to provide ethical knowledge to young technologists.

INTRODUCTION

Ethics is the **branch of Philosophy** also known as moral philosophy that involves systematizing, defending and recommending concepts of **right and wrong conduct.**[1] The term 'ethics' came from the ancient **Greek word 'ethos',** which means **'character'.** The Greeks used this term to explain a certain set of guiding principles, beliefs or ideas that qualify a community or a nation. The WordWeb Dictionary defines 'ethics' as 'a system of principles governing morality and acceptable conduct'.

Thus, ethics means **a set of beliefs, ideas, moral principles and values accepted as right and wrong or good and bad by a society, which conducts or governs human actions or behaviour.** For example, in the Indian society, stealing is accepted as wrong or bad and this value governs theft cases either legally or socially. Ethics is as old as human civilization and it changes with place and time. Ethics are governed under professional and legal frameworks.

---

[1] Internet Encyclopaedia of Philosophy: Ethics, available at http://www.iep.utm.edu/ethics

The word 'moral' should not be confused with the word ethics, though both are interchangeably used. The **'moral' or 'morality' means** a set of beliefs, ideas, principles and values accepted as right and wrong or good and bad **by an individual.** Morality is related to individual persons or one's inner concise, whereas **ethics is related to society.** So, **all moral values are not ethical** as individual's right/bad may not be socially right/bad. For example, killing innocent people may be morally right for a terrorist, but for the society it is unethical, as no society accepts killing innocent people as right.

Ethical theories are divided into three categories: **meta-ethics, normative ethics and applied ethics** (refer to footnote 1). Meta-ethics deal with the study of origin, concept, purpose and consequences of ethical values. Normative ethics is more practical, which is concerned with the standard ethical values to regulate the conduct of people. **Applied ethics** is related to the application of ethical theories into various fields, such as business ethics, medical ethics and engineering ethics and so on to study some specific ethical issues.

PROFESSION AND PROFESSIONAL ETHICS

The Oxford Dictionary defines 'profession' as 'the act or fact of professing'. A profession means 'vocation or occupation based on particular educational training'. According to the WordWeb Dictionary, 'professional' means, 'engaged in a profession or engaging in as a profession or means of livelihood' or 'characteristic of a profession or one engaged in a profession'.

The important **characteristics of profession** are as follows:

1. It requires **specialized knowledge and training.** For example, engineering profession requires an academic degree that provides engineering knowledge and a formal training.
2. Usually professions have **'monopoly'** with regard to providing professional service. Those people who possess medical knowledge and training can only give medical services to the people; engineers cannot provide such a service.
3. A professional enjoys considerable **'autonomy'** in his/her work field. Professionals have the freedom to take a decision and carry out their duty according to their discretion. They have freedom to choose their clients. For example, a doctor enjoys enough autonomy with respect to choosing his/her client and giving him/her a treatment.
4. All professionals have certain important **'responsibility'** concerning their work, and they are **accountable** for their professional acts.
5. All professions are **bound to 'ethical standards',** also known as **'professional ethics'.** Every profession prescribes its **own 'Code of Ethics'** and that is equally applicable to all concerned professionals in that field. The Code of Ethics also involves the provision of punishment in case of the violation of ethical standards by a professional person.

Professional ethics means, 'A set of beliefs, moral principles and rules that governs a profession.' In professional ethics, some set of beliefs, moral principles and rules determine what is right and what is wrong or what is good and what is bad in the profession and that is commonly applicable to all professionals of the same field. The professional ethics prescribes certain **personal, organizational and corporate standards** that need to be followed by all professionals involved, for example, engineering ethics, medical ethics, business ethics and so on.

The **important components of the professional ethics** are as follows:

1. Honesty
2. Liability
3. Integrity
4. Reliability
5. Responsibility
6. Transparency
7. Accountability
8. Safety
9. Confidentiality
10. Objectivity
11. Respectfulness
12. Obedience to the law
13. Loyalty

Basic duties: Professional codes of ethics are **referred to as 'basic duties'** because they prescribe a few **fundamental duties and obligations;** failure to fulfil those leads to punishment, such as reproach or sanctions.[2]

ENGINEERING ETHICS

Engineering ethics is a **kind of applied ethics** and it encompasses some moral principles that apply to the practice of engineering. It is the **study of moral issues** and decisions confronting individuals and organizations engaged in engineering. Engineering ethics is comprised of **some sets of beliefs, moral principles and rules that determine what is right and what is wrong or what is good and what is bad in the engineering profession, which are commonly applied to all engineers.** The engineering ethics **prescribes certain personal, organizational and corporate standards** that need to be followed by all engineers. The engineering ethics stipulate certain sets of **obligations by engineers** towards the **society and to the profession.** Usually, the engineering ethics are enforced by the **professional and legal frameworks.**

---

[2] Charles E. Harris, M. S. Pritchard and M. J. Rabins. 2005, *Engineering Ethics: Concept and Cases*, pp. 19–20.

For example, it is a moral principle or rule that engineers should not share sensitive defence technology with wrong persons like terrorists as it may be detrimental to the existence of humankind; hence, it is considered as wrong or bad. If any engineer does not follow this standard behaviour by violating it, he/she incurs legal or organizational punishment.

Engineering ethics deals with the ethical standards of an individual engineer or a group of engineers. It deals with the ethical standards of policy makers, decision makers, managers, scientists and so on. It is more related to the upper level of the organization.

Engineering ethics provides a detailed prescription about the standard of engineer's honesty, liability, integrity, reliability, responsibility, transparency, accountability, safety, confidentiality, objectivity, respectfulness, loyalty and obedience to the law and so on in engineering practice. In India, the **Institution of Engineers (India)** and **the National Society of Professional Engineers (NSPE)** formulated the **'Code of Ethics' for engineers.**

AIM OF ENGINEERING ETHICS

Important aims of the engineering ethics are as follows (refer to footnote 2):

1. **Stimulating moral imagination:** Imagination about a work or the problem and its consequences based on ethical standards providing the best options to an engineer to effectively and efficiently handle particular issues.
2. **Recognizing ethical issues:** Usually, engineering works are complex and complicated as many stakeholders' interests need to be considered by an engineer. In this kind of complex and complicated work, having knowledge of the ethics provides guidance to **identify what is right or wrong and good or bad.** Without the knowledge of engineering ethics, it would be difficult to recognize ethical issues involved in a work and it may affect the interest of the society.
3. **Developing analytical skills:** An engineer obliviously possesses technical skills and related analytical skills. The engineering ethics helps to broaden analytical skills of an engineer by means of providing the knowledge about justice, rights, social welfare, safety, legal education, responsibility and so on. In other words, it **connects the engineer's technical knowledge with social knowledge.**
4. **Eliciting a sense of responsibility:** Engineering is a subject that merely provides the technical knowledge, but it does not make an engineer aware of the various aspects of responsibilities, such as social and legal responsibilities, accountability and so on. So, the engineering ethics not only addresses this problem but also takes engineers beyond their formal duty and obligation by broadening their vision of responsibility.
5. **Tolerating disagreement and ambiguity:** If an engineering work is complex and complicated and there is no lack of consensus among diverse

stakeholders, it will lead to disagreement and ambiguity. The engineering ethics helps to **face and solve** such problems.

6. **Solving ethical dilemmas:** An **ethical dilemma** is a situation in which **one or more ethical values confront each other, leading to a mental conflict;** it is difficult to choose one ethical value as it could transgress another. The engineering ethics helps to solve such problems.
7. Promoting **moral integrity and professional integrity** among engineers.
8. Safeguarding **moral autonomy and moral consistency:** A moral autonomy means, sticking to our own inner voice for the righteous despite negative external pressure on a work. A moral consistency means, maintaining ethical values in work for a long time without compromising it for anything.

SCOPE OF ENGINEERING ETHICS

Mike W. Martin and Ronald Schinzinger[3] have listed out the scope of engineering ethics as follows:

1. **Engineering ethics are social experimentation:** A social experiment is a research project that is carried out on human matters in the real world or society. All projects in the engineering field are capable of generating comfort and harm to the people, and it is treated as a social experimentation. So, it creates new responsibilities for creating benefits, preventing harm and remarking danger.
2. **Moral values:** All engineering projects are embedded with moral values. All aspects of technological development include moral values. So, like in other professions, ethics and excellence in engineering too go hand in hand.
3. **Personal meaning and commitment:** An engineer's personal meaning and commitments do matter in engineering ethics. An engineer who has strong professional commitments cares for other human beings, maintains self-respect and generally motivates excellence in engineering.
4. **Promoting responsible conduct and preventing wrongdoing:** Engineering ethics seeks to promote a responsible conduct among engineers and prevents wrongdoing and also punishes wrong doers. However, **its first preference is to prevent wrongdoing, which is known as 'Preventative Ethics'.**
5. **Ethical dilemmas:** The engineering ethics may give rise to ethical dilemmas as moral values or ethical values are myriad, complex and can conflict.
6. **Micro and macro issues:** Micro issues are related to **the individual's or company's decisions,** whereas macro issues are related to **the national or global issues.** In engineering ethics, both are important and often interwoven. For example, the Cyber Security issue is related to the privacy of an individual, a company, national security and global debate.

---

[3] Mike W. Martin and R. Schinzinger. 2005, *Ethics in Engineering*. Wordsworth Publishing, Independence, KY, pp. 2–7.

7. **Cautions optimism about technology:** Pessimists point out negative aspects of technological development, such as pollution, war and so on. Optimists point out the positive aspects of technological development, such as connectivity, medical service, radio, TV, agriculture and so on. The engineering ethics must **be cautiously optimistic about technology.**

THREE KINDS OF INQUIRIES

There are three kinds of inquiries in engineering that help to find out ethics (refer to footnote 3). All of them are interrelated and complementary. They are as follows:

1. **Normative inquiry:** In this, one tries to find ethics based on the values that guide the individual and the group in their work. A certain set of pre-established norms or values help engineers to identify ethics. For example, in a public project like constructing a dam, an engineer need to consider many stakeholder values, such as farmers, businessmen, politicians, people and so on. That engineer needs to prioritize these values based on the welfare of all.
2. **Conceptual inquiry:** In this, one tries to find out ethics based on the concepts that guide the individual and the group in their work. For example, conceptualizing public safety while constructing a bridge on the river.
3. **Factual inquiry:** In this, one tries to find out ethics based on only the facts that guide the individual and the group in their work. This is also known as **'descriptive inquiry'.** For example, an engineer may verify the available geographical data and estimated loss of public property before constructing a dam and may take a moral decision.

ROLE MORALITY

Role morality can be **defined as 'claim(ing) a moral permission to harm others in ways that, if not for the role, would be wrong'.**[4] Each person has to play multiple roles, such as student, father, businessman, social servant and so on in life. Role morality **explains the morality of a person while playing different roles at a time.** In each role, **a person is associated with certain obligations and prerogatives (exclusive rights).** A person may claim the morality of his work in a role based on obligations and prerogatives associated with that role, but the same work may not be moral in his another role based on obligations and prerogatives associated with that role. This is referred to as 'role morality'.

For instance, a police inspector may roughly treat an innocent client believing that he is acting on behalf of the police department and so it is the right thing, but he may softly treat his own family members if they were in a similar situation like

---

[4] A. Applbaum. 1999. *Ethics for Adversaries: The Morality of Roles in Public and Professional Life.* Princeton University Press, Princeton, NJ, p. 3.

that of the innocent client. This is because the same man playing a dual role here. His associated obligations and prerogatives roles are different and conflicting.

What action will that police inspector take if his own daughter commits any crime? Will he, being a father, try to protect her without taking any legal actions? Or will he, as a police inspector, allow police inquiry against her? In such a situation, one must **adhere to the professional ethics.** The NPSE provided an ethical Code of Ethics to engineers to face such a situation.

CODE OF ETHICS FOR ENGINEERS BY THE NATIONAL SOCIETY OF PROFESSIONAL ENGINEERS

Preamble

Engineering is an important and learned profession. As members of this profession, engineers are expected to exhibit the highest standards of honesty and integrity. Engineering has a direct and vital impact on the quality of life of all people. Accordingly, the services provided by engineers require honesty, impartiality, fairness and equity, and they must be dedicated to the protection of public health, safety and welfare. Engineers must perform under a standard professional behaviour that requires adherence to the highest principles of ethical conduct.

I. **Fundamental Canons**
   Engineers, in the fulfilment of their professional duties, shall:

   1. Hold paramount the safety, health and welfare of the public.
   2. Perform services only in areas of their competence.
   3. Issue public statements only in an objective and truthful manner.
   4. Act for each employer or client as faithful agents or trustees.
   5. Avoid deceptive acts.
   6. Conduct themselves honourably, responsibly, ethically and lawfully so as to enhance the honour, reputation and usefulness of the profession.

II. **Rules of Practice**
   Engineers shall:

   1. Hold paramount the safety, health and welfare of the public.
   2. Perform services only in the areas of their competence.
   3. Issue public statements only in an objective and truthful manner.
   4. Act for each employer or client as faithful agents or trustees.
   5. Avoid deceptive acts.

III. **Professional Obligations**
   Engineers shall:

   1. Be guided in all their relations by the highest standards of honesty and integrity.
   2. At all times strive to serve the public interest.

3. Avoid all conduct or practice that is deceptive to the public.
4. Not disclose, without consent, confidential information concerning the business affairs or technical processes of any present or former client or employer, or public body to which they serve.
5. Not be influenced in their professional duties by conflicting interests.
6. Not attempt to obtain employment or advancement or professional engagements by untruthfully criticizing other engineers, or by other improper or questionable methods.
7. Not attempt to injure, maliciously or falsely, directly or indirectly, the professional reputation, prospects, practice or employment of other engineers. Engineers who believe others are guilty of unethical or illegal practice shall present such information to the proper authority for action.
8. Accept personal responsibility for their professional activities, provided, however, those engineers may seek indemnification for services arising out of their practice for other than gross negligence, where the engineer's interests cannot otherwise be protected.
9. Give credit for engineering work to those to whom credit is due, and will recognize the proprietary interests of others.

(For complete details, please visit http://www.nspe.org/resources/ethics/code-ethics)

CODE OF ETHICS FOR ENGINEERS BY THE INSTITUTE OF ENGINEERS (INDIA)

Code of Ethics for Corporate Members, effective from 1 March 2004:

I. **Preamble**

The Corporate Members of the Institution of Engineers (India) are committed to promote and practice the profession of engineering for the common good of the community bearing in mind the following concerns:

1. Concern for ethical standard
2. Concern for social justice, social order and human rights
3. Concern for protection of the environment
4. Concern for sustainable development
5. Public safety and tranquillity.

II. **The Tenets of the Code of Ethics**

1. A corporate member shall utilize his/her knowledge and expertise for the welfare, health and safety of the community without any discrimination for sectional or private interests.
2. A corporate member shall maintain the honour, integrity and dignity in all his/her professional actions to be worthy of the trust of the community and the profession.
3. A corporate member shall act only in the domains of his/her competence and with diligence, care, sincerity and honesty.

4. A corporate member shall apply his/her knowledge and expertise in the interest of his/her employer or the clients for whom he/she shall work without compromising with other obligations to these tenets.
5. A corporate member shall not falsify or misrepresent his own or his associates' qualifications, experience and so on.
6. A corporate member, wherever necessary and relevant, shall take all reasonable steps to inform him/herself, his/her employer or clients, of the environmental, economic, social and other possible consequences, which may arise out of his actions.
7. A corporate member shall maintain utmost honesty and fairness in making statements or giving witness and shall do so on the basis of adequate knowledge.
8. A corporate member shall not directly or indirectly injure the professional reputation of another member.
9. A corporate member shall reject any kind of offer that may involve unfair practice or may cause avoidable damage to the ecosystem.
10. A corporate member shall be concerned about and shall act in the best of his abilities for the maintenance of sustainability of the process of development.
11. A corporate member shall not act in any manner which may injure the reputation of the institution or which may cause any damage to the institution financial assets or otherwise.

III. **General Guidance**

The Tenets of the Code of Ethics are based on the recognition that

1. A common tie exists among the humanity and the Institution of Engineers (India) derives its value from the people, so that the actions of its corporate members should indicate the member's highest regard for the equality of opportunity, social justice and fairness.
2. The corporate members of the institution hold a privileged position in the community so as to make it a necessity for their not using the position for personal and sectional interests.

IV. **And, As Such, A Corporate Member**

1. Should keep his/her employer or client fully informed on all matters in respect of his/her assignment which are likely to lead to a conflict of interest or when, in his/her judgement, a project will not be viable on the basis of commercial, technical, environmental or any other risks.
2. Should maintain confidentiality of any information with utmost sincerity unless expressly permitted to disclose such information or unless such permission, if withheld, may adversely affect the welfare, health and safety of the community.
3. Should neither solicit nor accept financial or other considerations from anyone related to a project or assignment of which he/she is in the charge.

4. Should neither pay nor offer direct or indirect inducements to secure work.
5. Should compete on the basis of merit alone.
6. Should refrain from inducing a client to breach a contract and entered into with another duly appointed engineer.
7. Should, if asked by the employer or a client to review the work of another person or organization, discuss the review with the other person or organization to arrive at a balanced opinion.
8. Should make statements or give evidence before a tribunal or a court of law in an objective and accurate manner and express any opinion on the basis of adequate knowledge and competence.
9. Should reveal the existence of any interest—pecuniary or otherwise—which may affect the judgement while giving an evidence or making a statement.
10. Any decision of the Council as per provisions of the relevant Bye-Laws of the institution shall be final and binding on all corporate members.

(Source: https://www.ieindia.org/readmrCodeofethic.aspx)

CHAPTER

Responsibility of Engineers and Impediments to Responsibilities

INTRODUCTION

After the death of innocent people because of the collapse of a building, everybody asks: 'Who is responsible for it?' After the catastrophic Fukushima Daiichi nuclear disaster in Japan in 2011, everybody asked: 'Who is responsible for it?' So what is this responsibility?

Generally, responsibility indicates three things:

1. Acceptance to **successfully complete a work** within time
2. Acceptance of any **consequences or outcomes** (positive or negative) of that work
3. In case of failure to meet (1) and/or (2) (except positive outcome), **liable to punishment.**

Responsibility involves the **obligation** of an individual or a group to carry out his or their duties; **accountability,** that is, being answerable for one's acts or omission in doing accepted work; **reward** for the successful completion of work and **punishment** for mistakes or failure to complete the accepted work.

Suppose that an engineer has taken a responsibility to construct a nuclear power plant to produce electricity. It implies that he has accepted to successfully complete that work within the given time by considering all aspects of the work, that is, technological requirement, geographical area, impact on the environment and so on. He is obliged to carry out his duties; he is accountable or answerable for all his acts or omission with respect to that work. In case of any mistakes, for instance, radiation leakage, collapse of building, not following safety norms and so on, he is liable to punishment and if he successfully completes that work within the stipulated time, he deserves a reward.

The responsibility of engineers in the modern world is phenomenal and extraordinary because it has a direct impact on the welfare of humanity or its extinction. If an engineer fails to meet his responsibility, it will be catastrophic to society, for example, Fukushima Daiichi nuclear disaster, crash of the Space Shuttle Columbia, frequent train accidents in India, leakage of radiations from a nuclear power plant and so on.

Engineers have two kinds of responsibilities:

1. **Legal responsibility:** It means the responsibility of an engineer that can be **legally framed by law.** That is details of obligation, accountability, punishment and reward of an engineer working in writing in law or legal agreement.
2. **Moral responsibility:** It is the responsibility of an engineer that cannot be legally framed and that depends **on his moral values.** For example, an Engineer may resign from his job after the collapse of a building constructed by him in the past on moral grounds. Here he sincerely accepts the negative outcome of his work and resigns because he wanted to prevent such mistakes again in ongoing work, though legally his guilt is not proved yet. This is called the moral responsibility. A person having moral responsibility is referred to as a **'moral agent'.**

RESPONSIBILITIES TO CAUSE HARM

An engineer is responsible (either legal or moral) for causing harm to others while executing his work. There are three ways to cause harm:

1. **Intentional harm:** An engineer knowingly and purposefully may cause harm to others. Such an engineer is both legally and morally responsible for it. For example, an engineer intentionally manufactures low-quality railway tracks that may lead to the death of innocent people due to the derailing of a train.
2. **Negligent harm:** An engineer unknowingly and non-purposefully may cause harm to others by failing to take due care. Such an engineer is morally responsible, but may not be held legally responsible. For example, a mechanical engineer in Railways, although not having any ill intentions, may not seriously consider a mistake in the railway engine and that leads to the accident of that train.
3. **Reckless harm:** An engineer may not have any intention to harm others, but he is conscious that his actions may lead to harming others. Such an engineer is morally responsible. For example, an aeronautical engineer during a test trial of a chopper, although not having any intention to cause harm to anyone, may fly into a 'no fly zone' knowing the fact very well that it may cause harm to the people below that area if his chopper accidentally crashes down.

APPROACHES TO RESPONSIBILITY

All fingers are not of the same size. The same way, each engineer's approach to his responsibility is different. According to the **attitude of engineers,** the approaches to responsibility are classified into three categories:

1. **Minimalist view:** When it comes to an engineer having a minimalist view attitude, his approach to responsibility **is only concerned with his own work and related terms and conditions.** He takes as much minimum responsibility as he could by interpreting it in legal terms and on individual fault. This is a **negative approach** to responsibility. An engineer with an attitude to avoid hard work blames others and trouble others, usually takes this approach to responsibility. Usually, such kinds of engineers are found saying: **'I don't know'; 'I don't care about your work'; 'It is my job, not yours'; 'It is your job, not my fault'; 'That is not my problem'** and so on.

2. **Reasonable care:** An engineer having a reasonable care attitude is **not only concerned with his own work, but also about the people who are going to be hurt by his acts or omissions.** This is a higher level of degree of responsibility than the minimalist view. Mostly, **friends, relative and well-wishers** show such an attitude. For example, an engineer thinks about possible river pollution and its consequences on the people and environment before dumping the waste generated by his project work in a water body.

3. **Good work:** This is the **most superior level of approach to responsibility.** An engineer having a **good work** attitude **is not only concerned with his own work, but also goes above and beyond the call of duty while carrying out his responsibilities.** According to the duty or rules, he need not go to that extent while executing his responsibilities, but he still does such a work with a great positive attitude. Such engineers think about the welfare of all without any selfishness. Such people are very rare to see. Usually, saints, people with pure souls and parents show such an attitude.

   This is a higher level of degree of responsibility than those of the minimalist view and reasonable care. One of the best examples of this is an eminent engineer of India, **Sir M. Visvesvaraya.** In his work, he did not just thought of his duty, and its terms and conditions, but he also had a broad vision for the industrial development of our nation and the welfare of the people. That is why, we celebrate his birthday, **15th September,** as the **'Engineers Day'** in India.

IMPEDIMENT TO RESPONSIBILITY

The most common impediments to successfully complete a responsibility are as follows:

1. **Self-interest and self-centred attitude:** It is a human tendency to think about personal benefit over others, and engineers are no exception to that. A person who compromises his professional responsibility or his organizational interests for fulfilling his self-interests such as accepting bribe, unduly favouring his relatives and friends and so on cannot successfully complete his responsibility. Such a person not only risks his career, but also harms his

own organization and society at large. One's greed, jealousy, intention to take revenge on his boss, egoism and so on lead to a self-centred attitude to fulfil his self-interests. For example, an engineer, by compromising his responsibility, may build a low-quality road to gain personal benefit from the contractor that negatively affects the people; it is an unethical act.

2. **Lack of emotional intelligence:** Emotional intelligence means the ability to recognize the self and other people's emotions or feelings and use them for the maximum benefit for all. A person with the lack of emotional intelligence does not understand his own and other's feelings, which creates a conflict between them and that may lead to compromising with responsibility.

3. **Lack of communication skills:** A lack of ability to effectively express one's word or intention to others and listen to other carefully may lead to the misunderstanding and may affect one's responsibility. For example, A asks B to mix cement and sand in the 15 per cent and 13 per cent ratio, but B understands it as 15 per cent and 30 per cent because of the lack of listening skills. This will lead to the substandard work which will amount to compromising with responsibility.

4. **Dual personality:** An engineer may follow double standards: one for self and the other for others on the same issue. Suppose, for example, in a project work, the lunch break is just of 30 minutes. A senior engineer asks junior engineers to complete lunch within 30 minutes, but he himself takes more than 1 hour and expects no question from juniors in this regard. Such a person cannot earn respect and moral integrity.

5. **Fear, threats, cowardliness and distrust:** If an engineer surrenders himself to fear, threats, unreasonable distrust on colleagues and shows cowardliness emotions, he cannot successfully complete his responsibility because it disturbs his mental balance, concentration and diverts his attention to protect himself from these negative things by compromising his responsibility. For example, an engineer may give false safety certification for a big residential building because of threats from the owners of that building to kill his family members.

   Swami Vivekananda said, *'Fear is unrighteous, sin, death and hell. All the negative thoughts and ideas that are in the world have proceeded from the evil spirit of fear.'* A strong self-confidence, intelligence and high ethical standards help one overcome these negative things.

6. **Group behaviour:** Most men show different kinds (may be positive or negative) of responsibilities as an individual or a group member. Important issues that have an impact on the group behaviour are as follows:

   (i)   In a group, the management thinks of profit and the labour class thinks about fulfilling their basic needs. So there is a gap between both sections in the group that may affect the group responsibility.

   (ii) In a group, the labour class deliberately work below their potential just to maintain their demand for the management. This is called **'Natural Soldering'**.

(iii) Among a group, there is a tendency to **shift responsibility based on rationalization** to minimize one's workload and particularly avoid trouble in case of failure. An English proverb says, *'Everybody's responsibility, Nobody's responsibility.'*

(iv) An **illusion of morality,** in which group members tend to forget their personal moral principles for group's overall moral principles and lost the sense of individual right and wrong.

(v) A strong **'sense or feeling of I or us'** considers outsiders as enemies or adversaries and they may affect their self-interest.

(vi) In a group, informal relations have more impact on completing responsibility than formal relations.

(vii) An individual may assume that in case of failure of an assigned task, he may not be held personally accountable, but all members, that is, **the illusion of invulnerability** for failure.

(viii) A disagreed member may be suppressed by colleagues or higher level officers in a group.

(ix) Group members like status-quo and resist change.

(x) Level of morality is different from one member to another in a group. There are chances that high moral person may be demoralized in case of failure.

(xi) An **illusion of unanimity,** establishing the silence of a member as consent or expecting complete consensus among the group members.

(xii) A tendency of **self-censorship** makes a member of the group remain silent or restrain himself confining to the other member's private doubts or uncertainties related to group action.

(xiii) **Mindguarding,** in which a person preserves the ideas or principles of his group and protects it from internal and external disturbances.

7. **Overconfidence:** A person with overconfidence usually takes most decisions and executes his responsibility with the presumption that **'he knows all'**, **'him do only right work'**, **'he cannot be wrong'**, and so on without considering the situational difference and feasibility of his decisions. It may be okay in the short run, but in the long run, it will not work.

8. **Self-deception:** A self-deceptive person does not pay any heed to his 'inner voice' or 'inner selves' and wrongly believes that his acts are favourable for him, thereby misleading himself. Self-deception is an intentional act to avoid the truth. For example, one person smokes a cigarette with a disillusion that it will give him pleasure or relaxation, though his inner voice knows that smoking is injurious to health.

9. **Ignorance:** It means the lack of information, knowledge or education. A person cannot successfully complete his responsibility without the proper information, knowledge and education about his work. Reasons to become an ignorant are as follows:

(i) Inadequate information, due to the lack of resources or shortage of time

(ii) Lack of knowledge about work

    (iii) Laziness and a habit to enjoy rest

    (iv) Lack of consistence or perseverance in completing responsibility

    (v) Pressure to complete a work within given deadlines.

10. **Egocentric tendency:** It is natural for human beings to have ego. The egoist, egocentric and egomaniac are related words with some difference. An egocentric person is the one who has 'narrow mind' or 'parochial mind'. Such a person has misconception that he is superior to others **(superiority complex)** and others are inferior to him. An egocentric person does not accept his faults and gets angry with a person who points out his faults; he tries to justify his faults based on illogical or untruthful arguments and he does not easily praise others for good work and feel jealous of others. Such people often fail to successfully complete their responsibilities.

11. **Microscopic vision:** A person with microscopic vision pays his attention to a small amount of work which may not be that vital by considering his over-all responsibilities. An engineer should have 'macroscopic vision', in which he takes a much broader vision which covers scientific, technological, social, economical, cultural and political aspects with an intention to benefit people. Most successful engineers such as Sir M. Visvesvaraya, Man Mohan Sharma and so on had 'macroscopic vision' in their work.

12. **Surrender to boss:** A person who dedicates himself for his boss but not to the work or the responsibility, who always accepts boss as a 'right person' and does not use his intellect or discretion, and who tries to seek shelter in his boss for his mistakes is very unlikely to successfully complete his responsibilities.

13. **External pressure:** An engineer may bend to external pressures to compromise his responsibilities. For example, a builder may put pressure on his engineers to use low-cost materials to construct a building which may compromise with the safety of people.

30

CHAPTER _____

Risks, Safety and Liability of Engineers

RISK OF ENGINEERS

Some time, an action of a professional with good intention may result in negative consequences. For instance, an engineer builds an airplane with good intention, but it may end up by meeting an accident and kill passengers while flying. This is because **all consequences of an action are uncertain; uncertainty is unpredictable, potential, unmeasurable and uncontrollable. The risk lies in uncertainty**. **The risk is a probable negative consequence of an action taken despite of uncertainty.**

According to the WordWeb Dictionary, risk means 'source of danger, a possibility of incurring loss or misfortune' or 'expose to a chance of loss or damage'. **Risk is a potential loss of valuable thing,** such as loss of life; loss of physical health and harm to the body; polluting environment; economic loss; loss of job; loss of social status, such as prestige, reputation, trustworthiness and confidence in society; loss of time and effort (physical or mental); loss of emotional well-being, such as happiness, peace and so on.

Engineering also involves risk—risk for both: those who directly involve in engineering work (professionals), and those who enjoy the benefits of engineering work (public or consumers for society and the environment. All engineering works involve risk, but it **is very high in a few areas,** such as atomic field, mining, natural gas exploration, space technology, shipping industry, chemical manufacturing, cement industry, large-scale construction, such as building, metro and so on. Like all professionals, engineers also do tremendous work to study the various risks involved in each engineering field and try to mitigate risk as much as they can, but humans are still not the masters of uncertainty.

Classification of Risk

Risks are classified as follows:

1. **Voluntary Risk and Involuntary Risk**
   A voluntary risk means, taking a risk after **knowing** about it and its consequences. For example, astronauts know about the risk involved in a space

mission and its negative consequences, but still they do undertake that risk. An **involuntary risk** means, taking a risk **without knowing** about it and its consequences. For example, a person purchases a refrigerator at low price without about the knowledge of its poor quality. It is possible to take precautions to mitigate the consequence of voluntary risks, but not to involuntary risks.

2. **Expected Risk and Unexpected Risk**

   An **expected risk** is an **identified possible risk** that can be assessed and the probability of loss of value related to that risk can be estimated. For example, a tyre-manufacturing company gives a guarantee to its customer that the chance of its tyre getting burst is 1 out of millions. An **unexpected risk** is an **unidentified (or unknown) risk** that can neither be assessed nor estimated. For example, in Japan, unexpectedly both an earthquake and a tsunami simultaneously caused the Fukushima Daiichi nuclear disaster in 2011. It is possible to take precautions to mitigate the consequence of expected risks, but not against unexpected risks.

3. **Immediate Risk and Delayed Risk**

   An **immediate risk** is the one that is likely to cause harm or inflict loss of valuable things **in a short period of time or in the near future** or imminently; for example, rash bike driving. In case of an accident, it may cause the death of the bike rider. A **delayed risk** in the one that is likely to cause harm or inflict loss of valuable things in a **long period of time or in the long future;** for example, smoking that harms body over a long period of time, not immediately.

4. **Short-term Impact and Long-term Impact**

   In a short-term impact risk, the harm or loss of valuable things remains for a short period of time, and later it may be normalized; for example, cutting off the skin of a finger by a knife while cutting vegetables. **In a long-term impact** risk, the harm or loss of valuable things remains for a long period of time, and later it may not be normalized; for example, losing a leg due to a car accident.

5. **Reversible Effect and Irreversible Effect**

   Sometimes, a harm or loss caused by a risk is reversible—that is, it can be cured or recovered or it is possible to bring it to the original position or status sometimes—such a risk is referred to as **reversible effect** risks; for example, a damage caused by a knife to finger skin while cutting vegetables can be recovered in a short period of time. Sometimes, a harm or loss caused by a risk is irreversible—that is, something that can neither be cured nor recovered nor is it possible to bring it to the original position or status at any time—such a risk is referred to as the **irreversible effect** risk; for example, the loss of a leg due to a car accident.

6. **Threshold level of Risk-taking**

   Some kind of act involves a different level of risks based on the degree of probability of loss of a valuable thing or harm. A threshold level of risk means, taking risks beyond one's capacity or ability up to the maximum level, where the chances of harm or loss of the valuable thing are very high and severe. For example, Mr Malik's monthly salary is ₹20,000 and he is addicted to a horse race game. He usually spends ₹5,000–10,000 per month in the horse game. But one day he spends all of his ₹20,000 in the day; this is his threshold level of risk.

Difficulties in the Estimation of Risk

Professional engineers try to estimate the risk associated with their work, product or service so that they can avoid a risk or mitigate its negative consequences as much as possible. This is not easy, but very complex and hard. There are two well-known methods to estimate risk in engineering work: **'fault tree analysis' and 'event tree analysis'.**

1. **Fault Tree Analysis**
   A 'fault tree analysis' is a scientific tool to **identify, assess, estimate, analyse and prevent possible risk or accident in engineering.** Essentially, a fault tree **is a diagram;** it **estimates** about the possible ways of accident or malfunction that may occur. As its name suggests, it shows **possible faults** that may occur in a systematic manner. **It is a top-down method.** It is usually used to predict harm or hazards about a risk. There is little or no direct or first-hand experience available on such a risk, such as the meltdown of nuclear reactors (see Figure 30.1).

2. **Event Tree Analysis**
   Fault tree analysis is a top-down method to find the mode of failure, but event tree analysis is a **bottom-up method.** An event tree **starts with an initiating event, such as the component of failure, and tries to find out the reason of the system that led to that event.**

Despite the availability of some scientific tools to estimate risk, there are still **some difficulties** in estimating risks. Those are as follows:

1. It is very **difficult to predict** or find out all scientific reasons, such as physical, chemical, biological, mechanical, environmental and ethical, that lead to problems.
2. **Human errors are highly unpredictable;** despite being trained well, a pilot may make mistakes during the take-off or landing of a plane.
3. It is hard to be certain about **all the possible initiating events** that are included in the event tree diagram to make an analysis about the mode of failure.
4. Engineers can **deviate from standards** of safety and acceptable risks for too many times in their work, which increases the risk for the public. They make deviations from standards as normal over a period of time. This is referred to as **'normalizing deviance'.**[1]
5. An established probability of a risk is based on the analysis of experts. Sometimes it is **hard to prove it by experiments.** Even when it is practically

---

[1] Diane Vaugh. 1996, *The Challenger Launch Decision*, pp. 409–422.

FIGURE 30.1
FAULT TREE ANALYSIS OF A TWO-WHEELER MOTOR BIKE STARTING PROBLEM

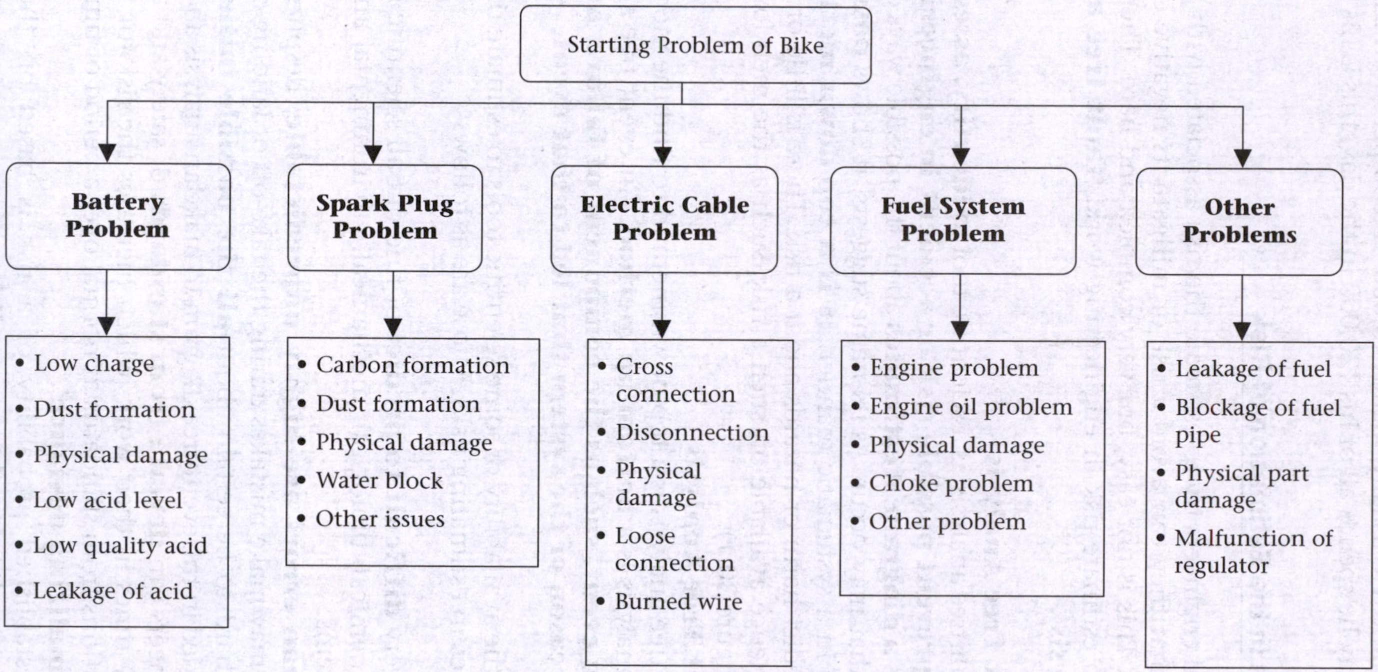

experimented, results may be much different from the real failure. For example, even though scientists may assess the possible meltdown of a nuclear reactor in a submarine, it is hard to experimentally prove it. In case it is proved, the experiment results may not match up the real meltdown of nuclear reactor in that submarine.

6. Some product involves too many components, especially in spacecraft, ships, fighter jets and so on, and it is difficult to predict the risks of all their small components. For example, in the 1980s an airplane met with an accident because of the improper fitting of a small bolt on its top body. It is very difficult for an aircraft engineer to predict such a risk.

Risk of Technology and Accidents

According to Charles Perrow,[2] there are two main characteristics of high-risk technology that increase the susceptibility of accident and also make it difficult to predict and control such accidents. Those characteristics are as follows:

1. **Tight and loose couplings**
   In a tight coupling, different parts or components of a system are arranged in such a manner that the process or function of a component **affects the process or function of the other components and thus the entire system is adversely affected within a short period of time.** In a system where the parts are tightly coupled, it is **very hard to prevent** the **damage** just by correcting the failure of one component because of their pre-arrangements. For example, in the Fukushima Daiichi nuclear disaster, the failure of boilers led to the damage of the entire nuclear reactor.

   On the other hand, in a **'loose coupling'**, the failure of the function or process of a component **does not have any effect on other components or on the entire system,** and there is enough time to prevent the adverse effect on the entire system. For example, in a college, the failure of one department may not affect other departments.

2. **Complex Interaction**
   In a 'complex interaction', a process or function of a system interacts **in unanticipated way**s. **No one can, therefore, predict that** the failure of A may also affect B in such a system. For example, chemical plants, nuclear reactors and so on.

Approach to Risk

Each person's perception about a risk may vary according to his/her education, social-economical background, experience and expertise. Accordingly, one's approach to

---

[2] Charles Perrow. 1984, *Normal Accidents: Living with High Risk Technologies*, Princeton Press, New Jersey, University of Chicago, pp. 3–4.

perceived risk may differ from those of the others. Some different approaches to risks are as follows:

1. **Common man approach:** Usually, the approach a common man or a layman to risk is **unplanned, emotional, irrational and vague.** A layman

   (i) Has the tendency of **'anchoring'** or **being biased** in estimating a risk with over-confidence; such estimations are likely to be substantially erroneous from the original estimate.

   (ii) Is mainly influenced by the **financial benefits or profit,** and also religion, cast, social norms and irrational thinking.

   (iii) Gives preference to his **safety** and tries to **protect** himself from a risk.

   (iv) **Combines concepts of risks** and does not try to distinguish them based on their particularity.

   (v) Prefers or accepts more **voluntary risks** than involuntary.

2. **Government's approach:** A government represents all sections of the society, so it **prefers to avoid or prevent a risk,** even a risk that causes harm to less number of people and benefit more number people; however, it does not happen all the time. A government considers the interest of all the people and nation, and carefully weighs harms and benefits (both long term and short term), and then proceeds with a calculated risk.

3. **Expert approach:** An expert approach to a risk is based on **proper understanding, rationality, planning and preciseness.** An expert

   (i) **Estimates** a risk properly in a scientific way and that may substantially be true.

   (ii) Makes a deep **study of history** of the concerned risk.

   (iii) **Does not combine the concepts of risks** and tries to distinguish them based on their particularity, such as real risks and perceived risks, immediate risks and delayed risks and so on.

   (iv) **Assesses** a risk using data and heuristics or intuitions and makes a proper judgement.

   (v) Is influenced by **professional motivation and public interests** before taking a risk.

   (vi) Tries to find accurate **'acceptability of risk'.** The acceptability of risk is measured by the **capacity of a person or an organization to reduce risk without jeopardizing its various benefits,** such as social, economic, and environmental.

   (vii) Usually follows the **'utilitarian' approach.** According to the **utilitarianism,** any moral question shall be answered by determining a **way of action** that maximizes welfare of the maximum number of people. In other words, an expert tries to find such a solution for a risk that gives maximum benefits by making the **'cost-benefit or risk-benefit'** analysis of that risk.

Engineer's Responsibility with Risk

A risk is associated with technology and its development. It is an ethical obligation or responsibility of engineers to reduce the risk as much as they can. With regard to this, an engineer

1. Should be aware of and be conscious about ethical responsibility towards a risk and should also remember the engineering professional Code of Ethics about a risk.
2. Must know the difficulties in estimating risks. Risks may be subtle, erroneous and treacherous.
3. Must not only consider quantifiable issues, but also human errors and non-quantifiable issues in the estimation of a risk.
4. Must be aware of legal liability, such as laws, rules, government regulations, judicial interpretation about a risk.
5. Must rightly determine the acceptability of a risk and the proper approach to a risk depending on the particularity of situations.
6. Must try hard to strike a balance between the harm and benefit of a risk.
7. Must consider public, society, workers, management, economy, environment and so on while defining an acceptable risk and then shall take a decision.
8. Must re-access an acceptable risk from time to time as its components may change with time.

SAFETY OF ENGINEERS

In any profession, the utmost important thing is the safety of life. However, the safety of the environment and property or assets must not also be neglected. The term safety denotes 'the state of being certain that adverse effects will not be caused by some agent under defined conditions'. As an engineering profession involves risk and associated threat and harm, it is the ethical responsibility of engineers to create a safe and conducive technological environment that could contribute to the prosperity of humanity.

In engineering, 'safety' implies that an engineer should **make sure that adverse effects will not be caused by some agent (internal or external) under the defined conditions.** For instance, old iron boards (home appliance) used to burn clothes when overheated because of the excess electric power supply. But modern iron boards do not burn clothes in case of excess electric power supply as they automatically prevent the electric supply after crossing a specific degree of temperature. Here, the manufacturer of the modern iron boards ensures that the overheating of the iron instruments does not have an adverse effect on clothes when there is an excess electric power supply. But a building may collapse due to a tremor while ironing may burn the skin of a person who was using it. It means that, it is very difficult for a professional to provide environmental and property-related safeguards to protect consumers, under undefined conditions.

Before the Fukushima Daiichi nuclear disaster in 2011, most nuclear countries considered nuclear technology as the safest technology to produce energy. But after witnessing that catastrophic disaster, many countries, such as Germany, Japan, France and so on have realized that nuclear technology is not safe to produce energy; instead, it is a great threat to humanity. They therefore abandoned or are in the process to abandon it. Still, some other countries, such as India, China, Russia, and so on continue to use nuclear technology to produce energy. Therefore, the concept of safety is a relative thing. The safety depends on time, place, perception and situation; it may change with these things. There is no universal concept of safety for all persons at all the times.

Responsibility of Engineers Regarding Safety

An engineer should give utmost importance to the safety of life, including that of the environment and assets with respect to design, manufacture and usage of a product and delivery of services. In this regard, the following things need to be considered:

1. A design and manufacturing of a product should be in accordance with **the law** in force, engineering **ethical codes** and international standard guidelines. Usually, in this regard, the engineering ethical codes prescribe laws to regulate safety standards of a product. Any compromise with these may lead to legal problems. For example, a law as well as an ethical code says that the radiations of a mobile phone should not be more than a particular level as it may affect the health of the person using that particular phone. An engineer must consider this while designing or manufacturing a mobile phone or else it may lead to a legal problem and loss of public trustworthiness.

2. Engineers need to prepare **multiple designs** and after carefully analysing all designs, one best design should be selected. This needs to be thoroughly tested from a safety point of view.

3. Engineers must consistently work to **explore and inculcate better design and manufacturing methods** that enhance the safe utilization of products and services.

4. Engineers should **be open to feedback, suggestions and advices** on the safety of their products and services, and they should seriously consider good feedback to improve safety standards.

5. Engineers should seriously work to **minimize or even eliminate risks**, such as accidents, and **maximize safe utilization** of products and services. Measures to prevent accidents or risks are called '**risk minimizers**' and measures to mitigate impacts or effects of accidents or risks are called '**impact minimizers**'.

6. A creator of a thing knows much better about its harm and benefits than others. So engineers should **formulate a safety policy** of a technology,

product and service, by considering the interest of all, such as public, environment, assets, nation and so on.

7. Some technologies are like two-edged scissors, with one edge representing good and another bad. Engineers should protect a technology, product and service from its **possible misuse** by mischiefs.

8. Engineers should clearly and in simple words explain the **safe usage method of a technology** or product to the consumer or the public. For instance, in electronic items, elevators, trains and so on you may find safety guidelines prepared by engineers.

9. If a product involves any danger that should be **thoroughly and immediately informed to the public.** For example, CFL bulbs include poisonous mercury; so most CFL bulb manufacturing companies give instructions to consumers about the safe disposal of CFL bulbs.

10. Engineers while providing services, particularly public services, should take care of all aspects of **public safety.** For example, an engineer needs to inform and warn the concerned people if the water level rises above the danger level in a dam.

11. Engineers should prepare immediate **harm management plans,** such as placing the first aid box, fire extinguishers and so on at an appropriate place.

12. Engineers are also social animals; they should give **safety education and build a safety culture** in organizations and society.

13. Last but not the least, engineers should give utmost importance to the **safety of their own life** and **other co-workers while working.** At work, they should strictly follow the safety guidelines and take necessary precaution to avoid any risks.

LIABILITY OF ENGINEERS

Liability means 'the state of being legally responsible for something' or 'state of being legally obliged or bound by law'. Like all other professionals, engineering is also bound by the law of the land and has legal obligations and responsibilities. All acts, omission and commission of engineers are subjected to the law and no engineer is above the law. For instances, usually in incidents such as collapse of a building, or a bridge, or a flyover, engineers are held accountable.

A **tort means, for any wrongdoing or civil wrong, an action for damage may be brought.** In other words, **there is a legal remedy for victims of harm or damage caused due to the wrongdoing** of a person. If an engineer's work causes harm or damage to any individual or public, a tort provides remedies for the victims. The **principal aim of the tort is to provide protection against wrongdoings and compensate the victims.**

Risk and safety are pre-incident, whereas **liability is post-incident.** Liability seeks to **fix responsibility** of a person who has committed wrong acts, intentionally or unintentionally. If an engineer is working for a company, his/her wrong acts cannot be transferred to company's liability; it is the liability of both the engineer and the company.

Engineers are subjected to '**tortuous liability**' when they breach their duty or responsibility as fixed by law and such a breach is redressable. Acts of engineers committed with negligence or carelessness, taking no or reckless action about a known risk, become wrongful and are liable.

Types of Liabilities

There are many types of liabilities; important among them are as follows:

1. **Primary liability:** If a person directly contributes to any wrongdoing that causes harm or damage others, then that person is legally responsible for that harm and must provide remedy or compensation to victims.
2. **Secondary liability:** When a person indirectly contributes to a direct wrongdoing of another person, then it is considered as a secondary liability.
3. **Vicarious liability:** It is a kind of secondary liability. In some situations, **one person (or superior officer) becomes liable for other's (subordinate's) wrongdoing.** Such a liability is called 'vicarious liability'. This can happen in the following situations:

    (i) **Liability by ratification:** If a person ratifies or approves other's work after it is being done, without the knowledge of any wrongdoings in it, or if it turns to be wrong later, then the ratified person becomes liable.
    (ii) **Liability by relationship:** It means wrongful acts done based on relation, such as master–servant, business relationships, parents and children and so on. For example, in some car accidents, the owner is liable even when the driver has actually committed the mistake.
    (iii) **Liability by abetment:** Intentional abetment of the tortuous act.

4. **Strict liability:** A person may be allowed to undertake risky or harmful activity on the condition that, irrespective of his/her fault, such a person will be made liable to provide remedy or pay for the damages. This is known as '**strict liability**'. Under strict liability, there is no necessity to prove a person guilty of wrongful acts. One may commit wrong acts **with or without negligence** and **bad intention,** but if any damage happens, then the concerned person must compensate the victims.

31
CHAPTER

Honesty, Integrity and Reliability in Engineering

HONESTY OF ENGINEERS

Honesty implies the quality of being fair, sincere, good, straightforward, morally correct, loyal, honest, truthful and trustworthy, and not being disposed of cheat, liar, theft, fraud, and deceptive, in attitude and behaviour. Being honest is a quality and virtue with oneself and others. It is valued and emphasized in many religions and cultures as well as in philosophy. An honest man upholds ethical and moral principles in his life and profession. An honest professional/scholar earns appreciation and respect from the society and inspires others; for examples, Sir M. Visvesvaraya, Swami Vivekananda and Mahatma Gandhi. Hence, 'Honesty is the Best Policy', both in professional and personal lives.

One of the **basic principles of the engineering Code of Ethics is 'honesty'.** It prescribes honesty as one of the **fundamental duties and obligations** of engineers; failure to fulfil it may lead to punishment, such as reproach or sanctions. It expects engineers to act as **'moral agents'.**

For the engineering profession, being honest is like **foundation;** no engineer will have professional success without being honest. An engineer is expected to be **honest and fair; self-disciplined;** committed to **moral values,** the profession and its ethics; **truthful** and **trustworthy** in expression and conduct towards his/ her clients and organization; not to get involved in or provoked into corruption, fraud, betrayal and other malpractices. A professional engineer is required to **seek, open and accept honest criticism** for self-improvement.

However, an engineer should behave honestly with caution, because there may be mischiefs who may try to exploit one's honesty for their personal gain. Also, an engineer requires to be honest with himself/herself, his/her profession, company, clients and so on. In case of a conflict between any of these, one must listen to his/ her inner voice, consider professional ethics, the Constitutional values and goodness of humankind with a rational thought, and then act.

Ways to Misuse Honesty or Truth

There are many ways to **misuse honesty or truths** by people; important among them are as follows:

1. **Lying:** Lie means, 'to tell an untruth; pretend with intent to deceive' or 'a statement that deviates from or perverts the truth'. The practice of communicating lies is called **lying.** A liar tries to tell an untruth as a truth with an intention to mislead or deceive the listener. Sometimes, a person may mistakenly speak untruth without any intention to mislead or deceive the listener; it is considered as untruth, not lying. Usually, fear, egoism, jealousy, greed and other negative emotions make a man telling lies.

2. **Deception:** Deception means, 'the act of deceiving' or 'a misleading falsehood'. It implies, telling or propagating belief of things that are not true or are half-truths. In deception, a person may not directly speak the untruth or the truth; he/she just manipulates that to mislead about truth or make wrong interpretation of the truth, which makes others believe it to be true. For example, an advertisement reads, 'Free local and STD calls offer', but below in terms and conditions, it prescribes that this offer is only valid for one month and to activate this offer you need to pay ₹50 per month.

3. **Withholding information:** Intentionally hiding or omitting truth or information to mislead or deceive someone is also considered as a kind of lying or deception. Here, a person does not directly lie, but he/she has the same ill-intention that of a liar, which is to mislead or deceive someone. **For example**, in a pre-survey of an XYZ project, an engineer came to know that he is going to make profit of ₹100 crore and that the project is also going to affect 10,000 people's livelihood. But that engineer intentionally withholds the information about the effect of the project on the people to a higher authority or public to make personal profit.

4. **Failure to disclose information:** An engineer is expected to disclose or reveal all relevant information about his/her work to the concerned people. For instance, in each battery, there is a clear instruction about its use, safety guidelines and disposal. A person with or without any intention does not disclose the true information to the concerned people. This may negatively affect them.

5. **Whistle-blower:** People who expose or provide information about illegal, dishonest or unethical activity within an organization (private or public) to the public are known as whistle-blowers. Whistleblowing is **an ethical act** as it helps identify the wrong activities of an organization. In India, 'the Whistle Blowers Protection Act 2011' provides protection to whistle-blowers.

6. **Failure to seek truth:** Without telling a lie and withholding or disclosing information, an engineer simply avoids finding out the truth; this is a form of incomplete honesty. Suppose a mobile battery explodes despite providing complete and detailed information about it by an engineer. In such cases, the engineer should find out what went wrong with the battery instead of considering it as accidental explosion.

7. **Revealing confidential information:** An engineer is likely to possess confidential information about his/her work, technology, clients, organization and nation. Sharing such information with others, such as the rival company, enemies, strangers and so on is considered as dishonesty and he/she will be liable to legal action. What happens if a military engineer in a nuclear power plant shares its security details with terrorists? Just imagine what a catastrophy this can bring!

8. **Corrupt judgement:** A corrupt judgement is the one in which a person compromises morality, ethics, efficiency and effectiveness in his/her judgement or decision **because of undue external factors.** For instances, an engineer simply judges a work as good without testing it, just because his brother has done it.

INTEGRITY OF ENGINEERS

The term 'integrity' came from the Latin word 'integer', which means 'whole or complete'. Integrity means, **the standard or quality of being honest and following sound moral principles,** and behaving with moral uprightness. A **'man of integrity'** implies that he has the following common moral principles that are equally applicable to all members of his organization. He contributes to protect the sanctity or unity of principles, ideas, rules and ethics of organizations. He becomes one among many or groups. For example, if an engineer in the Government of India accepts bribes, then he/she is not considered as an integral person, as he/she failed to uphold the NPSE Code of Ethics, government laws and his/her own morality; such persons are liable to legal action and punishment. Such a person will no longer be considered as one among many in his/her own group and earns disrespect from other members. An integral person behaves with honesty, trustworthiness, incorruptibility, loyalty, genuineness, morality with him/herself, others and the organization. The nation or society expects high standards of integrity from engineers, as they have a significant impact on the day-to-day life of the people and the future of humanity.

Integrity of Engineers with Some Issues

Integrity in Engineering's Research, Development and Testing

A case study of Ravi: The Government of Karnataka has appointed Mr Ravi, a civil engineer, to conduct a pre-survey to construct a new eight-storey building in Bangalore. Ravi's uncle Ram is a building constructor in Bangalore. Ram told Ravi that he would get a profit of ₹50 core if Ravi would secure that construction project for him. Considering the data of the survey, Ravi realizes that it is possible to construct a new building there and that building also affects around 10,000 people's livelihood.

Now, we consider the ways through which one may lose his/her integrity:

1. **Trimming or smoothing:** It means, **deliberately showing irregular or imprecise data as accurate and precise one.** Here, one intentionally **manipulates the truth** to make it suitable for his/her own needs. For example, in the above case, to make a profit for his uncle, Ravi may trim the data informing that it is feasible to construct the proposed building there as it affects no or just 100 people's livelihood.

2. **Cooking:** It means, **retaining or showing only those data or results that are suitable to a proposed theory or favourable to the project** and **omitting or discarding** other data or results. This is referred to as 'selective blindness or intelligent deafness'. For example, in the above case, Ravi may cook the data by reporting only about the feasibility of constructing the proposed building there and not mentioning anything about its effect on the people's livelihood so that his uncle may make a profit.

3. **Forging or fabricating:** It means, just **creating favourable data without doing any research** or doing that in an **inappropriate way.** Such data do not represent the truth. For example, in the above case, Ravi may forge or fabricate the data by without conducting a survey just to report to the Government on the feasibility of constructing the proposed building.

4. **Plagiarism:** It means, a piece of writing that has been **copied from someone else and is presented as being your own work.** In plagiarism, one person takes someone's **words or ideas** and shows or claims it to be his/her own original words or ideas. It is the use of other's intellectual property without a prior permission from him/her. This is just like the theft of other's ideas, words, writing work, musical composition and so on. This is very common in **theses, dissertations, books, articles, journal writing, song composition** and so on. The best way to prevent plagiarism is to use your own original work or idea. In case there is a need to take someone's words or ideas, give a **reference or quote** to that. By this, you will give credits to the original author and uphold your own morality.

5. **Multiple authorships:** It means, showing names of those persons as authors in a journal, article, book publication, who have made no contribution to such a work. It is claiming the authorship of a publication without writing anything. Usually, junior researchers, who would like to have more publications in their name, use the name of senior researchers, and this person earns free credit.

Intellectual Property Rights

According to the TRIPS,[1] 'Intellectual property rights (IPR) are the rights given to persons over the creations of their minds. They usually **give the creator an exclusive right over the use of his/her creation for a certain period of time.**'

---

[1] The Agreement on Trade-Related Investment Measures (TRIMS) is promoted by the WTO to regulate trade and investment affairs by foreigners in a member country.

The IPRs, **by law**, give **monopoly** to a person for his/her **intellectual creation or invention.** It is considered as **intangible property.** The IPRs cover **music, literature and other artistic works; words, phrases, symbols and designs; discoveries and inventions.**

'Infringement' is a violation of IPRs, which is considered to be a breach of the law of the land. The Government of India's **the Controller General of Patents, Designs and Trade Marks (CPGDTM) and the Copy Right Office** regulate and govern the IPR issues in India. An engineer or engineering-related organization must respect and follow the intellectual property-related laws and rules, or else it amounts to a breach of integrity.

Types of intellectual property rights

Depending upon the nature, subject, kind of creation or invention, there are many kinds of IPRs, such as

1. **Patent:** A patent is an **exclusive or monopoly right** granted by the Government to an inventor of a process for a limited period of time **(20 years).** A patent right allows the inventor to manufacture or sell his/her invention/ product in lieu of royalty and prohibits others from making, using, selling and importing that for a specific period of time, that is, **20 years.** To illustrate, if you invent a medicine for AIDS, the Government will grant you the patent right for the next 20 years. It means, no one, either a person or a company or any nation, can use or encash this medicine without your permission; if one does, it will amount to the breach of law. You can sell this right for others for economic benifits.

2. **Utility model:** A utility model is similar to the patent with a few differences. It is granted for the **marginal improvement of the invention or the relative marginal invention** for a period of **7–10 years.** The conversion of a patent into a utility model is always possible, but not vice versa.

3. **Copyright and related right:** The copyright protects the creative **literary, dramatic, musical and artistic** works, such as books, articles, pictures, sculptures, movies and sound recording, composition or tune of music, drawing and pictures and so on. It generally lasts for **the author's lifetime and after the author's death for 60 years.** Copyrights consider only the **way of expression, not an idea itself.** It prohibits the reproduction (printing, making photocopy or Xerox), communication and translation of an author's/artist's work.

   Related rights are granted to a few categories of people for their role in **communicating the original work** to the public, such as singers, translators for about 20 years. The **'Indian Copyright Act 1957' (amended in 2012)** governs the copyright and related issues in India.

4. **Geographical indication:** Geographical indication is **a name or sign** used to identify certain agricultural, handicraft and manufactured products **originating from a given geographical territory,** for example, a village, town, region or country. **Geographical indication is a community right, not an individual right.** It recognizes, protects and certifies the qualities of the

traditional method of manufacturing and the reputation of a product. Some Indian geographical indications are **Darjeeling tea; Mysore silk; Tirupati laddu; Channapatna toys and dolls; Coorg orange; Tanjavur painting; Mysore painting and so on.**

5. **Trade mark:** A trade mark is **a distinctive sign, design and expression in the form of 'a word, phrase, logo, and so on'** to show that the product is manufactured or service is provided by a given enterprise. For example, Nokia Phones' symbol, its logo, tag line (Connecting People); the symbol of Airtel, Vodafone, TATA DoCoMo telecom services and so on.

6. **Trade secret:** A trade secret **protects the valuable and confidential business information** in the form of data, manual, formula, compilation, design, process, pattern, instrument and so on from which a business firm makes a profit, for example, formula of MTR Masala, Pepsi, Dairy Milk Chocolates etc.

7. **Industrial design:** The **outward appearance of a product,** such as **design, configuration, shape and composition of pattern or colour** and so on. It may be a two- or three-dimensional product. For example, external shape/design of cars, bikes, fighter jet, the wrapper of Diary Milk chocolates and so on.

8. **Layout of design (topography) of integrated circuits:** Integrated circuit topography (ICT) is a **kind of electronically integrated circuits or products** that is assembled and interconnected. A **layout of design (topography)** of an integrated circuit provides protection to the creator of the ICT. It also provides a remedy in case of infringement.

9. **Plant breeders' rights:** A plant breeders' right (PBR) or plant variety right (PVR) is an exclusive **or monopoly right granted to the breeder of a new variety** of plant for commercial or other kind of purposes for a specific period of time, typically for 20–30 years.

The case of Sahana: Sahana is studying in her last semester Engineering course in Bangalore. She is a brilliant girl and invented a new design of a robot that is capable of helping a physically challenged person. She wanted to sell her robot design in the market so that it serves the needy people; so she approached a robot-manufacturing company. That company after examining her innovation told her, 'We have already planned to manufacture a similar kind of robot; so it's not a new kind of technology.' A few months later, that company launches the same kind of robot as invented by Sahana. So, what went wrong with Sahana, though she had invented a new kind of robot? What kind of precaution one should take after making any invention? Discuss with your Professors.

Integrity and Conflict of Interest

In a situation like **conflict of interest (COI),** an individual or an organization is involved in different or more than one interest, such as emotional, psychological, religious, social, economic and so on that could possibly corrupt the individual's or organization's core objective.

A professional following the professional duties and ethics is subjected to **loyalties, influences, temptations and other undue things** that may corrupt his/her professionalism or professional judgement and thus he/she may compromise on his/her integrity. A professional with COI may lose the trust of clients, employer or organization, and so his/her integrity. The NPSE code asks engineers to act as 'faithful agents or trustees' in a profession and **reveal the known or potential** COI to the concerned person, such as the employer or clients.

According to Charles Harris et al.,[2] a COI may be

1. **Actual:** That already exists and may corrupt the professional judgement.
2. **Potential:** That is capable of occurring and may corrupt the professional judgement in the near future.
3. **Apparent:** That seems to be exciting, but does not really exist. It may not corrupt the professional judgement, but affects the confidence and trustworthiness of a professional.

It is better for an engineer to avoid all kinds of COIs as much as possible to uphold integrity. **Accepting gifts** is one of the most common ways to fall into COI by engineers. Usually, a **'line-drawing method'** is used to analyse the effects of COI on one's integrity and honesty.

Integrity in the Client–Professional Relationship

An engineer may have clients and their confidential information. It is the ethical duty of each engineer to protect the confidential information and interest of their clients, in the same way as a doctor protect his/her patients' confidential matters.

An engineer should not share any confidential matters of his/her clients with third parties without any warrant; should share confidential matters of his/her clients with the government or other genuine authority when it is warranted to protect the larger interest of the public or society. Failure to do so, will amount to breach of integrity.

Integrity Shown as an Expert or Eye Witness

In case of a dispute between two or more persons or/and organization with regard to technical issues, such as patent infringement, defective product and so on, a legal court or any other competent authority takes the help of an expert person as a witnesses, who possesses good technical knowledge and experience that helps in solving disputes.

When an engineer is called upon as a witness, he/she should render honest, impartial and unbiased option to the court without bending for any influence, threat, temptations and so on. Failure to do so may amount to compromise his/her integrity.

---

[2] Harris, Charles E. (2009). *Engineering Ethics: Concepts and Cases*, 4th edition. Wadsworth Cengage Learning, Belmont, CA (pp.131–133).

He/she must also be capable of defending his/her opinion during cross-examination by the lawyers in the court. He/she must be credible and trustworthy to the court as his/her witness makes a significant impact on delivering justice.

It is good for an engineer to accept to be a witness to a case, when he/she has **enough time** for it. Believe that, the engineers have **enough expertise** after **consulting a concerned lawyer** and willing to accept new information at any time during the course.

Integrity and Failure to Inform the Public

It is another responsibility of engineers to provide timely and adequate information to the concerned public, authority or organization, so that the lack of information may not lead to a wrong decision or judgement from them that may affect the larger interest, such as health, safety and the life of the people. Deliberately not sharing adequate information or withholding information to the public may amount to the loss of integrity. Sometimes, the failure to disclose vital information by engineers in public may lead to a catastrophic event. For example, a few years ago, a bus-manufacturing company in India did not disclose all information to public authorities about accidental release of hazardous waste to the river because of the fear of legal litigation; later, a few people on the bank of that river used polluted water and died and health of some others deteriorated.

RELIABILITY OF ENGINEERS

What is the main difference between Chinese and Japanese products? The answer is 'reliability'. It is well known that Japanese products are more reliable than the Chinese.

The WordWeb Dictionary explains reliability as 'quality of being dependable or reliable'. Engineering reliability means, 'a **probability of dependability of a product (or a service) for a specific period of time in engineering'.** This applies to inception, design, manufacture, transportation, service, maintenance and disposal of a product. The main **object** of the engineering reliability is to **prevent or to reduce the failure of a product.**

The reliability of an engineering product or service implies that, it is trustworthy, safe, worth purchasing, can be used for a long time, is of the best quality, there is a guaranty or warranty in case of malfunction or deficiency and so on. One person or company need to put a lot of and consistent efforts to produce a quality product over a period of time. Then only they earn reliability from clients/consumers/public.

For example, consider a Nokia mobile phone and a non-branded Chinese mobile phone; the Nokia Company consistently produced high-quality mobile phones in India and gave a good quality of service for many years, and thus earned reliability or trust and confidence of the Indian consumers. But China's non-branded products are very infamous and highly unreliable. Hence, sincere, transparent, honest, ethical, oriented and consistent hard work to produce a good quality of product earns reliability over a period of time and benefit over a long period of time. That reliability will vanish only if the quality of the product is reduced. One well-known **method to measure the reliability of a product is 'consumer satisfaction'.**

Hence, one of the important ethical and moral responsibilities of an engineer is to give utmost importance to the reliability of his/her product or service. Without reliability, it is very hard to make economic profit as people want reliable products. So, a person or a company may suffer economic loss without reliability in their work/products. It is unethical for a professional engineer to get involved in cheating or deceiving people by giving a false promise about the reliability of his/her product or using someone else's reliability to manufacture a duplicate product; such a professional is unlikely to have any bright career development.

When people use elevators; use transportation such as bus, train, flights and ships or sits inside a building; a doctor uses a machine in an operation theatre; a military personnel uses defence technology; a country goes on a war with arms and ammunitions and so on—they all rely on and believe in engineers!! That is the significance of the reliability of engineers.

APPENDIX I:
SUBJECT MATTERS OF UNION, STATE AND CONCURRENT LISTS

LIST 1. UNION LIST

1. Defence of India and every part thereof including the preparation for defence and all such acts as may be conducive in times of war to its prosecution and after its termination to effective demobilization.
2. Naval, military and air forces; any other armed forces of the Union.
2A. Deployment of any armed forces of the Union or any other force subject to the control of the Union or any contingent or unit thereof in any State in aid of the civil power; powers, jurisdiction, privileges and liabilities of the members of such forces while on such deployment.
3. Delimitation of cantonment areas and local self-government in such areas, the Constitution and powers within such areas of cantonment authorities and the regulation of house accommodation (including the control of rents) in such areas.
4. Naval, military and air force works.
5. Arms, firearms, ammunition and explosives.
6. Atomic energy and mineral resources necessary for its production.
7. Industries declared by Parliament by law to be necessary for the purpose of Defence or for the prosecution of war.
8. Central Bureau of Intelligence and Investigation.
9. Preventive detention for reasons connected with Defence, Foreign Affairs, or the security of India; persons subjected to such detention.
10. Foreign affairs; all matters which bring the Union into relation with any foreign country.
11. Diplomatic, consular and trade representation.
12. United Nations Organization.
13. Participation in international conferences, associations and other bodies and implementing of decisions made thereat.
14. Entering into treaties, conventions and agreements with foreign countries and implementing treaties, agreements and conventions with foreign Countries.
15. War and Peace.
16. Foreign jurisdiction.
17. Citizenship, naturalization and aliens.
18. Extradition
19. Admission into, and emigration and expulsion from, India; passport and visas.
20. Pilgrimages to places outside India.

21. Piracies and crimes committed on the high seas or in the air; offences against the law of nations committed on land or the high seas or in the air.
22. Railways.
23. Highways declared by or under law made by Parliament to be National Highways.
24. Shipping and Navigation on inland waterways, declared by Parliament by law to be national waterways, as regards mechanically propelled vessels; the rule of the road on such waterways
25. Maritime shipping and navigation, including shipping and navigation on tidal waters; provision of education and training for the mercantile marine and regulation of such education and training provided by States and other agencies.
26. Lighthouses, including lightships, beacons and other provision for the safety of shipping and aircraft.
27. Ports declared by or under law made by Parliament or existing law to be major ports, including their delimitation, and the Constitution and powers of port authorities therein.
28. Port quarantine, including hospitals connected therewith; seamen's and marine hospitals.
29. Airways; aircraft and air navigation; provision of aerodromes; regulation and organization of air traffic, and of aerodromes; provision for aeronautical education and training and regulation of such education and training provided by States and other agencies.
30. Carriage of passengers and goods by railway, sea or air, or by national waterways in mechanically propelled vessels.
31. Posts and telegraphs; telephones, wireless, broadcasting and other like forms of communication.
32. Property of the Union and the revenue therefrom, but as regards property situated in a State subject to legislation by the State, save in so far as Parliament by law otherwise provides.
33. Omitted
34. Courts of wards for the estates of Rulers of Indian States.
35. Public debt of the Union.
36. Currency, coinage and legal tender; foreign exchange.
37. Foreign loans.
38. Reserve Bank of India.
39. Post Office Savings Bank.
40. Lotteries organized by the Centre or State.
41. Trade and Commerce with foreign countries import and export across customs frontiers definition of customs frontiers.
42. Inter-State trade and commerce.
43. Incorporation, regulation and winding up of trading corporations, including banking, insurance and financial corporations, but not including cooperative societies.

44. Incorporation, regulation and winding up of corporations, whether trading or not, with objects not confined to one State, but not including universities.
45. Banking.
46. Bills of exchange, cheques, promissory notes and other like instruments.
47. Insurance.
48. Stock exchanges and futures markets.
49. Patents, inventions and designs; copyright; trade-marks and merchandise marks.
50. Establishment of standards of weight and measure.
51. Establishment of standards of quality for goods to be exported out of India or transported from one State to another.
52. Industries, the control of which by the Union is declared by the Parliament by law to be expedient in the public interest.
53. Regulation and development of oilfields and mineral oil resources; petroleum and petroleum products; other liquids and substances declared by the Parliament by law to be dangerously inflammable.
54. Regulation of mines and mineral development to the extent to which such regulation and development under the control of the Union is declared by the Parliament by law to be expedient in the public interest.
55. Regulation of labour and safety in mines and oilfields.
56. Regulation and development of inter-State rivers and river valleys to the extent to which such regulation and development under the control of the Union is declared by Parliament by law to the expedient in the public interest.
57. Fishing and fisheries beyond territorial waters.
58. Manufacture, supply and distribution of salt by Union agencies; regulations and control of manufacture, supply and distribution of salt by other agencies.
59. Cultivation, manufacture and sale for export, of opium.
60. Sanctioning of cinematograph films for exhibition.
61. Industrial disputes concerning Union employees.
62. The institutions known at the commencement of this Constitution as the National Library, the Indian Museum, the Imperial War Museum, the Victoria Memorial and the Indian War Memorial, and any other like institution financed by the Government of India wholly or in part and declared by the Parliament by law to be an institution of national importance.
63. The institutions known at the commencement of this Constitution as the Benares Hindu University, the Aligarh Muslim University and the Delhi University; the University established in pursuance of Article 371-E; any other institution declared by the Parliament by law to be an institution of national importance.
64. Institutions for scientific or technical education financed by the Government of India wholly or in part and declared by the Parliament by law to be institutions of national importance.
65. Union agencies and institutions for technical training, research or detection of crime.

66. Co-ordination and determination of standards in institutions for higher education or research and scientific and technical institutions.
67. Ancient and historical monuments and records and archaeological sites and remains of, declared by or under law made by Parliament to be of national importance.
68. The Survey of India, the Geological, Botanical, Zoological and Anthropological Surveys of India; Meteorological organizations.
69. Census.
70. Union Public Service; All-India Services; Union Public Service Commission.
71. Union pensions, that is to say, pensions payable by the Government of India or out of the Consolidated Fund of India.
72. Elections to Parliament, to the Legislatures of States and to the offices of President and Vice-President; the Election Commission.
73. Salaries and allowances of members of the Parliament and presiding officers of the Parliament.
74. Powers, privileges and immunities of each House of the Parliament and of the members and the Committees of each House enforcement of attendance of persons for giving evidence or producing documents before committees of Parliament or commissions appointed by Parliament.
75. Emoluments, allowances, privileges, and rights in respect of leave of absence, of the President and Governors salaries and allowances of the Ministers for the Union; the Salaries, allowances, and rights in respect of leave of absence and other conditions of service of the Comptroller and Auditor General.
76. Audit of the accounts of the Union and of the States.
77. Constitution, organization, jurisdiction and powers of the Supreme Court (including contempt of such Court), and the fees taken therein persons entitled to practice before the Supreme Court.
78. Constitution and organization (including vacations) of the High Courts except provisions as to officers and servants of High Courts; persons entitled to practice before the High Courts.
79. Extensions of the jurisdiction of a High Court to and exclusion of the jurisdiction of a High Court from any Union territory.
80. Extension of the powers and jurisdiction of members of a police force belonging to any State to any area outside that State, but not so as to enable the police of one State to exercise powers and jurisdiction in any area outside that State without the consent of the Government of the State in which such area is situated; extension of the powers and jurisdiction of members of a police force belonging to any State to railway areas outside that State.
81. Inter-State migration; inter-State quarantine.
82. Taxes on income other than agricultural income.
83. Duties of customs including export duties.
84. Duties of excise on tobacco and other goods except alcohol liquors, opium, Indian hemp and other narcotic drugs and narcotics, but including medicinal and toilet preparations containing alcohol

85. Corporation tax.
86. Taxes on the capital value of the assets, exclusive of agricultural land, of individuals and companies; taxes on the capital of companies.
87. Estate duty in respect of property other than agricultural land.
88. Duties in respect of succession to property other than agricultural land.
89. Terminal taxes on goods or passengers, carried by railway, sea or air; taxes on railway fares and freights.
90. Taxes other than stamp duties on transactions in stock exchanges and futures markets.
91. Rates of stamp duty in respect of bills of exchange, cheques, promissory notes, bills of lading, letters of credit, policies of insurance, transfer of shares, debentures, proxies and receipts.
92. Taxes on the sale or purchase of newspapers and on advertisements published therein.
92A. Taxes on the sale or purchase of goods other than newspapers, where such sale or purchase takes place in the course of inter-State trade or commerce.
92B. Taxes on the consignments of goods in the course of inter-State trade or commerce.
93. Offences against laws with respect to any of the matters in this List.
94. Inquiries, surveys and statistics for the purpose of any of the matters in this List.
95. Jurisdiction and powers of all courts, except the Supreme Court, with respect to any of the matters in this List; admiralty jurisdiction.
96. Fees in respect of any of the matters in this List, but not including fees taken in any court.
97. Any other matter not enumerated in List II or List III including any tax not mentioned in either of those Lists.

LIST 2. STATE LIST

1. Public order.
2. Police.
3. Officers and servants of the High Court.
4. Prisons, reformatories, Borstal institutions and other institutions.
5. Local government.
6. Public health and sanitation; hospitals and dispensaries.
7. Pilgrimages, other than pilgrimages to places outside India.
8. Intoxicating liquors.
9. Relief of the disabled and unemployable.
10. Burials, burial and cremation grounds.
11. Omitted.
12. Libraries, museums and other similar institutions; ancient and historical monuments and records other than those of national importance.

13. Communications, that is, roads, bridges, ferries, and other means of communication not specified in List I; municipal tramways.
14. Agriculture, including agricultural education and research.
15. Preservation of stock and prevention of animal diseases; veterinary training and practice.
16. Pounds and the prevention of cattle trespass.
17. Water, that is, water supplies, irrigation and canals, drainage and embankments, water storage and water power.
18. Land, that is, rights in or over land, land tenures and collection of rents.
19. Omitted.
20. Omitted.
21. Fisheries.
22. Court of wards.
23. Regulation of mines and mineral developments.
24. Industries.
25. Gas and Gas-work.
26. Trade and Commerce within the State.
27. Production, Supply and distribution of goods.
28. Markers and fairs.
29. Omitted.
30. Money-lending and money-lenders; relief of agricultural indebtedness.
31. Inns and inn-keepers.
32. Corporations, other than those specified in List I, and universities; unincorporated trading, literary, scientific, religious and other societies and associations; co-operative societies.
33. Theatres and dramatic performances; cinemas, sports, entertainments and amusements.
34. Betting and gambling.
35. Works, lands and buildings of the State.
36. Omitted.
37. Elections to the Legislature of the State.
38. Salaries and allowances of Members and presiding officers of state legislatures.
39. Powers, privileges and immunities of state legislatures and of its members and the committees thereof.
40. Salaries and allowances of Ministers for the State.
41. State public services; State Public Service Commission.
42. State pensions.
43. Public debt of the State.
44. Treasure trove.
45. Land revenue, including maintenance of land records.
46. Taxes on agricultural income.
47. Duties in respect of succession to agricultural land.
48. Estate duty in respect of agricultural land.

49. Taxes on lands and buildings.
50. Taxes on mineral rights.
51. Duties of excise on alcoholic liquors, opium, Indian hemp and other narcotic drugs and narcotics, but not including medicinal and toilet preparations containing alcohol.
52. Taxes on the entry of goods into a local area.
53. Taxes on the consumption or sale of electricity.
54. Taxes on the sale or purchase of goods other than newspapers.
55. Taxes on advertisements other than advertisements published in the newspapers and advertisements broadcast by radio or television.
56. Taxes on goods and passengers carried by road or on inland waterway.
57. Taxes on vehicles.
58. Taxes on animals and boats.
59. Tolls.
60. Taxes on professions, trades, callings and employments.
61. Capitation taxes.
62. Taxes on luxuries.
63. Rates of stamp duty in respect of documents other than those specified in the provisions of List.
64. Offences against laws with respect to any of the matters in this List.
65. Jurisdiction and powers of all courts, except the Supreme Court, with respect to any of the matters in this List.
66. Fees in respect of any of the matters in this List, but not including fees taken in any court.

LIST 3. CONCURRENT LIST

1. Criminal law, including all matters included in the Indian Penal Code.
2. Criminal procedure, including all matters included in the Code of Criminal Procedure.
3. Preventive detention for reasons connected with the security of a State, the maintenance of public order, or the maintenance of supplies and services essential to the community.
4. Removal from one State to another State of prisoners, accused persons.
5. Marriage and divorce; infants and minors; adoption; wills, intestacy and succession; joint family and partition.
6. Transfer of property other than agricultural land; registration of deeds and documents.
7. Contracts.
8. Actionable wrongs.
9. Bankruptcy and insolvency.
10. Trust and Trustees.
11. Administrators-general and official trustees.

11A. Administration of Justice; Constitution and organization of all courts, except the Supreme Court and the High Courts.

12. Evidence and oaths; recognition of laws, public acts and records, and judicial proceedings.

13. Civil procedure, including all matters included in the Code of Civil Procedure.

14. Contempt of court, but not including contempt of the Supreme Court.

15. Vagrancy; nomadic and migratory tribes.

16. Lunacy and mental deficiency.

17. Prevention of cruelty to animals.

17A. Forests.

17B. Protection of wild animals and birds.

18. Adulteration of foodstuffs and other goods.

19. Drugs and poisons.

20. Economic and social planning.

20A. Population control and family planning.

21. Commercial and industrial monopolies, combines and trusts.

22. Trade unions; industrial and labour disputes.

23. Social security and social insurance; employment and unemployment.

24. Welfare of labour including conditions of work, provident funds, employers' liability, workmen's compensation, invalidity and old age pensions and maternity benefits.

25. Education, including technical education, medical education and universities.

26. Legal, medical and other professions.

27. Relief and rehabilitation of persons.

28. Charitable institutions, religious endowments and religious institutions.

29. Infectious or contagious diseases or pests affecting men, animals or plants.

30. Vital statistics including registration of births and deaths.

31. Ports other than major ports.

32. Shipping and navigation on inland waterways.

33. Trade and commerce in, and the production, supply and distribution of foodstuffs, including edible oilseeds and oils; cattle fodder, including oil-cakes and other concentrates; raw cotton, cotton seed and raw jute.

34. Price control.

35. Mechanically propelled.

36. Factories.

37. Boilers.

38. Electricity.

39. Newspapers, books and printing presses.

40. Archaeological sites and remains other than those of national importance.

41. Evacuee property (including agricultural property).

42. Acquisition and requisitioning of property.

43. Recovery in a State of claims in respect of taxes and other public demands.

44. Stamp duties other than duties or fees collected by means of judicial stamps, but not including rates of stamp duty.
45. Inquiries and statistics for the purposes of any of the matters specified in List 2 or List 3.
46. Jurisdiction and powers of all courts, except the Supreme Court, with respect to any of the matters in this List.
47. Fees in respect of any of the matters in this List, but not including fees taken in any court.

The table of precedence or the order of preference of the Republic of India is related to the rank and order of the officials of the Central and the state governments. It is given below.

Rank	Person
1.	President
2.	Vice-President
3.	Prime Minister
4.	Governors of States within their respective States
5.	Former Presidents
5A.	Deputy Prime Minister
6.	Chief Justice of India and Speaker of Lok Sabha
7.	Cabinet Ministers of the UTs, Chief Ministers of States within their respective States Deputy Chairman Planning Commission, Former Prime Ministers, Leaders of Opposition in Rajya Sabha and Lok Sabha
7A.	Holders of Bharat Ratna decoration
8.	Ambassadors Extraordinary and Plenipotentiary and High Commissioners of Commonwealth countries accredited to India, Chief Ministers of States outside their respective States, Governors of States outside their respective States
9.	Judges of Supreme Court
9A.	Chairperson of Union Public Service Commission, Chief Election Commissioner, and Comptroller and Auditor General of India
10.	Deputy Chairman of Rajya Sabha, Deputy Chief Ministers of States, Deputy Speaker Lok Sabha, Members of the Planning Commission, Ministers of State of the Union (and any other Minister in the Ministry of Defense for defense matters)
11.	Attorney General of India, Cabinet Secretary, Lieutenant Governors within their respective UTs
12.	Chiefs of Staff holding the rank of full General or equivalent rank
13.	Envoys Extraordinary and Ministers Plenipotentiary accredited to India
14.	Chairmen and Speakers of State Legislatures within their respective States. Chief Justices of High Courts within their respective jurisdictions
15.	Cabinet Ministers in States within their respective States, Chief Ministers of Union Territories and so on.
16.	Officiating Chiefs of Staff holding the rank of Lieutenant General or equivalent rank

17. Chairman, Central Administrative Tribunal. Chairman, Minorities Commission Chairperson, National Commission for Scheduled Castes Chairperson, National Commission for Scheduled Tribes Chief Justices of High Courts outside their respective and so on.

18. Cabinet Ministers in States outside their respective States Chairmen and Speakers of State Legislatures outside their respective States Chairman and so on.

19. Chief Commissioners of Union Territories not having Councils of Ministers, within their respective Union Territories and so on.

20. Deputy Chairmen and Deputy Speakers of State Legislatures and so on.

21. Members of Parliament

22. Deputy Ministers in State outside their respective States

23. Army Commanders/Vice-Chief of the Army Staff or equivalent in other services Chief Secretaries to State Governments and so on.

24. Officers of the rank of Lieutenant General or equivalent rank

25. Additional Secretaries to the Government of India. Additional Solicitor General Advocate Generals of States and so on.

26. Joint Secretaries to the Government of India and officers of equivalent rank. Officers of the rank of Major General or equivalent rank

I/II SEMESTER B.E. DEGREE EXAMINATION, JUNE/JULY 2015

(COMMON TO ALL BRANCHES)

Time: 2 hours   **Max. Marks: 50**

1. The Electoral system of India is largely based on the pattern of
   (a) France   (b) USA   (c) Great Britain   (d) Ireland

2. Election to the Lok Sabha and Rajya Sabha are conducted on the basis of
   (a) Adult franchise   (b) Single transferable vote
   (c) Proportional representation   (d) Limited suffrage

3. Engineering ethics is
   (a) Preventive ethics   (b) Developing ethics
   (c) Natural ethics   (d) Scientifically developed ethics

4. One of the characteristics of profession is
   (a) It demands high standard of honesty
   (b) It provides opportunity to help the poor and needy
   (c) Usually it is having monopoly
   (d) It is having tough competition

5. 'Good work' means
   (a) Work above and beyond the call duty   (b) Responsible work
   (c) Work involving high risk   (d) Superior work done with great care & skill

6. 'Ego-centric tendencies' means
   (a) Arrogant and irresponsible behaviour   (b) Habit of condemning the view of others
   (c) Interpreting situation from limited view (d) Superiority complex

7. One process or function of one component that affects the other and spreads the adverse effect to the entire system is observed in
   (a) Loosely coupled   (b) Tight coupled
   (c) Complexly interactive   (d) None of these

8. A fault tree is used to
   (a) Assess the risk involved   (b) Claim compensation
   (c) Take free consent   (d) Improve safety

9. Conflicts of interest may be
   (a) Created   (b) False   (c) Potential   (d) All of these

10. The owner of the 'Patent Right' retains his patent for
    (a) 20 years   (b) 50 years   (c) 75 years   (d) 100 years

11. Tendency of shifting responsibility will locally come down if there is a
    (a) Group think   (b) Microscopic   (c) Fear   (d) Obligation

12. The judges of the district court are appointed by
    (a) President   (b) Chief Justice   (c) Prime Minister   (d) Governor

13. Legislative council/Rajya Sabha is dissolved
    (a) Dissolved after 2 years   (b) Dissolved after 5 years
    (c) Dissolved after 6 years   (d) Is not subject to dissolution

14. 'To encourage the formation of co-operative societies'. This directive principle was added to the Constitution under
    (a) 42nd Amendment   (b) 44th Amendment
    (c) 97th Amendment   (d) 118th Amendment

15. The obligation and prerogative associated with specific role is referred as
    (a) Duty   (b) Role morality   (c) Responsibility   (d) Ethics

16. Which of the following shall not be introduced in Rajya Sabha?
    (a) Money Bill   (b) Union Budget
    (c) Constitution Amendments   (d) Finance Bill

17. Before entering upon the office President has to take an Oath before the
    (a) Chief Election Commissioner   (b) Vice-President
    (c) Chief Justice of India   (d) Lok Sabha Speaker

18. The President of India is elected on the basis of
    (a) Proportional representation by means of single transferable vote
    (b) Single member territorial representation
    (c) Adult franchise
    (d) Direct Election

19. Which Assembly is presided over by the non-member?
    (a) Lok Sabha   (b) Rajya Sabha   (c) State Assembly   (d) All of these

20. Power of the Supreme Court to decide dispute between the centre and the state falls under
    (a) Advisory Jurisdiction   (b) Original Jurisdiction
    (c) Appellate Jurisdiction   (c) Constitution Jurisdiction

21. How many judges are there in the Supreme Court including the Chief Justice of India
    (a) 15   (b) 19   (c) 26   (d) 31

22. The procedure for amending the Indian Constitution is
    (a) Partly Rigid and Partly Flexible   (b) Very Rigid
    (c) Very Flexible   (d) Occasionally Done

23. Who acts as a chief legal advisor to the government?
    (a) Union Law Minister   (b) Attorney General
    (c) Chief Justice of India   (d) None of these

24. Who is the executive Constitution lead of the State Government?
    (a) Chief Minister   (b) President   (c) Prime Minister   (d) The Governor

25. The ordinance issued by the Governor are subject to the approval by the
    (a) State Legislature   (b) President
    (c) Chief Justice of High Court   (d) Chief Minister

26. Bicameral means
    (a) Presence of no house in the state
    (b) Presence of one house in the state
    (c) Presence of two house in the state
    (d) None of the above

27. 73rd and 74th Constitution amendments are pertaining to
    (a) Local Self-Government
    (b) Extension of Reservation to SC & ST
    (c) Statehood of Goa
    (d) Land Reform

28. President can proclaim the emergency with the recommendation of
    (a) Vice-President   (b) Lok Sabha   (c) Prime Minister   (d) Union Cabinet

29. How many times National Emergency has been so far declared in India?
    (a) Once   (b) Twice   (c) Thrice   (d) Never

30. President made proclamation of emergency on the grounds of internal disturbance for first time in
    (a) 1975   (b) 1965   (c) 1962   (d) 1950

31. The Constituent Assembly was created as per the proposal of
    (a) Cabinet Mission
    (b) Simon Mission
    (c) Cripps Mission
    (d) Indian National Congress

32. The Preamble to the Indian Constitution is borrowed from
    (a) Britain Constitution
    (b) Objective Resolution
    (c) Canada Constitution
    (d) Australia Constitution

33. The Constitution of India provides for
    (a) Single citizenship
    (b) Double citizenship
    (c) Multiple citizenship
    (d) No citizenship

34. The final interpreter to the Indian Constitution is
    (a) Speaker of Lok Sabha
    (b) Parliament
    (c) President
    (d) Supreme Court

35. Parliamentary system in Indian is based on the pattern of
    (a) Great Britain   (b) USA   (c) France   (d) Canada

36. 26th November 1949 is a significant day in our Constitutional history because
    (a) The Constitution was adopted on that day
    (b) The India took pledge of complete independence on that day
    (c) India became republic on that day
    (d) The first amendment to the Constitution was passed on that day

37. Fundamental Rights can be claimed against
    (a) Judiciary   (b) Individual   (c) State   (d) All of these

38. The main objective of the Cultural and Educational Rights granted to the citizen is to
    (a) Preserve the rich cultural heritage of India
    (b) Help the minorities to conserve their culture
    (c) Evolve a single integrated Indian culture
    (d) All of these

39. This is not a ground to impose restriction on freedom of speech and expression
    (a) Morality or decency
    (b) Contempt of court
    (c) National security
    (d) Law and order

40. The writ of Habeas Corpus is issued
    (a) In the form of an order calling upon a person who has detained another person to bring that person before the court and show authority for such detention
    (b) By a superior court to a lower court not to exceed its jurisdiction
    (c) By a superior court to the subordinate court to do something in the nature of its allotted duty
    (d) In form of an order to stop proceeding in certain case

41. Right to primary Education guaranteed under the Article 21A was inserted to the Constitution by _____ Amendment
    (a) 61st Amendment   (b) 74th Amendment
    (c) 86th Amendment   (d) 97th Amendment

42. Right to freedom guaranteed under Article 19 _____ during emergency.
    (a) Can be restrained   (b) Cannot be restrained
    (c) Can be suspended   (d) Cannot be suspended

43. Which one of the writ literally means 'you may have the body'?
    (a) Mandamus   (b) Certiorari   (c) Quo-Warranto   (d) Habeas Corpus

44. The person arrested has to be produced before the magistrate within
    (a) One week   (b) 24 hours   (c) 72 hours   (d) 2 months

45. Who described the DPSP as the novel features of the Indian Constitution?
    (a) Dr B.R. Ambedkar   (b) Motilal Nehru
    (c) Madhav Rao N.   (d) L.M. Singhivi

46. The enforcement of DPSP depends on
    (a) The will of the government in power   (b) The judiciary
    (c) Resources available with the government   (d) All of these

47. 'Uniform Civil Code' means
    (a) A codified civil law applicable to all person of India irrespective of their religion
    (b) A code related to individual public life
    (c) A code meant for Hindus only
    (d) A code meant for Muslims only

48. Village Panchayat is the best example for India's _____ form of Government
    (a) Republic   (b) Democratic   (c) Sovereign   (d) Socialist

49. The Fundamental Duties of Indian Citizen were
    (a) Enshrined in original Constitution
    (b) Added to the Constitution by 42nd Amendment
    (c) Added to the Constitution by 44th Amendment
    (d) Added to the Constitution by 46th Amendment

50. Who acts as a President when neither the President nor the Vice-President is available?
    (a) Speaker of Lok Sabha   (b) Attorney General of India
    (c) Chief Justice of India   (d) Speaker of Rajya Sabha

(COMMON TO ALL BRANCHES)

Time: 2 hours   Max. Marks: 50

1. A person to be appointed as Governor of a state must have completed the age of
    (a) 30 years   (b) 35 years   (c) 45 years   (d) 50 years

2. Who acts as the channel of communication between the Governor and the state Council of Ministers?
    (a) Chief Minister   (b) Home Minister
    (c) Speaker of the Legislative Assembly   (d) Finance Minister

3. A Judge of High Court when he wants to resign should address his resignation letter to the
    (a) Chief Justice of the High Court   (b) Chief Justice of India
    (c) President of India   (d) Chief Minister of the State

4. The interval between two consecutive sessions of a State Legislative Assembly should not be more than
    (a) 2 months   (b) 3 months   (c) 4 months   (d) 6 months

5. Who decides the disputes regarding election of the President?
    (a) The Election Commission   (b) The Parliament
    (c) The Supreme Court   (d) The Prime Minister

6. Decision on question as to disqualification of membership of either house of Parliament rests with the
    (a) Election Commission   (b) Chief Justice of India
    (c) Parliament   (d) President after Consultation with the Election Commission

7. The Chief Election Commissioner holds office for a period of
    (a) 3 years   (b) 6 years
    (c) 5 years   (d) 6 years or till he attains the age of 65 years

8. Election Commission of Indian does not conduct elections to
    (a) State Legislature   (b) Vice-President
    (c) Municipalities   (d) Rajya Sabha

9. The procedure for amending the Constitution is detailed under
    (a) Article 360   (b) Article 368   (c) Article 352   (d) Article 301

10. Which Constitution Amendments Act limits the size of the Council of Ministers in the Union Government including Prime Minister to not more than 15% of the membership strength of Lok Sabha?
    (a) 42nd Amendments   (b) 44th Amendments
    (c) 86th Amendments   (d) 91st Amendments

11. Who decides whether a bill is a money bill or not?
    (a) President   (b) Chairman of Rajya Sabha
    (c) Speaker of Lok Sabha   (d) Minister of Parliamentary Affairs

12. The Judges of the Supreme Court of India now retire at the age of
    (a) 60 years   (b) 62 years   (c) 58 years   (d) 65 years

13. How many members are nominated to the Rajya Sabha by the President of India?
    (a) 10   (b) 12   (c) 14   (d) 20

14. In the Union Government the Council of Ministers is collectively responsible to the
    (a) Prime Minister   (b) President
    (c) Lok Sabha   (d) Lok Sabha and Rajya Sabha

15. When both offices of the President and Vice-President happen to be vacant simultaneously who will discharge the duties of the President?
    (a) Prime Minister   (b) Speaker of Lok Sabha
    (c) Union Home Minister   (d) Chief Justice of India

16. This is not a ground to declare Nation Emergency
    (a) Serious internal disturbance   (b) War
    (c) External aggression   (d) Armed rebellion

17. When the State Emergency is in operation, the President cannot interfere in the matters of
    (a) State Executive   (b) State Legislature   (c) State Judiciary   (d) All of these

18. Who is empowered to proclaim the Financial Emergency?
    (a) Finance Minister of the Union Government   (b) President
    (c) Prime Minister   (d) Parliament

19. Which one of the following is not the function of Municipalities?
    (a) Providing cattle ponds; prevention of cruelty to animals
    (b) Providing water supply for domestic, industrial and commercial purposes
    (c) Ensuring uninterrupted election power supply to homes
    (d) Collecting property taxes

20. Which one of the following is not the function of Gram Panchayats?
    (a) Promotion of cottage industries   (b) Care of public tanks
    (c) Supply of drinking water   (d) Primary education

21. Culture and Educational Rights have been incorporated under Fundamental Rights with the objective to
    (a) Preserve Indian culture   (b) Evolve a single culture
    (c) Eradicate illiteracy   (d) Help minorities to conserve their culture

22. Dr B.R. Ambedkar termed Article 32 of the Indian Constitution as the 'Heart and soul' of the Indian Constitution. Which one of the following Fundamental Rights it contains?
    (a) Right to freedom   (b) Right to Constitutional remedies
    (c) Right to education   (d) Right to freedom of religion

23. Prohibition of discrimination on grounds of religion, race, caste, sex or place of birth is a Fundamental right classifiable under
    (a) Right to freedom of religion   (b) Right against exploitation
    (c) Right to equality   (d) None of these

24. Which fundamental right of Indian Constitution has been deleted by 44thAmendment Act, 1978?
    (a) Right against exploitation   (b) Right to property
    (c) Right to strike and protest   (d) Right to speak

25. Writ of Mandamus can be issued on ground of
    (a) Non-performance of public duties (b) Unlawful detention
    (c) Unlawful occupation of public office (d) None of these

26. Protection of wild life comes under which of the following in India?
    (a) Fundamental Rights   (b) Fundamental Duties
    (c) Directive Principles of State Policy   (d) None of these

27. Which of the following is enforceable in a court of Law?
    (a) Preamble   (b) Fundamental Rights
    (c) Fundamental Duties   (d) Directive Principles of State Policy

28. Fundamental duties appearing in India Constitution are adopted from the Constitution of
    (a) Germany   (b) UK   (c) USA   (d) Russia

29. Which one of the following is not a Directive Principle of State Policy?
    (a) Free legal aid to poor   (b) Maternity relief
    (c) Improvement of public health   (d) None of these

30. Which of the following is a Fundamental Duty of the Indian citizen?
    (a) Strive to eradicate untouchability   (b) To cast his/her vote
    (c) To develop scientific temper   (d) To promote literacy

31. Which one of these is the primary source of Indian Constitution?
    (a) British Constitution   (b) Irish Constitution
    (c) Government of India Act 1935   (d) US Constitution

32. Who acted as chairman of the Drafting Committee of the Constituent Assembly?
    (a) Dr B.R. Amebedkar   (b) B.C Rajagopalachari
    (c) Dr Rajendra Prasad   (d) Jawaharlal Nehru

33. In the final form of the Constitution adopted by Constituent Assembly, how many Articles and Schedules were there?
    (a) 397 Articles and 7 Schedules   (b) 395 Articles and 4 Schedules
    (c) 400 Articles and 10 Schedules   (d) 395 Articles and 8 Schedules

34. The Preamble of the Indian Constitution does not contain
    (a) Democratic   (b) Adult Franchise   (c) Sovereignty   (d) Fraternity

35. The Emergency provisions incorporated in the Indian Constitution were influenced by the Constitution of
    (a) USA   (b) German Reich   (c) Russia   (d) Canada

36. Engineering ethics is _____
    (a) A macro ethics   (b) Business ethics
    (c) A preventive ethics   (d) A code of scientific rules based on ethics

37. Conflict of interest may be _____
    (a) False   (b) Imaginary   (c) Created   (d) Potential

38. The codes of ethics can be taken as guidelines by Engineers to _____
    (a) Overcome the work pressure   (b) Resolve the conflicts
    (c) Formulate the problem   (d) Escape from the responsibility

39. The use of intellectual property of others without permission or credit is referred as
    (a) Cooking   (b) Stealing   (c) Plagiarism   (d) Trimming

40. Which of the following is not a concept of responsibility?
    (a) Minimalist   (b) Maximalist   (c) Reasonable care   (d) Good Works

41. The Fault Tree is used to
    (a) Improve safety
    (c) Assess the risk involved
    (c) Take free consent
    (d) Claim compensation

42. An Expert Testimony does not demand _____
    (a) Consulting extensively with the lawyer
    (c) Expert legal knowledge
    (b) Adequate time for thorough investigation
    (d) Objective and unbiased demeanor

43. When an engineer abuses Client–Professional Confidentiality, it amounts to _____
    (a) Misusing the truth
    (c) Self-deception
    (b) Criminal breach of trust
    (d) None of these

44. An author retains copyright of his/her book for _____ after his or her death
    (a) 20 years   (b) 30 years   (c) 50 years   (d) 10 years

45. The formula of MTR Sambar Masala is an example of
    (a) Patent   (b) Trademark   (c) Copyright   (d) Trade secret

46. Mandal Commission deals with
    (a) Rights of the Minority
    (c) Reservation for backward class people
    (b) Laws relating to sexual harassment
    (d) Laws relating to child labour

47. At present, how many seats are reserved for Scheduled Castes and Scheduled Tribes in Lok Sabha?
    (a) 100 and 50   (b) 79 and 40   (c) 89 and 45   (d) 70 and 30

48. National Commission for Women was established in the year
    (a) 1985   (b) 1990   (c) 1995   (d) 2000

49. National Commissions for Scheduled Castes and Scheduled Tribes have to submit their annual reports on the working of the safeguards to
    (a) Prime Minister
    (c) President
    (b) Parliament
    (d) Chief Justice of India

50. No child below the age of 14 years
    (a) Shall be employed in any industry
    (c) Shall be employed in house-hold work
    (b) Shall be employed in any office
    (d) Can be employed anywhere

(COMMON TO ALL BRANCHES)

Time: 2 hours   Max. Marks: 50

1. One of the views on responsibility of engineers is
   (a) They should do good work
   (b) They should take reasonable responsibility
   (c) They should be strictly liable
   (d) They should be absolutely reliable

2. One of the impediments to responsibility is
   (a) Self-deception   (b) Rampant corruption at higher level
   (c) Interference by higher officers (d) Interference by politician

3. This does not amount to misusing the truth
   (a) Deliberation deception   (b) Biased professional information
   (c) Withholding information   (d) Failure to seek-out truth

4. 'Tight couple' means
   (a) Strong adhesive materials   (b) Process tightly coupled
   (c) Erecting two pillars side by side (d) Binding two beams tightly

5. Which of the following is not preserved as intellectual property?
   (a) Copyright   (b) Government regulations
   (c) Trade secrets   (d) Patents

6. 'Acceptable Risk' means
   (a) Inevitable risk
   (b) Risk is natural part of the process
   (c) Risk of harm equal to probability of producing benefit
   (d) Risk which cannot be avoided

7. An expert testimony does not demand
   (a) Adequate time for thorough investigation
   (b) Consultancy extensively with the lawyer
   (c) Expert legal knowledge
   (d) Objective and unbiased demeanour

8. What is morally wrong?
   (a) Can be legally right
   (b) Can be measured as constitutionally right
   (c) Cannot be measured as constitutionally right
   (d) Both b & c

9. Revealing confidential information means
   (a) Violation of patent right   (b) Criminal breach of trust
   (c) Breach of contract   (d) Misusing the truth

10. The tendency of interpreting situations according to their view and imposing view is
    (a) Confined vision   (b) Egocentric   (c) Self-interest   (d) None of these

11. Which of the following is not advised by NSPE code to engineers
    (a) To be honest   (b) Not to use firms home in dishonest business
    (c) Not to avoid deceptive acts   (d) To have professional obligations

12. Which of the following qualities and ethically responsible engineer should not have with regard to risk?
    (a) Dishonest in assessing
    (b) Be aware of different approaches to the determination
    (c) Not be deceiving
    (d) Aware of difficulty

13. Which of the following is not a democratic institution of the Rig Vedic era?
    (a) Samithi   (b) Sabha   (c) Grama   (d) Thaluku

14. Which act created for the first 'the Supreme Court'?
    (a) The Pitts India Act   (b) The Regulatory Act, 1773
    (c) The Amending Act   (d) The Act of 1976

15. Indian National Congress started 'Quit India Movement' after the failure of
    (a) Cripps Mission   (b) Sepoy Mutiny   (c) August Offer   (d) Wavell Plan

16. India borrowed the idea of incorporating fundamental rights in the Constitution form
    (a) China   (b) France   (c) USA   (d) UK

17. Which of the following is not a fundamental right?
    (a) Constitutional remedies   (b) Property   (c) Assemble peacefully   (d) Move freely

18. Who is authorized to lay down qualifications to acquire the citizenship?
    (a) Parliament   (b) President   (c) Speaker   (d) Prime Minister

19. Who quoted 'Child of today is the citizen of tomorrow'?
    (a) Dr B.R. Ambedkar   (b) Gandhiji   (c) Vallabhai Patel   (d) Jawaharlal Nehru

20. Right to equality is guaranteed under the article
    (a) 13   (b) 14   (c) 15   (d) 17

21. The directive principles of the state policy may be classified into
    (a) Socialist, Gandhian and liberal
    (b) Gandhian, liberal and communist
    (c) Socialist and communist
    (d) Liberal and communist

22. Which one of the following is a directive principle of the state policy?
    (a) The state shall not deny to any person quality before the law
    (b) The state shall endeavour to protect and improve the environment
    (c) The state shall not discriminate against any person on the grounds of religion, race, caste, sex or place of birth
    (d) Untouchability is abolished and its practice in any form shall be punishable by law

23. The directive principle of state policy
    (a) Can be enforced only by the Supreme Court
    (b) Can be enforced by the High Court
    (c) Can be enforced relating to SCs and STs only
    (d) Cannot be enforced by any court

24. The fundamental duties under the Indian Constitution are provided
    (a) An order of the President   (b) An amendment to the Constitution
    (c) A legislation by the parliament   (d) An order by the Supreme Court

25. The fundamental duties demand to
    (a) Abide by moral rules   (b) Avoid corruption
    (c) Work sincerely   (d) Abide by the Constitution

26. What is the main sanction behind the fundamental duties?
    (a) Legal   (b) Moral   (c) Social   (d) All of these

27. Which one of the following are fundamental duties?
    (a) To uphold and protect the sovereignty of India
    (b) To protect and improve environment
    (c) To safeguard the public property
    (d) All of these

28. The concept of judicial review has been borrowed from the Constitution of
    (a) Switzerland   (b) UK   (c) USSR   (d) USA

29. The President of the India is an integral part of the
    (a) LS   (b) Union cabinet   (c) Parliament   (d) Union

30. The chief justice and other judges of the High Court are appointed by the
    (a) Chief Justice of India   (b) President
    (c) Governor   (d) Chief Minister

31. Which article authorizes the President to seek an advice from the Supreme Court?
    (a) 142   (b) 124   (c) 134   (d) 143

32. Who appoints the Governor of the state?
    (a) Chief Justice of India   (b) Chief Justice of state
    (c) Chief Minister   (d) The President

33. The Governor of a state should
    (a) Be a member of Lok Sabha   (b) Not hold any other office of profit
    (c) Be residents of the State   (d) Have completed the age of 45 years

34. Who decide the number of judges in the High Court?
    (a) President   (b) State Legislature   (c) Governor   (d) Parliament

35. Salaries and other emoluments of the High Court judges shall be determined by the
    (a) Governor   (b) Parliament   (c) Chief Minister   (d) State legislature

36. In which year was 'Untouchability' abolished in India
    (a) 1952   (b) 1956   (c) 1950   (d) 1955

37. According to Marriage Act of 1954, the age is fixed at _____ years for men and _____ years for women.
    (a) 22 & 18   (b) 24 & 20   (c) 21 & 20   (d) 21 & 18

38. Minority groups are recognized on the basis of their
    (a) Population   (b) Religion   (c) Race   (d) Caste

39. Who is empowered to nominate Anglo-Indian community to Lok Sabha/Legislative Assembly?
    (a) Speaker of LS/LA   (b) President/Governor
    (c) Prime Minister/Chief Minister   (d) None of these

40. While proclamation of emergency is in operation, the President cannot suspend certain fundamental rights. They are
    (a) 32   (b) 14 & 15   (c) 14 & 16   (d) 20 & 21

41. President can proclaim emergency on the recommendation of the Union Cabinet. Such recommendation shall be
    (a) Oral recommendation   (b) Majority in the house
    (c) Written recommendation   (d) Sincere request

42. If a state fails to comply with the directives of the central government, the President can
    (a) Dissolve the state legislation and order fresh election
    (b) Declare breakdown of the Constitutional machinery in the state and assume responsibility for its government
    (c) Send reserve police force to secure compliance with directions
    (d) Do either (b) or (c)

43. Who has the duty to protect states against external aggression and internal disturbance?
    (a) Union government   (b) State government
    (c) Army   (d) Do such duty in federal state

44. The election system of India is largely based on the pattern of
    (a) France   (b) USA   (c) Britain   (d) None of these

45. The Chief Election Commissioner is
    (a) Appointed by the Union Home Minister   (b) Appointed by the Prime Minister
    (c) Elected by the Parliament   (d) Appointed by the President

46. Which article under the Constitution gives power to Election Commission to conduct elections?
    (a) 234   (b) 324   (c) 335   (d) 320

47. The party system in India can be describe as
    (a) Single-party   (b) Multi-party   (c) Bi-party   (d) A mixture of the all these

48. Professional ethics is
    (a) Set of rules relating to personal character of professionals
    (b) Traditional rules observed since a long time
    (c) Set of rules passed by professional bodies
    (d) Set of standards adopted by professionals

49. Engineering profession is considered to be like a building, its foundation is
    (a) Sound common sense & expert knowledge   (b) Hard and sincere work
    (c) Honesty   (d) Expert engineering knowledge and skill

50. One of the aims of Engineering Ethics is to
    (a) Stimulate the moral imagination
    (b) Inspire engineers to acquire in-depth knowledge in their field
    (c) Acquire new skills in engineering testing and research
    (d) Make engineers self-confident in discharging their duties

(COMMON TO ALL BRANCHES)

Time: 2 hours   **Max. Marks: 50**

1. The amendment procedure to the Constitution is borrowed from the Constitution of
   (a) South Africa   (b) United States   (c) Australia   (d) Britain

2. The idea of the Constitution of India was flashed for the first time by
   (a) Dr B.R. Ambedkar   (b) Dr Rajendra Prasad
   (c) Mahatma Gandhi   (d) Jawaharlal Nehru

3. The famous 'Dandi March' done by Gandhiji was against
   (a) British rule   (b) Untouchability   (c) Sati system   (d) Salt tax

4. The Indian Constitution came into force on
   (a) 21-11-1949   (b) 26-01-1950   (c) 15-08-1947   (d) 26-12-1950

5. The Preamble of Constitution of India has been amended so for
   (a) Four times   (b) Thrice   (c) Twice   (d) Once

6. A state which does not promote or interfere in the affairs of religion is referred as
   (a) Socialist   (b) Democratic   (c) Secular   (d) Sovereign

7. Our Constitution grants to the citizens _____ fundamental rights.
   (a) Six   (b) Five   (c) Ten   (d) Seven

8. Who are not entitled to form unions?
   (a) Students   (b) Police   (c) Teachers   (d) Entrepreneurs

9. Minority may be
   (a) Regional or National   (b) Linguistic or Religion
   (c) National or Racial   (d) Racial or Regional

10. Which one is not a fundamental right?
    (a) Right to against exploitation   (b) Right to freedom of religion
    (c) Right to strike   (d) Right to equality

11. The directive principles of state policies are
    (a) Social Rights   (b) Political Rights
    (c) Constitutional Rights   (d) Legal Rights

12. Which part of the Constitution aims at establishing a welfare state in the country?
    (a) Preamble   (b) Fundamental Rights
    (c) Fundamental Duties   (d) Directive Principles of State Policies

13. The phrase 'Economic justice' is found in
    (a) Preamble and fundamental rights
    (b) Preamble and directive principles
    (c) Fundamental rights and duties
    (d) Directive principles and fundamental duties

14. This is not a fundamental duty
    (a) To develop scientific temper   (b) To protect natural environment
    (c) Not to indulge in corrupt practice   (d) To abide by the Constitution

15. To respect the National Flag and National Anthem is a
    (a) Fundamental duty of every citizen
    (b) Fundamental right of every citizen
    (c) Directive principle of the state
    (d) None of these

16. Fundamental duties under the Indian Constitution are provided by
    (a) An order of the President   (b) An order of the Supreme Court
    (c) An amendment to the Constitution (d) A legislation by the Parliament

17. Which of the following is not one of the three organs of the union/state?
    (a) Executive   (b) Press   (c) Judiciary   (d) Legislative

18. Under the Indian Constitution the subjects of administration have been divided into
    (a) Two lists   (b) Four lists   (c) Five lists   (d) Three lists

19. How many Anglo-Indians and other members can be nominated by the President to the Lok Sabha and Rajya Sabha?
    (a) 2 & 12   (b) 1 & 10   (c) 2 & 10   (d) 1 & 12

20. Who will preside over the joint session of both houses of Parliament?
    (a) President   (b) Prime Minister   (c) Speaker   (d) None of these

21. 'Railways' is a subject under _____ list
    (a) Union   (b) State   (c) Concurrent   (d) Residuary

22. What is the minimum age in years for becoming an MP at Lok Sabha and Rajya Sabha?
    (a) 18 & 25   (b) 25 & 18   (c) 25 & 30   (d) 30 & 25

23. Full form of PIL is
    (a) Public interest legislation   (b) Public interest litigation
    (c) Private interest litigation   (d) Private interest legislation

24. When the office of the President falls vacant, the same must be filled within
    (a) 4 months   (b) 6 months   (c) 12 months   (d) 18 months

25. Who interprets the Indian Constitution?
    (a) Supreme Court (b) Parliament   (c) President   (d) Prime Minister

26. Which was the lengthiest Amendment to the Constitution?
    (a) 46th   (b) 44th   (c) 42nd   (d) 24th

27. Generally the Governor belongs to
    (a) Neighbouring state   (b) Same state
    (c) Some other state   (d) IAS officer

28. The emoluments, allowances and privileges of the Governor shall be determined by the
    (a) Chief Minister   (b) Prime Minister   (c) President   (d) Parliament

29. 'Bicameral' means
    (a) Presence of two Houses in the state
    (b) Presence of one House in the state
    (c) Presence of half House in the state
    (d) Presence of no House in the state

30. What is the effect of the resignation or death of the Chief Minister of the state?
    (a) New chief minister takes Oath   (b) Mid-term polls
    (c) Dissolves the Legislatives Assembly   (d) None of these

31. The minimum gap permissible between the two sessions of the legislature is
    (a) Three months   (b) Six months   (c) Two months   (d) Six weeks

32. Who is the neutral in the affairs of the party politics?
    (a) Chief Minister   (b) Home Minister   (c) Finance Minister   (d) Speaker

33. According to Marriage Act of 1954, the age is fixed at _____ years for men and _____ years for women
    (a) 22 & 18   (b) 24 & 20   (c) 21 & 20   (d) 21 & 18

34. Indian Constitution guarantees reservation to SCs and STs in
    (a) Legislative Assembly only   (b) Lok Sabha only
    (c) Legislative Assembly & Lok Sabha   (d) Rajya Sabha only

35. Jobs are reserved for Scheduled Castes and Scheduled Tribes people
    (a) Both at the time of appointment and promotion
    (b) On the basis of their annual income
    (c) At the time of appointment
    (d) At the time of promotion

36. Breakdown of Constitutional machinery in a state is popularly known as
    (a) National Emergency   (b) President's Rules
    (c) Financial Emergency   (d) All of these

37. The President can proclaim an emergency on the ground of
    (a) War   (b) Armed rebellion
    (c) External aggression   (d) All of these

38. Which one of the following types of emergency has not yet declared, till now?
    (a) State Emergency   (b) National Emergency
    (c) Financial Emergency   (d) None of these

39. Regional Election Commissioners may be appointed by the President with the consultation of the
    (a) Governor   (b) Prime Minister
    (c) Vice-President   (d) Election Commission

40. The Election Commission does not conduct election to the
    (a) Members of State Legislative Assembly   (b) Member of Parliament
    (c) President   (d) Speaker of Lok Sabha

41. What is the system used to elect the President of India?
    (a) Direct Election   (b) Proportional Representation
    (c) Secret Ballot   (d) Preferential System

42. Engineering Ethics is a
    (a) Developing ethics   (b) Natural ethics
    (c) Scientifically developed ethics   (d) Preventive ethics

43. This is not the aim of studying Engineering Ethics
    (a) Analyzing concepts   (b) Engaging sense of responsibility
    (c) Addressing unclarity   (d) Procuring faultless results

44. An Engineer may not be held legally liable for causing harm, when the harm is caused
    (a) Intentionally   (b) Ignorantly   (c) Negligently   (d) Recklessly

45. This is not an impediment to responsibility
    (a) Self-interest   (b) Self-respect   (c) Ignorance   (d) Fear

46. These are not trade secrets
    (a) Principles   (b) Patterns   (c) Formulas   (d) Devices

47. The use of intellectual property of others without their permission or credit is referred as
    (a) Trimming   (b) Cooking   (c) Forging   (d) Plagiarism

48. Patent holder does not allow others to use patented information for _____ years from the date of filing
    (a) 40   (b) 30   (c) 20   (d) 50

49. Which of the following does not depict the attitude towards responsibility?
    (a) Good works   (b) Protest   (c) Reasonable care   (d) Minimalist

50. Which of the following is not preserved as an intellectual property?
    (a) Government Regulations   (b) Copyrights
    (c) Patents   (d) Trade Secrets

(COMMON TO ALL BRANCHES)

Time: 2 hours   **Max. Marks: 50**

1. Can a person act as Governor of more than one state?
   (a) Yes   (b) No   (c) Only for period of six months   (d) Only for period of one year

2. An ordinance issued by Governor is subject to approval by
   (a) The President   (b) The State Council of Ministers
   (c) The State Legislature   (d) None of these

3. The member of Legislative Assembly of state varies between
   (a) 60 & 500   (b) 100 & 300   (c) 150 & 450   (d) 100 & 400

4. The High Court of state is directly under
   (a) The President   (b) The Supreme Court of India
   (c) The Governor of the state   (d) The Chief Justice of India

5. On what ground a judge of High Court can be removed
   (a) Prove misbehaviour or incapacity   (b) Insolvency
   (c) Insanity   (d) All of these

6. The amendment procedure of Indian Constitution has been modelled on the Constitution of
   (a) South Africa   (b) Canada   (c) USA   (d) Switzerland

7. In India, the citizens have been given the right to vote on the basis of
   (a) Age   (b) Education
   (c) Property qualification   (d) Duration of stay in country

8. Ethics is
   (a) Normative Science   (b) Natural Science
   (c) Both normative and natural   (d) Objective scheme

9. Work above and beyond full of duty means
   (a) Good work   (b) Reasonable work
   (c) Work involving high risk   (d) Responsible work

10. Engineering ethics
    (a) Stimulates to conduct research
    (b) Shine on time management
    (c) Acquire new skills in engineering, testing
    (d) Stimulates the moral imagination

11. Study of engineering ethics helps to
    (a) Recognize ethical issue   (b) Develop one's knowledge and skill
    (c) Develop one's moral character   (d) Provide satisfactory service to public

12. This is not impediment to responsibility
    (a) Fear   (b) Self-interest
    (c) Group thinking   (d) Critical acceptance of authority

13. This is not dishonesty in science and engineering
    (a) Forging   (b) Blending   (c) Trimming   (d) Cooking

14. Engineers can use Code of Ethics as guidelines to
    (a) Resolve the conflicts
    (b) Formulate the problem
    (c) Shift the responsibility
    (d) Overcome the work pressure

15. Engineers must protect the public from
    (a) Acceptable risk
    (b) Impending risk
    (c) Technical risk
    (d) None of these

16. How many types of emergencies have been envisaged by the Constitution?
    (a) Only one
    (b) Two
    (c) Three
    (d) Four

17. The President can proclaim national emergency only on written advice of
    (a) The Prime Minister
    (b) The Union Cabinet
    (c) The chief justices of India
    (d) The speaker of Lok Sabha

18. The tenure of Vice-President is
    (a) Co-terminus with that of the President
    (b) Five years
    (c) Dependent on the will of the President
    (d) Six years

19. Prime Minister is
    (a) The head of the state
    (b) The head of the government
    (c) The head of state as well as head of government
    (d) None of these

20. What can be the maximum strength of the Lok Sabha?
    (a) 500
    (b) 545
    (c) 552
    (d) 550

21. How many seats have been reserved for Union Territories in Lok Sabha?
    (a) 20
    (b) 25
    (c) 13
    (d) None of these

22. Rajya Sabha can have maximum strength of
    (a) 250 members
    (b) 225 members
    (c) 330 members
    (d) 350 members

23. What can be the maximum gap between two sessions of Parliament?
    (a) Three months
    (b) Six months
    (c) Four months
    (d) Nine months

24. The Supreme Court consists of Chief Justice and
    (a) Seven judges
    (b) Nine judges
    (c) 11 judges
    (d) 25 judges

25. Who is executive head of state?
    (a) Chief Minister
    (b) The Governor
    (c) The President
    (d) None of these

26. Preamble declares the objective of Constitution as
    (a) Secularism
    (b) Justice, liberty, equality & fraternity
    (c) Democratic socialist
    (d) Liberalism

27. Preamble declares that the Constitution of India was adopted on
    (a) 15th August 1947
    (b) 26th January 1950
    (c) 6th December 1945
    (d) 26th November 1949

28. Indian Constitution has
    (a) 410 articles
    (b) 358 articles
    (c) 444 articles
    (d) 395 articles

29. Indian Constitution has
    (a) 12 Schedules
    (b) 7 Schedules
    (c) 9 Schedules
    (d) 10 Schedules

30. Secularism means
    (a) Absence of state religion
    (b) Right to religious freedom
    (c) Equality of all religions
    (d) All of the above

31. Which article of India Constitution lays down the method of amendment?
    (a) Article 371
    (b) Article 368
    (c) 42nd Amendment
    (d) 44th Amendment

32. Which is not a fundamental right?
    (a) Right to Freedom
    (b) Right to Constitutional Remedies
    (c) Right to Property
    (d) Right to Equality

33. The Constitution lays down how many fundamental duties of a citizen
    (a) 6   (b) 11   (c) 15   (d) 20

34. Directive Principles of State Policy have been described in Articles
    (a) 36–51   (b) 1–11   (c) 12–35   (d) 19–27

35. Union list has
    (a) 95 subjects (b) 97 subjects (c) 105 subjects (d) 66 subjects

36. Centre can declare Constitutional emergency in a state under Article
    (a) 152   (b) 360   (c) 356   (d) 365

37. In India the Residuary powers are with
    (a) State Government
    (b) Union Government
    (c) Local Government
    (d) Government of Union Territories

38. India has a
    (a) Democracy
    (b) Presidential System
    (c) Direct Democracy
    (d) Parliamentary Democracy

39. President of India is elected by
    (a) Elected MPs
    (b) All elected MPs and all elected MLAs
    (c) Elected MLAs
    (d) All MPs and MLAs

40. Who has the emergency power?
    (a) Prime Minister
    (b) Union Cabinet
    (c) President of India
    (d) Union Parliament

41. Who appoints the Prime Minister?
    (a) The President of India
    (b) The Lok Sabha
    (c) The majority party in the Lok Sabha
    (d) The people of India

42. Meghalaya has how many seats in Rajya Sabha?
    (a) One   (b) Two   (c) Three   (d) Four

43. Which is exclusive power of Rajya Sabha?
    (a) To intimate money bills
    (b) To impeach the President
    (c) To declare a subject of state list as subject of National importance
    (d) To remove Prime Minister

44. The Constitution of India is
    (a) Rigid
    (b) Flexible
    (c) Partly rigid and partly flexible
    (d) Very rigid

45. The Fundamental Rights of Indian citizens are contained in
    (a) Part III of Constitution   (b) Part IV of Constitution
    (c) The seventh schedule of the Constitution (d) None of these

46. Supreme Court of India has how many judges?
    (a) 24   (b) 25   (c) One Chief Justice and 25 other judges   (d) 13

47. What is the tenure of member of Rajya Sabha?
    (a) 6 years   (b) 3 years   (c) 5 years   (d) No fixed tenure

48. The Chief Justice of India is appointed on principle of
    (a) Merit   (b) Will of President   (c) Seniority   (d) Election by the Judge

49. The Directive Principles of State Policy are
    (a) Justifiable
    (b) Non-justifiable
    (c) Only some directive principle are justifiable
    (d) None of these

50. To be eligible for election as President, a candidate must be
    (a) Over 35 years of age   (b) Over 65 years of age
    (c) Over 60 years of age   (d) There is no age limit

(COMMON TO ALL BRANCHES)

Time: 2 hours   **Max. Marks: 50**

1. For how many years, months and days did the constituent assembly work on the framing of the Constitution of India?
    (a) 2 years 11 months and 18 days
    (b) 13 years 2 months and 16 days
    (c) 4 years 2 months and 18 days
    (d) 1 years 11 months and 15 days

2. Equality of opportunity in matters of public employment under Article
    (a) 14   (b) 15   (c) 16   (d) 19

3. Abolition of untouchability in matters of public employment under Article
    (a) 17   (b) 19   (c) 21   (d) 32

4. Classification of fundamental rights is in Part
    (a) I   (b) II   (c) III   (d) IV

5. Unnikrishnan v/s State of Andhra Pradesh regarding
    (a) Public Interest litigation   (b) Abolition of Capital fee
    (c) Smoking in public place   (d) Noise pollution due to blaring of music during religion activities

6. The directive principles of state policy under article:
    (a) 16–30   (b) 31–51   (c) 61–76   (d) None of these

7. How many fundamental duties are there?
    (a) 5   (b) 6   (c) 10   (d) 11

8. The fundamental duties have been included during the tenureship of
    (a) Dr Ambedkar   (b) Gandhiji
    (c) Dr Rajendra Prasad   (d) Indira Gandhi

9. The President of India is
    (a) The real ruler of India
    (b) The Constitutional head of the state
    (c) The leader of majority party which forms the government
    (d) The head of the state as well as the government

10. The President of India is elected for
    (a) 3 years   (b) 4 years   (c) 5 years   (d) 6 years

11. The financial emergency under Article
    (a) 352   (b) 354   (c) 360   (d) 364

12. National emergency was proclaimed first time during the year
    (a) 1952   (b) 1956   (c) 1962   (d) 1971

13. How many emergencies are there?
    (a) One   (b) Two   (c) Three   (d) Four

14. The term of Lok Sabha and Legislative Assemblies the period was extended for 6 years in Amendment
    (a) 26th   (b) 42nd   (c) 44th   (d) 46th

15. Reservation for Anglo-Indians in Karnataka Legislative Assembly is
    (a) 1   (b) 2   (c) 3   (d) 4

16. Which of the States is having highest members in Lok Sabha?
    (a) Andhra Pradesh   (b) Madhya Pradesh
    (c) Uttar Pradesh   (d) Karnataka

17. The Upper house is called
    (a) Lok Sabha   (b) Rajya Sabha   (c) Vidhan Sabha   (d) None of these

18. Who appoints the Chief Election Commissioner?
    (a) Prime Minister   (b) President   (c) Parliament   (d) A.I.C.T.E

19. The Chief Justice of India is appointed by
    (a) Parliament   (b) Government   (c) Vice-President   (d) President

20. The smoothing of irregularities to make data to look extremely precisely done researched is called
    (a) Trimming   (b) Cooking   (c) Plagiarism   (d) Forging

21. Tendency of shifting responsibility will logically come down if there is
    (a) Group thinking   (b) Microscopic vision   (c) Fear   (d) Both b and a

22. Considering an engineering profession as building then, is its foundation of
    (a) Honesty   (b) Creativity   (c) Imagination   (d) Both b and c

23. Which of the following is not conflict of interest as applied to making judgement?
    (a) Actual   (b) Potential   (c) Apparent   (d) Virtual

24. The formulae of a soft drink are an example of
    (a) Trade secret   (b) Patent   (c) Copyright   (d) Trade marks

25. Which of the following are not the concepts of responsibility?
    (a) Minimalist   (b) Utilitarianism   (c) Reasonable care   (d) Good works

26. How many Articles included while making Indian Constitution?
    (a) 300   (b) 368   (c) 395   (d) 448

27. The Indian Council Act, 1909 is called as
    (a) Montague and Chelmsford reforms   (b) Minto-Morley reforms
    (c) Cripps Mission Act   (d) British Act

28. British Parliament passed the Indian Independence Act on
    (a) 15th August 1947   (b) 18th July 1947
    (c) 26th January 1950   (d) 14th August 1947

29. The Act of 1935 abolished
    (a) Diarchy in the provinces   (b) Provincial autonomy
    (c) Diarchy at the centre   (d) None of these

30. Indian Constitution is flexible, that is
    (a) Cannot amended easily
    (b) Can be amended only after undergoing a special procedure
    (c) Can be amended easily
    (d) Does not allow frequent changes

31. Which of the following words were added to the preamble of the Indian Constitution by the 42nd amendment?
    (a) Secular   (b) Socialist   (c) Integrity   (d) All of these

32. The Ultimate source of authority of India
    (a) The Government   (b) The Constitution
    (c) The Parliament   (d) The People

33. According to the marriage Act of 1954 the age is fixed at 21 years for men and for women
    (a) 16 years   (b) 17 years   (c) 18 years   (d) 21 years

34. Which of the following is no longer a fundamental right?
    (a) Right to freedom of religion   (b) Right to equality
    (c) Right to liberty   (d) Right to property

35. The concept of welfare state is included in the Constitution of India in the
    (a) Preamble   (b) Fundamental rights
    (c) Fourth schedule   (d) The directive principled of state policy

36. The President of India can be removed from his office only on ground of
    (a) Accepting bribe   (b) Disobedience of the Parliament
    (c) Violating the Constitution   (d) Showing favours to his party members

37. The disputes regarding the election of the President of India are decided by
    (a) The Supreme Court   (b) The Parliament
    (c) The Lok Sabha   (d) The High Court

38. Who appoints the advocate general?
    (a) Governor   (b) President   (c) Prime Minister   (d) Chief Minister

39. The first President election held during the year
    (a) 1950   (b) 1947   (c) 1951   (d) 1952

40. In Indian Constitution the subject of administration have been divided into
    (a) Two lists   (b) Three lists   (c) Four lists   (d) Five lists

41. How many members retired in legislative council for every two years?
    (a) 1/4   (b) 1/3   (c) 1/5   (d) 1/6

42. How many members are there in Karnataka Legislative Assembly?
    (a) 120   (b) 220   (c) 225   (d) 235

43. The Council Minister and Prime Minister should not exceed the total strength of the parliament
    (a) 5%   (b) 10%   (c) 12%   (d) 15%

44. The Prime Minister shall be selected from
    (a) President   (b) Vice-President
    (c) Majority Party of Lok Sabha Members   (d) None of these

45. The Vice-President is elected by electoral college consist of
    (a) Adult franchise of the constituency   (b) Lok Sabha and State Assembly
    (c) Rajya Sabha members   (d) Lok Sabha and Rajya Sabha members

46. The Greatest impediment to responsibility is
    (a) Rampant Corruption   (b) Self-interest
    (c) Interference by politicians   (d) Interference by higher officials

47. Conflict of interest may be
    (a) Actual   (b) Imaginary   (c) Produced   (d) True

48. The patent holder does not allow other to use patent information for years
    (a) 10   (b) 15   (c) 18   (d) 20

49. Fear is _____ to responsibility
    (a) a way to shift   (b) an impediment   (c) conflict   (d) both a and c

50. Risk estimation can be done by using
    (a) Cooking   (b) Trimming   (c) Event tree   (d) Both a and b

(COMMON TO ALL BRANCHES)

Time: 2 hours   **Max. Marks: 50**

1. Which amendment to the Constitution of India added the words 'Socialist and Secular' to the preamble?
   (a) 42nd Amendment   (b) 43rd Amendment
   (c) 44th Amendment   (d) 45th Amendment

2. The Constitution of India came into effect on ———
   (a) 26th November 1949   (b) 26th January 1950   (c) 15th August 1950   (d) 15th January 1950

3. The preamble of the Constitution reads as follows
   (a) We the member of Parliament   (b) We the people of India
   (c) We the members of Cabinet   (d) We the members of Association

4. The main objectives of Directive Principles of state policy is to
   (a) Establish Political Democracy   (b) Establish a Police state
   (c) Establish Economic Democracy   (d) Establish a Welfare state

5. The Fundamental Rights are enshrined in
   (a) Chapter I   (b) Chapter II
   (c) Chapter III   (d) Chapter IV

6. At present the Fundamental Duties of Indian Citizens are
   (a) 8   (b) 9   (c) 10   (d) 11

7. The President of India is elected for
   (a) Four years   (b) Five years   (c) Six years   (d) Seven years

8. The Oath of office of the President is conducted by
   (a) The Vice-President   (b) The Prime Minister
   (c) The Chief Justice of India   (d) None of these

9. The President of India can be removed from his office before the expiry of his term by
   (a) The Chief Justice of India   (b) The Prime Minister
   (c) The two houses of parliament   (d) The Vice-President

10. Article 352 of the Constitution deals with
    (a) National Emergency   (b) Financial Emergency
    (c) State Emergency   (d) None of these

11. Who presides over the joint session of the two houses of parliament?
    (a) The Speaker   (b) The Deputy Speaker
    (c) The President   (d) The Vice-President

12. The Judges of Supreme Court are appointed by
    (a) The President   (b) The Vice-President
    (c) The Prime Minister   (d) The Law Minister

13. The Parliament of India consists of
    (a) Lok Sabha & Legislative Council
    (b) Rajya Sabha & Legislative Council
    (c) Lok Sabha & Rajya Sabha
    (d) Legislative Assembly & Zila Panchayat

14. The Chairman of Rajya Sabha is
    (a) The Vice-President
    (b) The Deputy Speaker
    (c) The Prime Minister
    (d) The Home Minister

15. Who has the power to pardon in case of death sentenced by the courts in India?
    (a) The President
    (b) The Vice-President
    (c) The Prime Minister
    (d) The Auditor General

16. The Governor may resign for his post by addressing to
    (a) The President
    (b) The Vice-President
    (c) The Prime Minister
    (d) The Chief Minister

17. The total number of seats in Legislative Assembly of Karnataka is
    (a) 200   (b) 224   (c) 240   (d) 250

18. Which Article gives special provisions to the state of Jammu and Kashmir?
    (a) 350   (b) 360   (c) 370   (d) 380

19. Which of the following is not a Fundamental Right?
    (a) Right to Religion
    (b) Right to Equality
    (c) Right against Exploitation
    (d) Right to Strike

20. The Chief Minister is appointed by the
    (a) The Prime Minister
    (b) The President
    (c) The Governor
    (d) The Judge of High Court

21. A person arrested by police has to be produced before magistrate within
    (a) 12 hours   (b) 24 hours   (c) 48 hours   (d) 72 hours

22. One of the aims of studying Engineering Ethics is to
    (a) Inspire engineers to acquire in-depth knowledge in their field
    (b) Stimulate moral imagination
    (c) Acquire new skills in Engineering testing
    (d) Make engineers self-conflict in discharging their duties

23. 'Being safe or blaming others' is ——— type of attitudes of responsibility of engineers
    (a) Reasonable care   (b) Minimalist   (c) Good works   (d) None of these

24. This is not Dishonesty in engineering
    (a) Trimming   (b) Blending   (c) Negligently   (d) Intentionally

25. An author retains copyright of his book for
    (a) 25 years   (b) 50 years   (c) 60 years   (d) 100 years

26. Who was the Chairman of Drafting committee of the Constituent Assembly?
    (a) Jawaharlal Nehru
    (b) Sardar Patel
    (c) Dr Babu Rajendra Prasad
    (d) Dr B.R. Ambedkar

27. Who was the chairman of the Constituent Assembly?
    (a) Dr B.R. Ambedkar
    (b) Dr Babu Rajendra Prasad
    (c) Jawaharlal Nehru
    (d) Sri Krishna Wqamy Ayyer

28. For how many years, months and days did the Constituent Assembly work of the framing the Constitution
    (a) 2 years 11 months 18 days
    (b) 4 years 12 months 20 days
    (c) 3 years 3 months 29 days
    (d) 5 years 5 months 10 days

29. In the final form of the Constitution adopted by the Constituent Assembly, how many articles and schedules were there?
    (a) 398 Articles and 7 Schedules (b) 319 Articles and 10 Schedules
    (c) 315 Articles 9 Schedules (d) 395 Articles 8 Schedules

30. The Constitution of India is
    (a) One of the briefest constitution
    (b) One of the bulkiest constitution
    (c) A medium sized constitution
    (d) An evolved constitution

31. The total fundamental rights are at present
    (a) Six (b) Seven (c) Eight (d) Nine

32. Which of the below rights is deleted from the list of fundamental rights?
    (a) Right to Quality (b) Right to Freedom
    (c) Right to Life & Liberty (d) Right to Property

33. Which of the following writs is issued by the court in case of an illegal detention of a person by police?
    (a) Habeas corpus (b) Certiorari (c) Mandamus (d) Quo-warranto

34. The Fundamental Rights can be suspended during
    (a) Elections (b) State Emergency
    (c) National Emergency (d) Financial Emergency

35. Who is the First Citizens of India?
    (a) The President (b) The Vice-President
    (c) The Prime Minister (d) The Governor

36. 'Legislature' means
    (a) Body of Law making (b) Body of Ministers
    (c) Body of Judges (d) Body of Administrators

37. The Prime Minister and Council of Ministers are responsible to
    (a) The President (b) The Vice-President
    (c) The Parliament (d) The Supreme Court

38. The maximum strength of Lok Sabha is
    (a) 545 (b) 575 (c) 590 (d) 600

39. The maximum strength of Rajya Sabha is
    (a) 200 (b) 225 (c) 250 (d) 275

40. The members of Rajya Sabha re-elected for a term of
    (a) 4 years (b) 5 years (c) 6 years (d) 7 years

41. Which is the highest court of 'Appeal' in India?
    (a) Military Court (b) High Court (c) The Supreme Court (d) District Court

42. What is the minimum age to become a legislative member of Assembly?
    (a) 21 years (b) 23 years (c) 25 years (d) 30 years

43. Who appoints the Governor of a state?
    (a) The Home Minister (b) The Law Minister
    (c) The Prime Minister (d) The President of India

44. Who appoints the Vice Chancellors of the State Universities?
    (a) The Prime Minister   (b) The Judge of High Court
    (c) The Governor   (d) The Chief Minister

45. Who is the executive head of a State Governor?
    (a) Governor   (b) Chief Minister   (c) The Minister   (d) None of these

46. The Code of Ethics can be taken as guidelines by Engineers to
    (a) Resolve the Conflict
    (b) Overcome the work pressure
    (c) Formulate the problem
    (d) Escape from the responsibilities

47. To overcome as impediment 'Uncritical Acceptance', what step an engineer has to take?
    (a) Analyse and Accept   (b) Accept and Analyse
    (c) Always say 'yes' Boss   (d) None of these

48. Corrupt Professional Judgement leads to
    (a) Conflict of Interest   (b) Integrity in R & D
    (c) Reliability   (d) None of these

49. Stealing of Intellectual property means
    (a) Cooling   (b) Forging   (c) Plagiarism   (d) Trimming

50. Which one is not the way of misusing truth?
    (a) With holding information
    (b) Failing to adequately promote the dissemination of information
    (c) Deliberate deception
    (d) Patenting

(COMMON TO ALL BRANCHES)

Time: 2 hours   **Max. Marks: 50**

1. The basic feature of Indian Constitution is found in
   (a) Fundamental Duties   (b) Fundamental Rights
   (c) Preamble   (d) Directive Principles of State Policy

2. Original Constitution classified fundamental rights into seven categories but now there are
   (a) Eight   (b) Six   (c) Regrouped into social, economic and political   (d) Five

3. The final stage of the election process is
   (a) Polling   (b) Counting of votes
   (c) Announcing the results   (d) None of these

4. The Indian Federal system is based on the Federal system of
   (a) Canada   (b) USA   (c) France   (d) New Zealand

5. Engineers must
   (a) Recognize the value of a Code of Ethics
   (b) Support a Code of Ethics
   (c) Look upon a Code of Ethics as a sacred writ
   (d) Both (a) & (b)

6. The President of India takes the oath of office before the
   (a) Vice-President   (b) Prime Minister
   (c) Chief Justice of Supreme Court   (d) Speaker of Lok Sabha

7. 'Judicial Review' means
   (a) Reviewing the lower court judgment
   (b) Reviving the laws passed by the legislature
   (c) Examining the actions of executives
   (d) Advising the President of India

8. India is known as parliamentary democracy because
   (a) Powers have been clearly distributed between center and states
   (b) President is elected indirectly
   (c) MPs are directly elected by the people
   (d) Executive is responsible to the parliament

9. One of the basis attitudes towards responsibility is
   (a) Vigilant view   (b) Minimalist view
   (c) Moralistic view   (d) Maxima List view

10. The Foreign policy of the Government is shaped by the
    (a) Cabinet   (b) Parliament   (c) Prime Minister   (d) Vice-President

11. The First Session of Parliament is called
    (a) Primary   (b) Winter   (c) Budget   (d) Monsoon

12. Uniform civil code means
    (a) A code related to individual's public life
    (b) A codified law applicable to all persons of India irrespective of their religion
    (c) A civil procedure code
    (d) A code meant for Hindu only

13. The Vice-President is having power
    (a) To sign bills passed by Rajya Sabha   (b) To preside over Rajya Sabha
    (c) To nominate two members to Rajya Sabha   (d) To promulgate ordinance

14. Parliament of India consists of
    (a) Lok Sabha   (b) Lok Sabha and Rajya Sabha
    (c) Only Rajya Sabha   (d) Lok Sabha, Rajya Sabha and the President of India

15. The tenure of members of Legislative Council is
    (a) 3 years   (b) 5 years   (c) 6 years   (d) 4 years

16. 'Respite' means
    (a) Awarding lesser punishment   (b) Death due to suffocation
    (c) Painless death   (d) Death due to drowning

17. This is not dishonesty in science and engineering
    (a) Cooking   (b) Forging   (c) Trimming   (d) Blending

18. A National emergency can remain in operation with the approval of parliament for
    (a) An indefinite period   (b) A maximum period of six months
    (c) A maximum period of one year   (d) A maximum period of three years

19. As applied to engineering research and testing retaining the contradictory statement, discarding the rest is called
    (a) Trimming   (b) Scanning   (c) Cooking   (d) Skimming

20. The Chief Justice and other Judges of the High Court are appointed by
    (a) President   (b) Chief Minister
    (c) Prime Minister   (d) Governor

21. The Concept of secular state implies
    (a) No religion   (b) Dictatorship
    (c) Neutrality of religion   (d) Adoption of a single religion

22. The other name of Rajya Sabha is
    (a) Upper house   (b) Council of state
    (c) A Federal house   (d) All the above

23. The term 'Ethics' is derived from
    (a) Ethical in English   (b) 'Ethic' in Latin
    (c) Custom   (d) Ethics in Greek

24. The Governor of a State acts as
    (a) Real executive of a state   (b) Agent of President
    (c) Secretary of President   (d) Advisor to central government

25. Jobs are reserved for SCs and STs
    (a) For promotion   (b) For appointment
    (c) For appointment and promotion   (d) On the basis of their annual income

26. How many subjects are there in the central, state and concurrent list
    (a) 97, 66 & 47   (b) 47, 66 & 98
    (c) 97, 47 & 65   (d) 47, 96 & 55

27. Village Panchayats Article-40 are the best examples for India's _____ form of government
    (a) Republican   (b) Secular   (c) Sovereign   (d) Democratic

28. The Fundamental duties of Indian citizens were incorporated in the Constitution in
    (a) 1952   (b) 1976   (c) 1980   (d) 1985

29. The aim of the Directive Principles of State policy is to establish
    (a) Capitalist state in our country   (b) Communist state in our country
    (c) Welfare state in the country   (d) All of these

30. Sexual harassment of working women in working places in violation of
    (a) Right to profession   (b) Right to reputation
    (c) Right to personal liberty   (d) Right to life

31. The 'Chief Minister' of a state is appointed by the
    (a) Speaker   (b) Chief Justice of High Court
    (c) Prime Minister   (d) Governor

32. Exclusion of creamy layer makes a backward class
    (a) Socially backward   (b) Truly backward
    (c) More backward   (d) Economically backward

33. Special majority means more than
    (a) 50% majority   (b) Two-third majority
    (c) 75% majority   (d) 60 majority

34. One of the ways of misusing the truth is
    (a) Exaggerating the truth   (b) Making wrong statement
    (c) Making confused statement   (d) Failure to seek out the truth

35. The Constitution empowers state government to make special law for
    (a) Workers   (b) Teachers   (c) Women & children   (d) Farmers

36. The controller and Auditor General act as the
    (a) Guardian of Public Finances   (b) Chief Legal Advisor of the government
    (b) Guardian of Public interests   (d) Guardian of Fundamental Rights

37. The system of Legislature in the state of Karnataka is
    (a) Bicameral   (b) Unicameral   (c) Cameral   (d) Multicameral

38. Voting age of citizens from 21 to 18 years by _____ Constitutional Amendment Act
    (a) 42nd   (b) 56th   (c) 61st   (d) 76th

39. Writ of Prohibition cannot be issued against the
    (a) Judicial functions   (b) Legislative functions
    (c) Acts of lower courts   (d) Quasi-judicial functions

40. 'Fault Tree' is used
    (a) To trace the risk   (b) To assess the accuracy
    (c) To trace the result   (d) To assess the risk

41. State emergency is declared by the
    (a) Chief minister   (b) Governor   (c) Lok Sabha   (d) President

42. The Mandal Commission for backward classes was setup in
    (a) 1987   (b) 1978   (c) 1996   (d) 1986

43. According to 44th Amendment of 1978 the right to property was emitted as a fundamental right and made it a
    (a) Social Right   (b) Legal Right   (c) Universal Right   (d) None of these

44. Group thinking
    (a) Gives a good result   (b) Leads to better result
    (c) Widens our knowledge   (d) Is an impediment to responsibility

45. Our Constitution prohibits
    (a) Untouchability   (b) Freedom   (c) Liquor   (d) Politics

46. The President can appoint to Lok Sabha from Anglo-Indian Community
    (a) Two persons   (b) One person   (c) Five persons   (d) Three persons

47. 74th Amendment of the Constitution refers to
    (a) Rural Local Bodies   (b) Right to Property
    (c) Urban Local Bodies   (d) None of these

48. Which article of the Constitution provides protection to the civil servants?
    (a) 315   (b) 311   (c) 368   (d) 388

49. The Party System in India can be described as
    (a) Bi-Party   (b) Majority Party   (c) Single Party   (d) Multi Party

50. The Phrase economic justice is found in
    (a) Fundamental rights and fundamental duties
    (b) Preamble and directive principles of state policy
    (c) Fundamental duties and directive principled of state policy
    (d) Fundamental rights and fundamental duties

(COMMON TO ALL BRANCHES)

Time: 2 hours   Max. Marks: 50

1. Passing Criminal Law with retrospective effect is called as
   (a) Expost facto law   (b) Post facto law
   (c) Post facto law   (d) None of these

2. Which of the following writ is issued by the court in case of illegal detection of a person?
   (a) Certiorari   (b) Mandamus
   (c) Habeas corpus   (d) Quo-warrants

3. The sole channel of communication between President and his council of ministers is
   (a) Speaker of Lok Sabha   (b) Prime Minister
   (c) Vice-President   (d) Opposition leader

4. Article 19 provides
   (a) Seven freedom   (b) Five freedom   (c) Two freedom   (d) Six freedom

5. 'Respite' means
   (a) Awarding lesser punishment in place of originally awarded
   (b) Temporary suspension of death sentence
   (c) Reducing the length of punishment without changing the character of punishment
   (d) Substituting one form of punishment for another of a lighter character

6. Equality before law permits
   (a) Legislation based on race, religion, caste, sex and birth place
   (b) Legislation classification and prohibits class legislation
   (c) Class legislation and prohibits legislature classification
   (d) Legislative classification based on caste but prohibits class legislation based on religion

7. Legally permissible age for boy and girl is
   (a) 25 & 23   (b) 21 & 18   (c) 16 & 18   (d) 20 & 18

8. This is not the function of Election Commission
   (a) Selection of candidates
   (b) Preparation of electoral rules
   (c) Determine code of conduct of candidates
   (d) Allotment of symbols

9. The minister holds office during the pleasure of President which in fact means during the pleasure of
   (a) The Parliament   (b) The Lok Sabha
   (c) The Prime Minister   (d) None of these

10. Magna Carta is a written document of 13th century assuring liberties awarded to
    (a) Indian citizen   (b) French citizen
    (c) British citizen   (d) Citizen of world by U.N.O

11. Directives principled come under _____ of the Constitution
    (a) Part II   (b) Part III   (c) Part IV   (d) Part I

12. The ground for the impeachment of the President
    (a) Failure to follow the advice given by the Prime Minister
    (b) Unable to discharge his duties due to old age
    (c) Violation of Constitution
    (d) Misbehaviour with foreign dignitaries

13. The Speaker of Lok Sabha is
    (a) Appointed by the President   (b) Elected by members of Parliament
    (c) Appointed by the Vice-President   (d) Elected by members of Lok Sabha

14. The number of members nominated by the President to Rajya Sabha is
    (a) 12   (b) 10   (c) 14   (d) 8

15. Revealing confidential information amount to
    (a) Violation of patent   (b) Misuse of truth
    (c) Breach of truth   (d) Criminal breach of truth

16. Which amendment deals with establishment of municipalities as a part of constitutional system?
    (a) 74th   (b) 76th   (c) 86th   (d) 44th

17. To become a judge of the High Court, one must be practicing advocate of High Court for a period of at least _____ years
    (a) 20   (b) 10   (c) 15   (d) 5

18. Creamy layer means
    (a) Upper cast peopled
    (b) Highly endured people
    (c) Persons holding high post and having higher income of backward class of people
    (d) Educated people

19. Voting age of citizen is reduced from 21 to 18 years by _____ constitutional amendment
    (a) 42nd   (b) 61st   (c) 7th   (d) 55th

20. Under the Indian Constitution, the subject of administration have been divided into
    (a) 3 list   (b) 2 list   (c) 4 list   (d) 5 list

21. The total number of ministers in the council of ministers of the union shall not exceed
    (a) 21% of the total members of Lok Sabha
    (b) 12% of the total members of Lok Sabha
    (c) 15% of the total members of Lok Sabha
    (d) 15% of the total members of Lok Sabha & Rajya Sabha

22. Right against exploitation seeks to protect the weaker section of society by
    (a) Giving equal pay for equal work for both men and women
    (b) Proving compulsory education for children below the age of 14 years
    (c) Prohibiting human trafficking and beggar
    (d) None of these

23. One-third of the members of Rajya Sabha retire
    (a) Every year   (b) Every two years
    (c) Every three years   (d) Every four years

24. The directive principles of the state policy do not direct the state to endeavour to protect
    (a) Environment   (b) The objectives of artistic of national importance
    (c) Forest   (d) The interest of minorities

25. The Chief Justice of the state High Court hold office until they attain the age of
    (a) 58 years
    (b) 60 years
    (c) 65 years
    (d) 62 years

26. The Vice-President of India is ex-Officino Chairman of
    (a) Rajya sabha
    (b) Law commission
    (c) Planning commission
    (d) Finance commission

27. Cooking means
    (a) Boiling under pressure
    (b) Retaining result which fit the theory
    (b) Making deceptive statements
    (d) Misleading the public about the quality of product

28. Egocentric tendencies mean
    (a) Superiority complex
    (b) Retaining result from limited view
    (c) Arrogent and irresponsible behaviour
    (d) Habit of condemning views of others

29. This is not a fundamental duty
    (a) Respect to National Flag and National Anthem
    (b) Safeguard public property
    (c) Respect to elders and teachers
    (d) Renounce the practices insulting

30. Total number of articles in Indian Constitution
    (a) 445
    (b) 420
    (c) 400
    (d) 395

31. Financial emergency can be proclaimed under the article
    (a) 256
    (b) 356
    (d) 360
    (d) 352

32. According to Indian Constitution, the power of amending the Constitution are vested with
    (a) Parliament of India
    (b) President of India
    (c) People of India
    (d) The Prime Minister of India

33. In the Indian Constitution, the fundamental rights
    (a) Were added by the first amendment
    (b) Formed part of the original Constitution
    (c) Were added by 42nd amendment
    (d) Were added by the 24th amendment

34. The Chief election commissioner is appointed by
    (a) Chief Justice
    (b) President
    (c) Prime Minister
    (d) Governor

35. To declare national emergency a decision must be taken by the
    (a) Rajay Sabha
    (b) Lok Sabha
    (c) Union Cabinet
    (d) Both by Lok Sabha and Rajya Sabha

36. There is no provision for impeachment of
    (a) Judges of Supreme Court and High Court
    (b) Vice-President
    (c) President
    (d) Governor

37. Who is the President of India?
    (a) Mrs Prathibha Patil
    (b) Mr Pranab Mukharjee
    (c) Dr A.P.J. Abdul Kalam
    (d) Mr S.M. Krishna

38. Fear is _____ responsibility
    (a) A way to shift
    (b) An impediment
    (c) Both A and B
    (d) A way of corrupt

39. If one considers Engineering profession as a building then the following is its foundation
    (a) Accepting the risk
    (b) Imagination
    (c) Honesty
    (d) Creativity

40. A fault tree is used to
    (a) To improve safety
    (b) To claim compensation
    (c) Assess the risk involved
    (d) Take free consent

41. Legislature council is
    (a) Dissolved after 6 years
    (b) Dissolved after 3 years
    (c) Dissolved after 5 years
    (d) Not dissolved

42. What is the minimum age for becoming MP to Lok Sabha and Rajya Sabha?
    (a) 25 & 18   (b) 25 & 30   (c) 18 & 25   (d) 30 & 35

43. Lying is
    (a) Dishonesty
    (b) One of the way of misusing the truth
    (c) Cheating
    (d) None of these

44. One of the salient features of our Constitution is
    (a) It is partly rigid partly flexible
    (b) Fully flexible
    (c) Fully rigid
    (d) None of these

45. Right to religion is not subject to
    (a) Public order   (b) Public morality   (c) Public welfare   (d) Public health

46. A person arrested has to be produced before the magistrate within
    (a) 24 hours   (b) 48 hours   (c) 72 hours   (d) 96 hours

47. The owner of the patent right retains it for
    (a) 100 years   (b) 20 years   (c) 50 years   (d) 75 years

48. This is not the dishonesty in the engineering
    (a) Forging   (b) Trimming   (c) Blending   (d) Cooking

49. The Constitution empowers state government to make special law for
    (a) Unemployed youth   (b) Formers   (c) Workers   (d) Women and children

50. Which state among the following has no two houses?
    (a) Tamil Nadu   (b) Andhra Pradesh   (c) West Bengal   (d) Karnataka

ANSWER KEYS

JUNE/JULY 2015

1.	c	11.	a	21.	d	31.	a	41.	c
2.	a*	12.	d	22.	a	32.	b	42.	c
3.	a	13.	d	23.	b	33.	a	43.	d
4.	c	14.	c	24.	a	34.	d	44.	b
5.	a	15.	b	25.	a	35.	a	45.	a
6.	d	16.	a	26.	c	36.	a	46.	a*
7.	b	17.	c	27.	a	37.	c	47.	a
8.	a	18.	a	28.	d	38.	b	48.	b
9.	c	19.	b	29.	c	39.	d*	49.	b
10.	a	20.	b	30.	a	40.	a	50.	c

December 2014/January 2015

1.	b	11.	c	21.	d	31.	c	41.	b
2.	a	12.	d	22.	b	32.	a	42.	c
3.	c	13.	b	23.	c	33.	d	43.	b
4.	d	14.	c	24.	b	34.	b	44.	c
5.	c	15.	d	25.	a	35.	b	45.	d
6.	d	16.	a	26.	b	36.	c	46.	c
7.	d	17.	c	27.	b	37.	d	47.	c
8.	c	18.	b	28.	d	38.	b	48.	b*
9.	b	19.	c	29.	d	39.	c	49.	c
10.	d	20.	b	30.	c	40.	b	50.	a

December 2010

1.	A	11.	c	21.	a	31.	d	41.	C
2.	A	12.	a	22.	b	32.	d	42.	B
3.	B	13.	d	23.	d	33.	b	43.	A
4.	B	14.	b	24.	b	34.	a	44.	C
5.	B	15.	a	25.	d	35.	b	45.	D
6.	C	16.	c	26.	b	36.	c	46.	B
7.	C	17.	b	27.	d	37.	d	47.	B
8.	C	18.	a	28.	d	38.	a	48.	D
9.	B	19.	d	29.	c	39.	b	49.	C
10.	B	20.	14	30.	b	40.	d	50.	A

JUNE/JULY 2011

1.	a	11.	a	21.	a	31.	b	41.	b or c
2.	c	12.	d	22.	c	32.	d	42.	d
3.	d	13.	b	23.	b	33.	a	43.	c
4.	b	14.	c	24.	b	34.	c	44.	b
5.	d	15.	a	25.	a	35.	a	45.	b
6.	c	16.	c	26.	c	36.	b	46.	a
7.	a	17.	b	27.	c	37.	d	47.	d
8.	b	18.	d	28.	d	38.	c	48.	c
9.	b	19.	a	29.	a	39.	d	49.	b
10.	c	20.	c	30.	a	40.	d	50.	a

JUNE 2012

1.	a	11.	a	21.	a	31.	b	41.	a
2.	c	12.	d	22.	a	32.	c	42.	a
3.	a	13.	b	23.	b	33.	b	43.	c
4.	b	14.	a	24.	d*	34.	a	44.	c
5.	a	15.	c	25.	a	35.	b	45.	a
6.	a	16.	c	26.	b	36.	c	46.	c*
7.	a	17.	b	27.	d	37.	b	47.	a
8.	a	18.	b	28.	c	38.	d	48.	c
9.	a	19.	b	29.	a	39.	b	49.	b
10.	d	20.	c	30.	d	40.	c	50.	a

JANUARY 2013

1.	a	11.	c	21.	a	31.	d	41.	b
2.	c	12.	c	22.	a	32.	d	42.	c
3.	a	13.	c	23.	d	33.	c	43.	d
4.	c	14.	b	24.	a	34.	d	44.	c
5.	b	15.	a	25.	b	35.	d	45.	d
6.	d	16.	c	26.	c	36.	c	46.	b
7.	d	17.	b	27.	b	37.	a	47.	a
8.	d	18.	b	28.	b	38.	b	48.	d
9.	b	19.	d	29.	a	39.	d	49.	b
10.	c	20.	a	30.	C	40.	b	50.	c

JUNE/JULY 2013

1.	a	11.	a	21.	B	31.	a	41.	c
2.	b	12.	a	22.	B	32.	d	42.	c
3.	b	13.	c	23.	B	33.	a	43.	d
4.	d	14.	a	24.	b*	34.	c	44.	c
5.	c	15.	a	25.	C	35.	a	45.	b
6.	d	16.	a	26.	D	36.	a	46.	a
7.	b	17.	b	27.	B	37.	c	47.	a
8.	c	18.	c	28.	A	38.	a*	48.	d
9.	c	19.	d	29.	D	39.	c	49.	c*
10.	a	20.	c	30.	A	40.	c	50.	D

DECEMBER 2013/JANUARY 2014

1.	C	11.	C	21.	C	31.	D	41.	D
2.	B	12.	B	22.	A	32.	C	42.	B
3.	D	13.	B	23.	D*	33.	B	43.	B
4.	A	14.	D	24.	B*	34.	D	44.	D
5.	D	15.	C	25.	C	35.	C	45.	A
6.	C	16.	A	26.	A*	36.	A	46.	A
7.	B*	17.	D	27.	D	37.	A	47.	C
8.	D	18.	C	28.	B	38.	C	48.	B
9.	B	19.	C	29.	C	39.	B	49.	D
10.	C	20.	D	30.	D	40.	D	50.	B

JUNE/JULY 2014

1.	A	11.	C	21.	C	31.	C	41.	D
2.	C	12.	C	22.	C	32.	A	42.	B
3.	B	13.	D	23.	B	33.	C	43.	B
4.	D	14.	A	24.	D	34.	B	44.	A
5.	A	15.	B	25.	D	35.	C	45.	D
6.	A*	16.	A	26.	A	36.	D	46.	A
7.	B	17.	B	27.	B	37.	B	47.	B
8.	A	18.	C	28.	A	38.	B	48.	C
9.	C	19.	B	29.	C	39.	C	49.	D
10.	C	20.	A	30.	A	40.	C	50.	D*

* The given question may be wrong or the given key options are wrong or there may be more than one correct options or the question is not according to the latest changes in the Constitution of India.

INDEX